# The Contextualized Psalms
(Punjabi *Zabur*)

# The Contextualized Psalms (Punjabi *Zabur*)

A Precious Heritage of the
Global Punjabi Christian Community

YOUSAF SADIQ

*Foreword by Peter G. Riddell*

WIPF & STOCK · Eugene, Oregon

THE CONTEXTUALIZED PSALMS (PUNJABI *ZABUR*)
A Precious Heritage of the Global Punjabi Christian Community

Copyright © 2020 Yousaf Sadiq. All rights reserved. Except for brief quotations in critical publications or reviews, no part of this book may be reproduced in any manner without prior written permission from the publisher. Write: Permissions, Wipf and Stock Publishers, 199 W. 8th Ave., Suite 3, Eugene, OR 97401.

Scripture quotations taken from The Holy Bible, New International Version® NIV® Copyright © 1973 1978 1984 2011 by Biblica, Inc.TM
Used by permission. All rights reserved worldwide.

Wipf & Stock
An Imprint of Wipf and Stock Publishers
199 W. 8th Ave., Suite 3
Eugene, OR 97401

www.wipfandstock.com

PAPERBACK ISBN: 978-1-7252-7152-4
HARDCOVER ISBN: 978-1-7252-7151-7
EBOOK ISBN: 978-1-7252-7153-1

11/06/20

# Contents

| | | |
|---|---|---|
| Foreword by Peter G. Riddell | | vii |
| Acknowledgments | | xi |
| List of Abbreviations | | xiii |
| Introduction | | xv |
| I | The Making of the Punjabi Psalter | 1 |
| II | The Contributors for the Punjabi Psalter | 21 |
| III | The Punjabi Psalms: Causes for Their Success and Delayed Preparation | 47 |
| IV | The Present-Day Usage of the Punjabi Psalms | 64 |
| V | Missiological Aspects of the Psalms in an Islamic Context | 77 |
| VI | The Sociolinguistic Circumstances Facing Pakistani Punjabi Christians: Their Effect on the Punjabi Translation of the Scriptures and the Future of the Metrical Psalms | 106 |
| Conclusion | | 129 |
| Bibliography | | 145 |
| Subject Index | | 159 |
| Scripture Index | | 167 |

# Foreword

WITH A VAST POPULATION of around 220 million, Pakistan is the fifth-most populous country on earth. Of this number, some 96 percent are Muslim, so it might be assumed that at only 2 percent of Pakistanis, the country's four million Christians would struggle to survive, let alone thrive.

However, Christians tend to cluster in particular locations in Pakistan, constituting majorities in some neighborhoods. Indeed, almost two-thirds of the Pakistani Christian community live among a vast Muslim majority in the province of Punjab, which itself is home to around half of Pakistan's population. So Punjabi Christianity represents a substantial part of Christianity in Pakistan and it is to this particular community that Dr. Yousaf Sadiq has devoted his attention in this fascinating book.

Christianity came early to the Indian subcontinent and can be traced to the arrival of Saint Thomas to Kerala around twenty years after the crucifixion of Christ, leading to the establishment of the Seven Churches.[1] As for Protestant Christianity, it traces its roots in the area of present-day Pakistan to the middle of the nineteenth century, when North American Presbyterian missionaries established themselves in the Punjab on invitation from the Church Missionary Society. Little time was lost in sharing the gospel with local communities, and these early Protestant pioneers found fertile ground among the Hindu Dalits or untouchables. Individual conversions were followed by conversions of entire communities of Dalits and, in that way, the church grew in the Punjab.

---

1. Stephen A. Missick, "Mar Thoma: The Apostolic Foundation of the Assyrian Church and the Christians of St. Thomas in India," *Journal of Assyrian Academic Studies* 14 (2000) 35ff.

Several centuries before, as the Protestant Reformation was underway in Europe, a fresh form of worship emerged in the newly reformed Swiss and French communities. Certain early Protestants put the text of the psalms to musical forms that were metrically regular. These new metrical psalms, sung in familiar melodies, won favor especially among the Presbyterian and Reformed traditions. A particularly famous version, the Genevan Psalter that was developed by the Huguenots, is still in use among some French Protestant churches.

So with the arrival of Presbyterian missionaries in the Punjab in the mid-nineteenth century, the way was clear for metrical psalms to find a new home.

In this book, Dr. Yousaf Sadiq closely studies the important role of Rev. Dr. Imam-ud-Din Shahbaz, who can justly be identified as the father of metrical psalms in the Punjab. Dr. Sadiq begins by looking into the socio-historical and missional context in which the Punjabi Psalter was prepared. He then explores the life of Rev. Shahbaz and the important work by him and others to take the metrical psalm format and adapt it to Punjabi language and native Punjabi musical forms.

After considering the important work of the pioneers of the metrical psalm format in the Punjab and the reason why they became so popular among Punjabi Christians, Dr. Sadiq turns his attention to the extent to which the psalms can and do serve as a bridge between the Christian minority and the surrounding Muslim majority community.

Indeed, the text of the Qur'an is itself highly metrical and lends itself well to chanting, a very developed art form in Muslim communities around the world. Qur'anic recitation is a skill that is much sought after, with international and local competitions attracting vast interest among Muslims the world over. The practice of Islam includes various dimensions of orality, including both recitation of sacred text and a system of calls to prayer, which becomes an area of great specialization.

Dr. Sadiq's discussion of the sociolinguistic issues facing the Punjabi Christians in Pakistan is both interesting and important. He draws attention to issues of linguistic hierarchy involving negative attitudes toward mother-tongue use in Pakistan, which represent a threat to the long-term survival of the Punjabi Psalms. Dr. Sadiq suggests practical steps for overcoming such negative attitudes toward mother-tongue use through preservation of the Punjabi *Zaburs*.

All in all, this book by Dr. Yousaf Sadiq offers multiple dimensions of interest. It provides a window into sociocultural and missional history in the region of present-day Pakistan. It also highlights a process of transmission from Europe to Asia of a particular worship form within the Protestant tradition. The book additionally raises a number of interesting and important questions relating to Christian-Muslim relations in Pakistan. These questions offer potential bridges between the faiths rather than focusing on awkward differences.

Thus this book looks into the past, the present, and the future, and in doing so, it represents an invaluable addition to Christian scholarly literature.

PROFESSOR PETER G. RIDDELL
*Senior Research Fellow, Australian College of Theology*
*Professorial Research Associate, History, SOAS University of London*

# Acknowledgments

Throughout the thinking, research, and writing of this book many people have been an invaluable aid to me. There is no room to mention everybody, but a few people do deserve special mention.

I would like to thank Professor Peter G. Riddell. His advice, guidance, and willingness to make himself available has been invaluable, as has his patience in wading through draft after draft of many chapters. He never stopped believing in me and showed great confidence in my work. I greatly admire him for his sensitivity, thoroughness, and wisdom.

I would like to express my earnest gratitude to Kayoko Ishii and her husband, Katsuro, for their generous support and inspiration that has realized my dream of becoming a Christian scholar. I'm thankful to them for the recognition of my efforts; without their support this book would not be in your hand at this time.

Some friends have also been of great help in the writing of this book, and their help means a lot to me. I'm indebted beyond words to Stephan Fairfield, Ken and Rita Pearson, Dan and Katy Forshaw, Stefan Amstutz, Stephan Hertig, Dr. Timothy Farrell, Dr. Richard Hoyle, Tim Clifford, Ted Foster, and my dear friend Hazel Oberst for their many prayers, dedication, and generous time.

I am immensely grateful for the support of my parents, Sadiq and Piyari Masih, my beloved wife, Ruth, who kept me focused and remains as excited as I am about the subject, and my beautiful daughters, Abigail Y. Sadiq and Elianna-Zebel Y. Sadiq. Without their love, encouragement, prayers, and many sacrifices this book would probably never have seen the light of day.

I also express my appreciation for the careful editorial work done by the staff at Wipf and Stock, especially Matthew Wimer, editorial production manager, for his flexibility in working with me on this project.

Above all, I am grateful to God, who allowed me to participate in this study and granted me peace and health to finish this work. Without him in my life, I could not have written this book, and it is my prayer that through this book God's glory in some way will be more greatly manifested.

# List of Abbreviations

| | |
|---|---|
| AM | Asian Music |
| BDB | Brown, Drivers and Briggs, *Hebrew and English Lexicon of the Old Testament* |
| BFBS | British and Foreign Bible Society |
| BT | *Bible Translator* |
| CBCP | Catholic Bible Commission Pakistan |
| CC | *Christian Century* |
| CMI | *Church Missionary Intelligencer* |
| CMS | Church Missionary Society |
| ER | *The Ecumenical Review* |
| HBT | *Horizons in Biblical Theology* |
| JPCS | *Journal of Postcolonial Studies* |
| JPS | *Journal of Punjab Studies* |
| JQR | *Jewish Quarterly Review* |
| MIR | *Missiology: An International Review* |
| MW | *The Muslim World* |
| NIV | New International Version |
| OESAC | *Oxford Encyclopaedia of South Asian Christianity* |
| PBS | Pakistan Bible Society |

| | |
|---|---|
| PCUSA | Presbyterian Church in the United States of America |
| PHS | Presbyterian Historical Society |
| R&S | *Religion & Society* |
| SFM | *St. Francis Magazine* |
| TJMC | *Touchstone: A Journal of Mere Christianity* |
| UPBFM | United Presbyterian Board of Foreign Missions |
| VT | *Vetus Testamentum* |

## BIBLICAL BOOKS ABBREVIATIONS

| | |
|---|---|
| Ps/Pss | Psalms |

# Introduction

As a child, I learned many of the psalms in my native language, Punjabi. Early in the morning, my father would sing them melodiously, the tunes and the beautiful words of these psalms would bring unexplainable peace and comfort to my mind and heart. My house was facing the main mosque in the area, the call to prayer would be made loud through the speakers installed in the minarets, but listening to the psalms from my father would fade the call to prayer from reaching my ears. Before going to school or work, it was a regular practice in our family in Pakistan to begin our day by listening to the Psalms in Punjabi being played on a cassette recorder. These were recorded by the Pakistan Christian Recording Ministries. The Psalms in Punjabi, from the beginning, were a vital part of my personal and communal life, and it continues to be so. The only difference is that they are now being played on compact discs and modern digital devices.

Growing up in an atmosphere where the Psalms were much cherished, many of the questions I had with regard to the Punjabi Psalter, I could not find their answers both from people around me and from the books that were available to me. I often wondered why do we make frequent use of the Psalms at home and at church? Where do they come from? Who prepared them? Where did my parents learn them from, especially since both of my parents never had the opportunity to go to school due to economic reasons? I was curious to discover the answers. My profound interest and curiosity ultimately became the basis for conducting a comprehensive study on the Psalms in Punjabi. The findings are recorded in this book.

This book aims to study the cultural, sociohistorical, missiological, and sociolinguistic aspects of the Punjabi Psalms (*Zabur*), shared heritage of the Punjabi-speaking Christians in the Indian subcontinent and around the globe. The first objective for writing this book is to esteem this heritage by exploring its fascinating story of contextualization and to appreciate the hard work of several individuals tied to the account of the Punjabi Psalter. Likewise, the intent is to introduce the Punjabi Psalms both to the global Punjabi Christian community and the international community. The second purpose is to consider the value and availability of Psalms in poetic form for the Muslim community in a Pakistani context, to see its bridge-building and evangelistic elements. And the third aim of this book is to highlight the risks involved in the continuing use of the Punjabi *Zabur* due to the precarious sociolinguistic issues facing the Punjabi Christians in Pakistan.

The first three chapters of this book investigate the social, historical, and missional context of the Psalms in Punjabi and the life of Rev. Dr. Imam-ud-Din Shahbaz. The first chapter looks at the historical context of the Psalms in Punjabi, its versions and methodology employed in their contextualization. The focal point of the second chapter is on individuals who contributed to the making of the Punjabi Psalms. Particular focus is given to the leading figure, Rev. Dr. Imam-ud-Din Shahbaz, who played an integral role in the compiling of these psalms. An attempt is made in the second chapter to uncover aspects of the life and poetry of Dr. Shahbaz. The third chapter endeavors to explore the key factors behind the spread and success of the Punjabi Psalms, and study the reasons for which these psalms rapidly became popular among the ordinary people. Attention is drawn to elements that hindered their preparation and caused a delay in the making of the Punjabi Psalms. The devotional, liturgical, and cultural ways in which the Punjabi Psalms are used, and the unity these psalms create among all denominations as one body of Christ are discussed in the fourth chapter.

A careful observation of the Psalms in Punjabi reveals that these psalms have a number of terms and expressions that are Muslim-friendly or familiar to Islam. The fifth chapter attempts to draw attention to how particularly the poetic form of the Psalms in Punjabi seems fitting to bridge gaps between Christians and Muslims in an Islamic context, and how the Psalms, in a culturally appropriate style, are pertinent for sharing with the Muslim community. The final chapter concentrates on the present-day sociolinguistic situation among the Punjabi-speaking churches, and the effects it is likely to bring to the metrical translation of the Punjabi Psalms. The British and Foreign Bible Society's correspondence held at Cambridge University regarding the Punjabi New Testament is surveyed to make concluding comments on this matter.

The late Rev. William Galbraith Young, a graduate of the University of Glasgow and a former missionary and bishop in Sialkot, was inspired by the singing of psalms and hymns in the Punjabi congregations. He wrote a

Introduction                                                                 xvii

small book with the title *Sialkot Convention Hymn Book: Notes on Writers and Translators* that was published from Daska, Pakistan, in 1965. Its Urdu translation with the title *Sialkot Convention Git Ki Kitab: Giton Ke Musanafin O Mutrajamin*, done by W. A. Singh, was published by the *Masihi Ishat Khana* (Christian Publishing House) from Lahore, Pakistan. Although it focuses on those who wrote and translated songs found in the Sialkot Convention hymn book, the first few pages provide information on the story of the Punjabi Psalms. Bishop Young's book serves as the key resource on the Punjabi Psalms, available in Urdu, the official language of Pakistan. However, Young expresses a struggle with regard to the availability of resources on this subject; for example, he did not have access to the original versions of the Psalms in Punjabi.

At present, inaccurate information is circulated with reference to the life of Rev. Dr. Imam-ud-Din Shahbaz, the leading figure in the making of the Psalms in Punjabi. This is due to ignorance, as Bishop Young in his book *Days of Small Things? A Narrative Assessment of the Work of the Church of Scotland in the Punjab in "The Age of William Harper, 1873–1885"* talks about another Muslim convert from Sialkot, named Imam-ud-Din. Although it is not difficult to conclude that this Imam-ud-Din is different from Imam-ud-Din of the Psalms, people get confused by the similarity of name and place. For example, a few years ago, a book in Urdu was published in which history on the life of Dr. Shahbaz was erroneously taken from Young's aforementioned book published in 1991 from Rawalpindi by the Christian Study Centre, in which the author writes of a different Imam-ud-Din.

Lack of resources and scattered information on this topic caused difficulties in the investigation of this topic. Unexpectedly, very little was discovered from Gujranwala Theological Seminary, the oldest and one of the major seminaries in Pakistan. Valuable and useful resources were found at the British Library, Church Missionary Society archives held in the Cadbury Research Library at the University of Birmingham, Church Missionary Society archives held at the Crowther Centre Library in Oxford, the Centre for Muslim-Christian Studies Library in Oxford, University of Glasgow Library, the British and Foreign Bible Society archives held at the University of Cambridge Library in Cambridge, and archival records held at the Presbyterian Historical Society in Philadelphia, Pennsylvania. In addition, relevant materials were generously provided electronically by Gordon-Conwell Theological Seminary Library in South Hamilton, Massachusetts, and the Pittsburgh Theological Seminary Library in Pittsburgh, Pennsylvania.

The details on individuals who contributed in contextualizing the Psalms in Punjabi, the poetic features of the Punjabi *Zaburs*, themes of the personal poetry of Dr. Shahbaz, and key factors that played a vital role in the spread of these psalms and delayed in their preparation have never before been surveyed. Besides, this book looks into sociohistorical aspects of the Punjabi Psalms and of the life of Dr. Shahbaz that have not been explored before.

A study on the Muslim-friendly terms in the Punjabi *Zaburs* and the notion of poetic psalms for bridge-building in Pakistan have been thoroughly investigated here. Attention is drawn to how particularly the poetic form of the Psalms in Punjabi seems fitting to bridge gaps between Christians and Muslims in the Pakistani Islamic context, and how the Psalms, in a culturally appropriate style, are pertinent for sharing with the Muslim community. Moreover, the sociolinguistic challenges facing the Punjabi Christians in Pakistan have never been studied. This book for the first time investigates the present-day complexities of attitude to the Punjabi language within the church circles, emphasizing its effects and possible risks on the continuing use of the Psalms in Punjabi.

It is my earnest prayer that through this book, the global Punjabi Christian community may be richly blessed, and that they may come to have a deeper appreciation for the precious heritage that they have in the form of the Punjabi *Zabur*. I pray that they may continue to cherish the beautiful melodies of the Punjabi Psalter, make an effort to pass them on to the next generations, and grow in loving and valuing their mother tongue, the Punjabi language. May God's glory in some way be more greatly manifested through this book.

# I

# The Making of the Punjabi Psalter

THE PSALMS TRANSLATED INTO the Punjabi language in versified form can unequivocally be regarded as the most accustomed, read, sung, recited, and memorized part of Scripture by the body of Christ in Pakistan. This chapter endeavors to explore the historical and sociocultural context in which the Psalms were translated into Punjabi, the methodology that was taken up by the Psalms committee in preparing them, and the past links of Christian missions with the Sialkot region of Punjab, where the story of the Punjabi Psalms originated. Furthermore, the Urdu metrical psalms that led to the preparation of Psalms in the Punjabi language are discussed.

## 1. SIALKOT AND THE EARLY CHRISTIAN MISSIONS

The account of the Punjabi Psalms dates back to the 1890s from Sialkot, a diminutive city situated in the northeast of present-day Pakistan, then British India. Before proceeding further, it is beneficial to briefly divulge a few historic connections between Sialkot and the preceding Christian missions, as the name Sialkot will recur over the following pages in relation to the Punjabi metrical psalms and the different characters attached to it. Today, the city is proud to produce world-class sports goods, preeminently hand-stitched footballs, and surgical instruments par excellence. It also generates the largest revenue for the country after Karachi, the largest city and the commercial nucleus of Pakistan. Moreover, Sialkot is famous for producing cordon bleu rice in the country. Doctor John Youngson, a missionary of the Church of Scotland in the Punjab, regarded the city as a key municipality in a highly productive and densely inhabited region.[1] The contributions of the Christian missions toward the present-day business status and economic stability of the city does require some comprehensive research.

Many people appear ignorant and some are refusing to accept reality by calling the contribution of Christian missions to the present-day economic strength of Sialkot a mere coincidence, while others acknowledge the truth that the present-day surgical industry in Sialkot was developed due to the presence of the Christian hospital. It remains a fact that, toward the end of the nineteenth century, the Christian missionaries opened up business opportunities for the inhabitants of Sialkot, and encouraged them in the hand-working skills for which the city is today renowned. In regard to this, Robert Stewart, an American missionary of the United Presbyterian Mission in Sialkot, writes: "Another method adopted for the advancement of the people in worldly prosperity is that of industrial training," it was considered an important area on which the Christian missions were focusing in making arrangements to help the locals to receive training.[2] Today, several Christians living in Sialkot are involved in manufacturing world-class surgical instruments at a small scale.

Besides, the Christian missions contributed considerably in the areas of health and education in Sialkot. The Memorial Christian Hospital (commonly known as the Mission Hospital), was built by the American Presbyterians and inaugurated by the principal English representative Major Montgomery in 1889 and has been serving the people of Sialkot without any discrimination.[3] It is fascinating to know that the surgical industry in Sialkot was born at the Christian hospital where in the early days "broken instruments" were being repaired at the recommendation of the missionary surgeons; the surgical products made by the locals were acquired by other Christian hospitals in India and abroad. Moreover, Murray College (then known as Mission College) a renowned academic institution, was built by the Scottish Presbyterians, and the national poet and philosopher Dr. Mohammad Iqbal, the first person to present the idea of Pakistan as a separate country, had the honor of studying there. The Church of Scotland commenced its mission work in Sialkot between 1856 and 1857 under the

---

1. Youngson, *Panjab*, 7.
2. Stewart, *Life*, 324–31.
3. Anderson and Campbell, *Shadow*, 209.

direction of Rev. Thomas Hunter, a graduate of the King's College, Aberdeen, who was martyred in Sialkot during the Indian revolt.[4] Today, there is a beautiful Hunter Memorial Church and a small town known as "Hunter Pura," literally meaning "land of Hunter" in Sialkot.

The region of Punjab was annexed to the British administration in 1849; Sialkot, a city "within sight of the great mountains to the north" came forward as an imperative military location, and the Christian missionaries were drawn to the area realizing its rising value.[5] This is evident by the words of Captain John Mill, a military officer of the British army: "This field, Sialkot, is looked upon by different Christian bodies as an inviting one."[6] The United Presbyterian mission was quite keen on concentrating on evangelistic activities in Sialkot district. Rev. Dr. Andrew Gordon, an American missionary of the United Presbyterian Mission, was the first Christian missionary to arrive in Sialkot on August 8, 1855, with the purpose of evangelizing among the heathen, and the work was known as the Sialkot Mission.

## 2. CONTEXTUALIZATION OF THE PUNJABI ZABUR

The Punjabi *Zabur* is the versified translation of Psalms into the Punjabi language. It is imperative to describe the words *Punjabi* and *Zabur*. Punjabi, or Panjabi, is an "Indo-Aryan language" from the family of Indo-European, Indo-Iranian languages.[7] It is primarily spoken in the most populated province of Pakistan, i.e., Punjab, and it is estimated that approximately over a hundred million people, more than half of the population of Pakistan, speak Punjabi as their first language.[8] Likewise, Punjabi is chiefly spoken in the Indian province of Punjab where it holds provincial language status. Besides, a large number of Punjabi speakers can be found across the globe and Punjabi has been stratified in the list of top twenty "widely spoken languages in the world."[9]

Punjab or Panjab is the combination of two Persian words: *Panj*, meaning "five," and *ab*, meaning "water." In other words, Punjab is the land of five rivers, namely Ravi, Sattlaj, Chennab, Jehlum, and Beas. The language spoken in the Punjab is known as Punjabi and the speakers of this language are called Punjabis or "Punjabees." *Zabur* is an Arabic word that is used to

---

4. Berner, "Pakistan," 630.
5. Neil, *Christianity*, 331.
6. Anderson and Campbell, *Shadow*, 19.
7. Bhatia, "Punjabi," 299.
8. Weiss, "Population," 238.
9. Bhatia, "Punjabi," 886.

refer to the Psalms in the Old Testament. The same word has occurred in the Qur'an in reference to "the Psalms of David."[10] Besides *Zabur*, the word *Mazmur*, meaning "a psalm," or *Mazamir* (plural) is sometimes used for the Psalms. The Roman Catholic translation of the Bible in Urdu, the national language of Pakistan, uses *Mazamir* as a title for the book of Psalms. Nevertheless, in Pakistan, the word *Zabur* is commonly used and understood as a generic term to refer to the book of Psalms.

## 2.1. The Urdu Metrical Psalms

Before moving onto the Punjabi translation of Psalms in verse, it is essential to address this question: what was used before the Punjabi Psalter became available, particularly among the Presbyterian congregations in India? Robert Stewart mentions that until 1883, the singing among the United Presbyterian churches was done mostly by the use of hymns and psalms set to meter that were chanted or sung to Western melodies. He continues that *Zabur aur Git* (Psalms and Hymns) was used largely for this purpose and that the "metrical versions" prepared by other Christian missions were also being used.[11] The editions with the title *Zabur aur Git* were published by the Presbyterian Mission Press from Allahabad for the Ludhiana Mission, in the years 1842, 1855, and 1859. The materials in the 1842 edition of *Zabur aur Git* were for the most part provided by Rev. Bowley, and it was not furnished with Western notations.

Rev. William Bowley was from an Anglo-Indian background and served with the Church Missionary Society in India. The first section in the 1842 edition consisted of all 150 metrical psalms in Roman Urdu, with the name of the tune on which the psalms was to be sung and a short title explaining the content for each psalm, and similar information was provided for 276 hymns in the second part. For example, the following details were provided for the first psalm:

- *Pehla Zabur—Pehla Hisa* (Ps 1, part 1)
- L. M. Euphrates, Wells, Winchester (tune for the psalm)
- *Sharir aur Dindar ki chal aur anjam* (Walk and end of the upright and the wicked)

The general hymns were divided according to topics such as Praise, Trinity, Christ, Holy Spirit, Faith, Teaching, New Year, Judgment, Heaven,

---

10. Hughes, *Islam*, 698.
11. Stewart, *Life*, 303.

and Baptism, whereas a list of special hymns and psalms had been provided separately. Moreover, a detailed list of tunes was being provided in the 1842 edition.[12]

The 1859 edition, arranged by Rev. Rudolph, was published in Persian script. It consisted of 150 psalms and 200 hymns in Urdu, each with a title at the beginning.[13] Rev. Adolph Rudolph was a Presbyterian missionary from the States who served in India with the Ludhiana Mission. A rather smaller edition, "*Ragmala*," meaning "garland of melody," was published from London in 1872 by William Clowes and Sons. It was arranged by Rev. Julius Fredrick Ullmann, a German missionary in India who first served with the Berlin Mission and later with the Farukhabad Mission of the United Presbyterians. It consisted of seventy-two psalms and hymns in Roman Urdu with Western notations. However, it is significant to note that all these versions were not considered to be in complete accordance with the Hebrew text of the Psalter.

*Swar Sangrah* (a "collection" of tunes) or the Hindustani Choral Book, published by the Baptist Mission in Roman Urdu from Benares in 1861 and compiled by John Parsons, was furnished with Western notations. Similarly, *Masihi Git Ki Kitab* (The Christian Hymn Book), printed in Lucknow by the American Methodist Press in 1866 demonstrated a similar style in terms of its presentation. There were 179 hymns in Roman Urdu that were divided according to the topics, and names for Western tunes to which they were supposed to follow. It indicates that in general a similar approach to church worship was taken up by the various Christian missions. In other words, the hymns and the metrical psalms were sung to Western tunes; and in the above-mentioned cases, the language used was Urdu. During the years 1882–83 the United Presbyterian Mission formed various committees for its different activities; with the purpose of fostering the overall work and training of the local Christian workers so that they could be equipped to take up further roles.[14]

Stewart mentions that, although the committee for the Urdu Psalms was formed in 1882, the plans for an accurate and new translation of the Psalter had been established long before. However, Stewart draws attention to an indispensable issue when he gives the reason for the delay: "Those interested in the work oscillated between the adoption of Eastern and Western

---

12. *Zabur aur Git*, 1842 ed.
13. *Zabur aur Git*, 1859 ed.
14. Gordon, *India*, 493.

meters."[15] This was a very crucial matter which needs a somewhat lengthy discussion, and therefore will be taken care of at a later stage.

The committee for the Urdu translation of Psalms was formed in January 1882. The task given to this committee was to work on a metrical translation of Psalms into Urdu that could be sung to Western melodies, and that the translation should correspond to the original text.[16] The exact number of members on this special committee for the Psalter remains unknown; however, three names have been mentioned by Stewart in this regard: Rev. Dr. Andrew Gordon, who served as the head of this committee from January 1882 to spring 1885; Dr. Samuel Martin, who took over the responsibilities as head of the committee in 1885 after Gordon left for the United States; and Rev. Imam-ud-Din Shahbaz, who served as a poet and put these psalms into verse. The work was rather slow as, after one year of its formation, the committee approved only seven versified psalms in 1883, although they were in use immediately after their publication.[17] In the second year, the progress was comparatively faster as another thirty-six metrical psalms were approved.[18]

Stewart mentions that the Persian script was used in preparing the first sixteen psalms in the year 1884. It is not clear if the remaining twenty psalms were published with Persian or Roman script the same year. In 1885 the total number of psalms approved by the committee was twenty-five, since the progress was slow in the first quarter in which only six psalms were approved. However, the work was steady in the year 1886, and the committee managed to prepare another thirty-two metrical psalms in that year. This brought the total of the number of psalms to one hundred, which were published in the year 1887 in Roman Urdu.[19] The same were published in Persian script in 1889. The committee finished the task of translating all 150 psalms to Western meters in October 1891, and the work was published first in Persian and later in the Roman script.[20] This shows that from 1882 to 1885, a total of sixty-eight psalms were approved by the Psalms committee under the supervision of Gordon. The remaining eighty-two psalms were supervised by Martin from 1885 to the final publication in 1891. Moreover, it took almost ten years for the committee to prepare the translation of all 150 metrical psalms in Urdu. The later project of the Psalter in Punjabi verse

---

15. Stewart, *Life*, 303.
16. Young, *Sialkot*, 3.
17. Stewart, *Life*, 303.
18. Young, *Sialkot*, 3.
19. Stewart, *Life*, 303.
20. Young, *Sialkot*, 3.

derived from the Urdu version. The poet Rev. Imam-ud-Din Shahbaz will be discussed in length later, as he continued to serve on a committee for the Punjabi metrical psalms. Here it is worth noting briefly Rev. Dr. Andrew Gordon and Rev. Dr. Samuel Martin, who supervised the entire project of the metrical translation of Psalms into Urdu.

As a pioneer missionary to Sialkot, Gordon led and served in the mission field for thirty years, from 1855 to 1885. Preaching the good news, helping the poor, and development of the local population through practical ways were on the heart of Gordon.[21] He stressed the importance of training and education of converts. The converts being trained under him came from educated and non-educated backgrounds; Aziz-ul-Haq, Abdullah, Karam Dad, Maulvi Muhammad Alim, Chaughatia, Ditt, Prem Masih, and Rahmat Masih were among notable names. The well-known Gordon College built by the American Presbyterians in Rawalpindi, a city adjoined to the capital of Pakistan, was named after Gordon in 1895 by the United Presbyterian mission in recognition of his immense services.[22] His admiration for the simple and uneducated converts is reflected through his words:

> *I have grown to entertain a profound respect, even though they are so illiterate as to be barely able to read, their worldly condition being little above that of day laborers. . . . Fundamental truths presented in their simplicity reach the hearts of the sons of poverty, and are blessed of God to their conversion.*[23]

---

21. Berner, "Pakistan," 629.
22. Webster, "Gordon," 251.
23. Gordon, *India*, 445–46.

Rev. Dr. Andrew Gordon.

It is sad to mention that the Christian educational institutions in Pakistan were nationalized by the government in 1972, and except for the Forman Christian College in Lahore, all other institutions, including the Gordon College, have not been returned to the church yet. At present, efforts are being made for the return of this historic institution.[24]

Martin played a major role in serving the untouchables of the society, and had the privilege to baptize the first convert from the depressed class—namely, Mr. Ditt.[25] It has been reported that in a single year, fifteen thousand new Christians were baptized by Martin.[26] He took particular interest in the settlement of the new converts. In Scot Garh (literally meaning Scotland) near Sialkot, where he was based, the settlement of converts took place through his efforts. Likewise, a large piece of land allocated for the new

---

24. Other institutions include Murray College in Sialkot and Edwards College in Peshawar.

25. Pickett, *Mass Movement*, 44.

26. Campbell, "Church," 151.

converts, called "Martinpur," was named after him.²⁷ This large Christian village in the Punjab province of present-day Pakistan is an example of his love and concern for converts from underprivileged background. Being acquainted with biblical Hebrew, Dr. Martin helped Rev. Shahbaz to make sure that the translation of the Urdu Psalms corresponded to the original text.²⁸ He also translated portions from the "explication of the shorter catechism" into Urdu, for the boarding schools for girls in Sialkot. Martin entered the mission field in 1867 and went to be with the Lord in 1910.

**Rev. Dr. Samuel Martin.**

## 2.2. The Punjabi Metrical Psalms

It is crucial to note that a year before the final publication of the Urdu metrical psalms, initiatives were started for a separate committee in January

---

27. Forrester, *India*, 79.
28. Martin, *Father*, 46.

1890; the reason of this new committee has been explained by Stewart: "Less cultured of our people like native meters and native airs better than those of occidental origin, and it was found necessary to prepare versions of the bhajan form, and that, too in the Punjabi tongue-the language which they love most and know best."[29]

When efforts were taking place to form this new committee, one hundred psalms had already been published and the entire 150 metrical psalms in Urdu were about to be published the following year. The first cycle of Urdu metrical psalms published in 1883 was already in use, yet it took almost eight years before it was realized that a new translation was needed.

Rev. Young mentions that by 1890, the Christian hymns and the psalms were already in use in the Punjabi language and were sung to local tunes, although they were fewer in number.[30] It is not known who prepared these Punjabi Christian songs but it seems that they were beginning to have an influence on ordinary people. Was it the increasing popularity of those existing Christian songs in Punjabi that created a need for the translation of the Psalter into Punjabi, or was it due to the unpopularity of the Urdu metrical psalms, or a bit of both? Although this needs further investigation, it cannot be ignored that the former must have played an integral role in highlighting a need for the availability of Psalms in Punjabi. In a supplementary note in his book, Rev. Young writes that it had been brought to his knowledge that the melody and wordings of Psalm 24 (vv. 7–10) were prepared by Rev. G. L. Thakur Das (1845–1910). He continues that it had also been stated that this psalm was prepared even before the metrical translation of the Punjabi Psalms took place. However, Rev. Young asserts: "I have not been able to verify this from any other source."[31] Rev. George Lawrence Thakur Das was a bright convert from Hindu religion who served as a UP evangelist in Sialkot, later becoming professor at the newly established theological seminary of the same mission.

None of the locals were part of the newly formed committee for the translation of Psalms into Punjabi; rather the committee consisted of missionaries alone. It seems a little strange and difficult to understand why no local had been included on the committee, considering the fact that a native had already served on a similar project for the translation of Urdu metrical psalms, and it had been proven that this work could not be done without the help of a local. It is not clear why the new committee did not consider the pros and cons of such a vital project without the inclusion of a native. Was

---

29. Stewart, *Life*, 304.
30. Young, *Sialkot*, 3.
31. Young, *Sialkot*, 5.

the committee unable to find a suitable local for this task? Was it felt that it was doable without any help from a native, or was the committee simply waiting for Rev. Imam-ud-Din Shahbaz to be released from his first project? Nevertheless, the progress made by this committee amounted to very little as it lacked the services of a native poet, and soon it was realized that the work could not go any further without the help of a local person gifted in the area of poetry.[32]

The committee for the metrical translation of the Psalter into Punjabi consisted of Rev. Imam-ud-Din Shahbaz, Miss Mary Rachel Martin, Rev. Robert Cummings, and Dr. David Smith Lytle, the head of the committee.[33] However, Emma Dean Anderson asserts that Miss Mary Jane Campbell was also part of the Psalms committee. Moreover, Miss Mary Rachel Martin was added to the committee at a later stage along with her sister Josephine Martin, Mrs. William McKelvey, and Henrietta Cowden.[34] Miss Emma Dean Anderson came to India with Mr. and Mrs. Lytle and Miss Calhoun in 1881.

Nevertheless, the roles of Henrietta Cowden, Josephine Martin, and Mrs. William McKelvey at later stages of the Punjabi metrical psalms has also been affirmed by Rev. Young.[35] One thing that seems to be doubtful is the mention of Rev. Robert Cummings as a committee member by Rev. Young.

The records of missionaries who served in India, provided by Emma Dean Anderson, show that Rev. Robert Cummings entered the mission field in 1920, which means that he joined the mission long after the committee for the Psalter had been established in 1890. However, it seems very probable that Rev. Robert Cummings has been mixed up with his father, Rev. Dr. Thomas Cummings, who served with the United Presbyterian Mission in India from 1889 to 1907.[36] The formation of the Psalms committee and the publication of the first cycle of Punjabi metrical psalms took place between 1890 and 1892. Not only the dates indicate that it was probably Thomas Cummings who served on the committee for Psalms, but his excellent skills and unique gifting in language-related matters are also noteworthy in this regard. After his arrival in 1889 Miss Anderson writes of him: "In Pasrur he was compelled to take up the study of the Punjabi by ear, quite without the aid of eye."[37] Dr. Thomas Cumming's son, Rev. Robert Cummings, was

32. Stewart, *Life*, 304.
33. Stewart, *Life*, 304.
34. Anderson and Campbell, *Shadow*, 114.
35. Young, *Sialkot*, 4–5.
36. Anderson and Campbell, *Shadow*, 361.
37. Anderson and Campbell, *Shadow*, 175.

also known as an expert in language-teaching matters, who, while using his father's methodology, taught a large group of missionaries belonging to various missions in India at the Landour Language School in 1939. The Psalms committee members will be discussed briefly later, and some important aspects of the life of Rev. Imam-ud-Din Shahbaz will be focused on in detail.

The first work of the committee for the Punjabi Psalter was published in 1892; it was a collection of fifty-five psalms that had been furnished with musical notations mainly being prepared by Dr. Lytle. The title given to the first publication was: *Zabur Punjabi Nazm Men Tarjuma Kiya Gaya* (Psalms Translated in Punjabi Verse).[38] This selection of psalms was published in Roman script; and the preface indicates that there were plans for its publication in Persian script before long. The selections of fifty-five psalms are found in the following sequence:

| 1. Ps 1 | 2. Ps 2 | 3. Ps 3 | 4. Ps 4 | 5. Ps 5 |
|---|---|---|---|---|
| 6. Ps 19 | 7. Ps 117 | 8. Ps 23 | 9. Ps 14 | 10. Ps 130 |
| 11. Ps 15 | 12. Ps 22 | 13. Ps 23 | 14. Ps 100 | 15. Ps 95 |
| 16. Ps 113 | 17. Ps 31 | 18. Ps 96 | 19. Ps 51 | 20. Ps 22 |
| 21. Ps 91 | 22. Ps 127 | 23. Ps 34 | 24. Ps 36 | 25. Ps 27 |
| 26. Ps 24 | 27. Ps 146 | 28. Ps 103 | 29. Ps 103 | 30. Ps 136 |
| 31. Ps 22 (vv. 11–22) | 32. Ps 5 | 33. Ps 8 | 34. Ps 24 (v. 7–10) | 35. Ps 67 |
| 36. Ps 85 (vv. 8–13) | 37. Ps 51 (vv. 6–14) | 38. Ps 11 | 39. Ps 33 | 40. Ps 33 (vv. 18–22) |
| 41. Ps 30 | 42. Ps 1 | 43. Ps 18 | 44. Ps 18 | 45. Ps 18 |
| 46. Ps 91 (vv. 9–16) | 47. Ps 96 (v. 8–13) | 48. Ps 16 | 49. Ps 22 (vv. 11–21) | 50. Ps 90 |
| 51. Ps 72 (vv. 17–20) | 52. Ps 19 (vv. 7–14) | 53. Ps 51 (vv. 15–19) | 54. Ps 146 (vv. 6–10) | 55. Ps 122 |

The arrangement of psalms in the 1892 edition is not done according to the sequential number but according to the tune on which they have been set. For example, Psalm 117 comes after Psalm 19, which means that the tune for Psalm 19 should be used for Psalm 117, as well. Although different sections from a single psalm (e.g., Ps 18) are found in this edition, exact verse numbers are not provided for all psalms. An alphabetical index of psalms has been provided at the end. The musical notations are not provided for

---

38. The first edition of the Punjabi Psalter was published from Benares by Medical Hall Press in 1892.

each psalm—for example, Psalms 8, 33, 91, and 122 are without notations, but it is suggested that they be sung to the same tune as Psalm 2 or 3. Psalm 22 (vv. 1–10) is the only one that is in the Urdu language but has still found a place among the Punjabi Psalms. What could be the possible reason for the inclusion of an Urdu psalm in the first publication of the Punjabi Psalter is unclear.

The minutes of the United Presbyterian General Assembly of 1894 records that "selections from the Psalms have been published in the Punjabi" and that, as a result, the Punjabi Psalms gained huge popularity as they were warmly welcomed and greatly appreciated by the ordinary people.[39] Stewart describes their popularity in this way: "Their use at present is even more extensive. Scarcely anything else is now sung in our village congregations, at melas, or in bazaar work."[40] The esteem of the *Bhajans* is further described by Miss Angus of the *Zenana* (women) mission: "*Bhajans* are a wonderful assistance in opting both houses and minds, particularly in country districts. The singing proves an irresistible attraction to those who would refuse to listen to the Scriptures; and the learning of a hymn lays the founding for teaching."[41] It seems that the first publication was done on a trial basis, yet after seeing its enthralling popularity the committee was reactivated in 1895 so that the entire Psalter could be translated into Punjabi and sung to local tunes.[42] Rev. Young writes that the entire Punjabi metrical psalms were accomplished in 1916 and that in 1905 two thousand copies of the first edition were published, but later in a correcting note he writes: "Since writing the above I have seen a music edition of the Punjabi Psalm dated 1908." It is very likely that he was referring to the 1908 edition when he mentions the 1905 edition. As a matter of fact, it was the 1908 edition that was published with two thousand copies. This was printed at the medical hall press in Benares with the title: *Punjabi Zabur: Desi Ragan Vich* (Punjabi Psalms: In Local Melodies).

This was published in Roman Urdu with Western notations. The arrangement and distribution of Psalms was done according to the American Psalter.[43] For example, Psalm 119 is divided into twenty-two parts, whereas parts 1 and 3 of the same psalm are set to more than one tune. The preface to the 1908 edition of the Punjabi Psalms states that out of all the books that have been written for God's praise to this day, the book of Psalms in

---

39. UPCUSA, *Minutes of the Thirty-Sixth General Assembly*, 507.
40. Stewart, *Life*, 304.
41. Murdoch, *Manual*, 473.
42. Young, *Sialkot*, 3.
43. UPCNA, *Annual Report*, 216.

the Bible is the best. It is the only book for divine praise. It is the only book that has been set aside by God for praise. It is the only one that is appropriate for all ages, territories, generations, languages, and human conditions. Only this suits equally to the young and the old, rich and poor, scholars and illiterates, sick and healthy, those full of joy and mourners, weak and strong, and the living and those facing death. This is the only book that Christ himself used for praise.[44]

The selection of fifty-five psalms that had been published in the 1892 edition is specified as an old edition in the 1908 edition, and contrary to the 1892 edition, the numbering of psalms in 1908 is found in sequence. Moreover, at the end of Psalm 150, alternative tunes for Psalms 37 (part 1), 5 (part 1), and 9 (part 1) have been introduced, while the list of doxologies and meters are provided toward the end. However, the poetry of the first psalm in the 1892 and 1908 editions differs, as the words have been changed and rearranged, although the number of stanzas remains the same. Moreover, the tune has also been modified. Similarly, slight changes and rearrangements can also be observed in the poetry of Psalms 14 and 23. Along with the old tunes for Psalms 4, 5, 15, 19, and 23, the new tunes have also been introduced in the 1908 edition, whereas the tune for Psalm 14 has been maintained as the 1892 edition. In the 1892 edition the notation for each psalm was not provided. For example, it was suggested that Psalm 130 be sung to the same tune as Psalm 14. However, a notation for each Psalm has been provided in the 1908 edition. Contrary to the 1892 edition where verse numbers were provided for some psalms, verse numbering has not been provided in the 1908 edition.

Two psalms are found in Urdu instead of Punjabi in the 1908 edition: Psalm 22 (parts 1 and 2), both parts set to different tunes, and Psalm 119 (part 10). Psalm 22 (part 1) had been published in the 1892 edition in Urdu; in the 1908 edition it has been highlighted as an old edition. It is interesting to observe that both parts of Psalm 22 in Urdu have been omitted in the recent editions of the Punjabi Psalms. In the following year, the Punjabi Psalms were published in the Persian script in 1909. Five thousand five hundred copies were printed at Nol Kishore Printing Press in Lahore; these were published without the Western notations.[45] The preface in this edition is the same as the one found in the 1908 edition published in the Roman script. A list of psalms sung on the same meters is provided in the 1909 Persian script edition: Psalms 8, 12 (part 2), 31 (parts 2 and 3), 37 (part 1), 39 (part 2), 49

---

44. The 1908 ed. of the Punjabi Psalms, with the title *Punjabi Zabur: Desi Ragan Vich*, was published from Benares by Medical Hall Press in 1908; translation mine.

45. The Punjabi Psalm in the Persian script, with the title *Zabur: Desi Ragan Vich*, was published from Lahore by Nol Kishore in 1908; transliteration mine.

(part 1), 54, 56 (part 1), 69 (part 1), 69 (part 3), 70, 71 (parts 4 and 5), 74 (part 4), 79 (part 3), 80 (parts 2 and 3), 85 (part 1), 89 (parts 2 and 4), 90 (part 2), 97 (part 2), 98, 102 (part 1), 104 (parts 4 and 5), 108 (part 3), 109 (part 2), 111 (part 1), 118 (part 2), 119 (parts 2, 4, 6, 7, 9–11, 13, 19 21), 125, 132 (part 1), 137, 140 (part 2), 141 (part 1), 143 (part 1), and 145 (part 2).

Moreover, a list of verses from the psalms suggested to be sung at the end of a worship meeting is also provided: Psalms 28 (part 2, vv. 6–10), 67 (vv. 6–8), and 72 (part 4, entire psalm).

The 1908 edition of the Punjabi *Zabur* is a rare book. In 2009 I visited a Baptist church in London. After the service, the pastor said he has a book that he would like to show me. I could not believe that he was showing me the 1908 edition of the Punjabi *Zabur* that was given to him by a deceased missionary who had served in India. He was very kind to gift me the book so that I can make use of it for my study on the Punjabi *Zabur*.

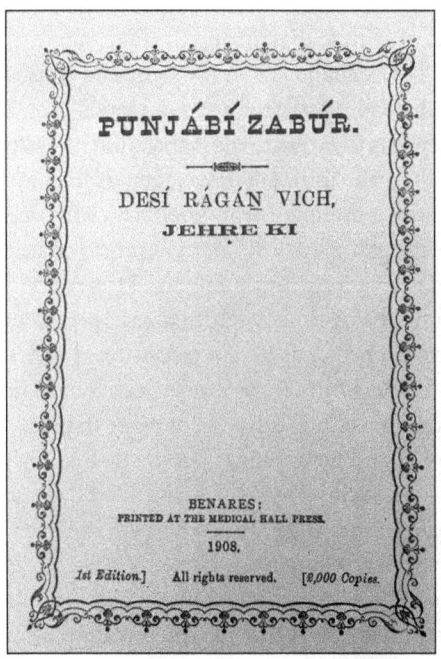

**1908 Edition of the Punjabi** *Zabur*.

## 2.3 The Methodology

It is crucial to look at the methodology and procedures that were taken up by the Psalms committee in preparation of the Punjabi metrical psalms. In general, the psalms were first translated into the Punjabi language in a versified form; this step was dependent upon and carried out by Rev. Imam-ud-Din Shahbaz, the poet and translator. Rev. F. Y. Pressly of the Associate Reformed Presbyterian Church, who had gathered the data on the Punjabi Psalms and gladly shared it with Rev. Young, says:

> It is the writer's privilege to know, personally, Babu Sadiq, who, as a young man, acted as a reader for Dr. Shahbaz. Babu Sadiq recounts that he would read over and over a portion from the Psalms to Dr. Shahbaz. Then, verse by verse, and paragraph by paragraph, Dr. Shahbaz would in this way work out the correct Punjabi metre.[46]

It is significant to note that during the later stages of the Punjabi Psalter, Rev. Imam-ud-Din Shahbaz lost his sight and thus was unable to read for himself, so Babu Sadiq assisted him as a reader.[47]

The next step was to evaluate the translation of psalms using the original text of the Psalter. The third and last stage was the musical arrangements of the Punjabi metrical psalms. The missionaries with musical skills worked tirelessly to collect data. Fredrick Stock mentions that, in order to collect data and listen to the various commonly used tunes, the missionaries spent a considerable amount of time at ordinary shopping and eating places.[48] Rev. Young adds that help was also received from the *mirasis*, a group of nomadic singers.[49] The *mirasis* have always been looked down on by society. Living in groups in tents, they travel from place to place. Their only source of income is singing and entertaining people by making jokes, particularly on special occasions such as weddings and birthdays, and they normally carry musical instruments with them wherever they go.[50] In rural areas in the Punjab province they can often be seen at *melas*, fairs, and festivals. These can be annual festivals in remembrance of local saints, seasonal festivals or purely entertaining events in which eating, shopping, and amusement spots are provided.

---

46. Pressly, "Zabur," 9.
47. Young, *Sialkot*, 3.
48. Stock, *People*, 120.
49. Young, *Sialkot*, 4.
50. Sauli, "Circulation," 191.

The involvement of *mirasis* in the musical arrangements of the psalms could put many Punjabi Christians in a rather shocking and embarrassing situation today. The majority of Punjabi Christians would be unaware of this, and those who know would either hesitate or avoid mentioning it. It is not so much because of the inferior social class of this wandering group, but primarily due to the sole identity of *mirasis* as entertainers.[51] As a matter of fact the word *mirasi* is often used as a term of insult in the Pakistani society.[52] However, their participation in setting up some of the local tunes of psalms is a fact that cannot be ignored, although some Punjabi Christians in Pakistan would simply deny it. This is understandable, since Punjabi Christians would not like the Psalter to be viewed as entertainment.

A gifted missionary in music, Mary Rachel Martin, with the help of Miss Henrietta Cowden, Josephine Martin, and Mrs. William McKelvey, wrote down the musical tunes in Western notations so that the Western missionaries could also sing and play them.[53] In an introductory note in the 1908 edition of the Punjabi Psalms that was published with Western notations, it has been mentioned that as the Eastern and the Western musical tunes and system differ considerably, an attempt has been made to provide a close resemblance, and thus the notations are to be regarded as a guide rather than a work of total accuracy.[54] It is essential to mention that the Indian music is not written. Rather, it is learned by ear and practice.[55]

In this regard, the account of Miss Henrietta Cowden is noteworthy:

> *An Indian, Radha Kishan, a professional Hindu singer, was found who agreed to give time and come to our aid. He said he knew all the tunes of India very well. This proved to be true, I believe. He went to Dr. Shahbaz who had already prepared some of the poems. The two would read the poem together until the singer caught the rhythm, then he would fit a tune to that rhythm and meter, and come back to Dr. Shahbaz and sing it to him. If he accepted it, the singer brought the copy to me and sang it until I got it into my ear. Sometimes ten time were required, sometimes fewer, sometimes with many repetitions for one phrase. I then wrote it, as I had heard it, on music paper and sang it to him. If he approved, that particular Psalm was ready to go to the printers. If not satisfactory, then it had to be corrected.*[56]

51. Nayyar, "Punjab," 764.
52. Qureshi, "Destigmatising," 183.
53. Anderson and Campbell, *Shadow*, 114.
54. *Punjabi Zabur*, vi.
55. Reck, "India," 195.
56. Young, *Sialkot*, 4.

In general, it is likely that the psalms were translated first and the tunes were chosen later. However, it was also done vice versa, the meter being selected first, and later the poetry adjusted to the meter. The methodology used in the selection of tunes for some of the psalms faced resistance, as certain tunes were viewed to have an association with worldly music and it was anticipated that the use of such tunes could cause harm to the Christian testimony.[57] In a way, it was a genuine concern, as this could have put the Psalter as religious songs in the category of worldly music. Surprisingly, such doubts were found to be baseless. It seems that, in spite of the fact that some of these psalms were set to folk tunes, the focus was on the content and the Psalms were regarded with reverence and great respect by the Punjabi believers. Nevertheless, there is no doubt that at that time the use of popular folk tunes for some of the psalms assisted in the singing and memorization of these psalms.

Today, the melodies of the Punjabi Psalms cannot be associated with the current popular tunes found in Pakistani secular music. The compositions of the Punjabi Psalms can clearly be recognized as unique, although at that time they were feared to be associated with the secular tunes of that time. Today there is a strong resistance in using secular tunes for religious purposes among the Protestant denominations in Pakistan. With the advance of media and technology it is not difficult to identify a musical composition with something that already exists, and the concerns about using secular tunes for religious purposes remain the same, as it is viewed as a possible hindrance to the Christian witness. Although this method worked for some of the Punjabi psalms, it has generally been discouraged in Pakistan to avoid the possible harm involved. However, among some circles, especially in the rural Punjab, such a practice is still followed to some extent where various Christian songs are put to popular folk tunes. It is interesting to note that a few of the Punjabi psalms that were put on the Western tunes are today still sung to Western melodies. Rev. Young mentions that Psalms 99 (vv. 1–5), 139 (vv. 1–6), 145 (vv. 8–13), and 150 are set to Auld Lang Syne, Nettleton, Follow Me, and Clementine, respectively. Moreover, Psalms 47 and 85 (vv. 8–13) are partially sung to Western tunes.[58]

The Punjabi Psalms were regarded as *bhajans*, as their melodies were composed on *bhajana* style.[59] The word *bhajana* with Sanskrit origin means "adoration, worship." According to Herbert Arthur: "The *Bhajana* is a favorite form of religious musical recital, in which a choir sings after a

---

57. Stock, *People*, 120.
58. Young, *Sialkot*, 5.
59. Stewart, *Life*, 304.

leader, accompanied by an orchestra."[60] The *bhajana* style is commonly used in India for religious worship and consists of singing for devotional and meditational purposes.[61] James Massey mentions that the first occurrence of the root *bhaj* is found in the Hindu Scriptures, namely Upanishad, and that the word for religious worship, *bhakti*, comes from the same root.[62] Writing of the Punjabi Psalter, Campbell asserts that some of these *Zaburs* have similarities with *Kirtans* in terms of their melodies; the *Kirtans* are regularly sung by the followers of Sikhism in Gurdwaras, their worship places.[63] A group of missionaries in Ahmednager are said to have successfully used the Christian songs in *Kirtan* style.[64]

It is worth noting that the language used in the Gurdwara for singing and teaching is Punjabi. Although *bhajana* and *kirtan* style of worship carries similarity, the latter is more of an activity in which the religious instructor explains words by pausing between phrases. Moreover, *bhajan* can be performed by anyone whereas *kirtan* has to be led only by the religious instructor.[65] The Punjabi Psalms fits better into the category of *bhajans* than *kirtans*, as words are not explained by pausing while singing and they do not have to be led by the religious instructor alone.

Among the Punjabi congregations in Pakistan, the word *bhajan* is not used anymore for making a reference to the Psalms, since *Zabur* is the common term in use. However, among the churches in the rural parts of Sindh province in the south of Pakistan, the word *bhajan* is preferred for Christian songs, including the Psalter. These churches consist of believers converted from a tribal Hindu background, and their languages belong to the family of Rajasthani and Gujarati language that are used on both sides of the Thar Desert.[66] Contrary to the Punjabi congregations in Pakistan, among the Indian Punjabi churches some use the term *bhajan* in reference to the Punjabi Psalms.[67] With regard to the Indian melodies, William Hunter asserts that this music may sound odd to strangers; however, "some of its tunes are most delighted. Their very weirdness, wildness, plaintiveness and curious

60. Popley, *Music*, 91.
61. Acharya, "Bhajan," 435.
62. Massey, "Bhakti," 138.
63. Campbell, "Church," 160.
64. Murdoch, *Manual*, 139.
65. Thompson, "Gujurat," 1018.
66. Jacobsen, *Christians*, 116.
67. Massey, "Bhakti," 135.

repetitions chain the attention and entrance the heart even of a foreigner, and to a native are as irresistible as the songs of paradise."[68]

In sum, it was the pioneering work of Andrew Gordon and Samuel Martin on the Urdu metrical psalms that paved way for the poetic psalms in Punjabi. The success of the 1892 trial version led to the availability of the entire book of Psalms in the versified form in 1908. The beautiful melodies of these psalms were put after the *bhajan* style. Cultural fondness was given preference in gathering musical data for these psalms. The United Presbyterian missionaries prepared the musical notations, the Muslim convert Imam-ud-Din Shahbaz put them in versified form, and a Hindu singer named Radha Kishan and the wandering minstrels assisted with tunes of the psalms in Punjabi.

---

68. Stewart, *Life*, 304.

# II

# The Contributors for the Punjabi Psalter

THIS CHAPTER FOCUSES ON individuals who contributed to the making of the Punjabi Psalms. Who were these individuals, where did they come from, and what specific role did each of them play in the story of the Punjabi *Zaburs*? The committee for the Punjabi Psalms consisted of Rev. Dr. David Smith Lytle, Miss Mary Jane Campbell, Rev. Dr. Thomas Fulton Cummings, Rev. Dr. Imam-ud-Din Shahbaz, and the lady musicians including Miss Mary Henrietta Cowden, Mrs William Mckelvey, Miss Mary Rachel Martin, and Miss Emma Josephine Martin. Particular attention will be given to the leading figure, Rev. Dr. Imam-ud-Din Shahbaz, who played an integral role in the compiling of these psalms. An attempt has been made in this chapter to uncover aspects of the life and poetry of Dr. Shahbaz that have not been explored before. In general, when people talk about the making of the Punjabi Psalms, there is no mention of the contributions made by the missionaries. This is simply due to the lack of information available on the individuals who had been involved in this work. The following pages will help to appreciate and acknowledge the teamwork of missionaries and Dr. Imam-ud-Din Shahbaz in the making of the Punjabi Psalter.

## 1. REV. DR. DAVID SMITH LYTLE

Dr. Lytle, a graduate of Monmouth College and Xenia Theological Seminary, was born in Pennsylvania and joined the mission field in India with the United Presbyterian Mission in 1881. He was ordained shortly before his arrival in India; besides teaching he had spent considerable time in farming as his family business. After his arrival in India he was based in Sialkot where he was in-charge of the United Presbyterian mission work. The focus of his work was the village people of Sialkot district. Traveling on camels and living in tents, he went from village to village in Sialkot preaching the gospel along with a few other missionaries and native evangelists.[1] His personal diaries show that he was enthusiastic about preaching, baptizing those who confessed their faith, and making use of the Psalter for public worship as he traveled from village to village. On one occasion, about his visit to Mahanwala village and talking about an old man, he writes: "When he heard us singing a psalm, he said: 'That is one they sing at Mirali', thus showing the close attention paid." On another occasion in Sabzkot village he writes, "On Saturday evening took our camp chairs, lanterns and candles with us, and dedicated the new church-singing on this occasion the 127th Psalm."[2] He was often found engaged in discussions with seekers of the truth, providing them guidance.[3] This became even more important as the numbers of inquirers were beginning to become greater than those already Christians. Lytle was head of the committee formed for translating the psalms into Punjabi and putting them into Eastern melodies. The notations found in the 1892 edition of the Punjabi Psalms were prepared by Lytle, a selection of fifty-five psalms. Mary Jane Campbell writes: "Mr. Lytle did an excellent work when he prepared these psalms in Punjabi, and he has done more perhaps than any other person to make the psalms popular with the common people in the Punjabi."[4]

---

1. Gordon, *India*, 454.
2. Gordon, *India*, 454–60.
3. Stewart, *Life*, 302.
4. PCUSA Archives—letter dated June 11, 1892, from Mary Jane Campbell.

**Rev. Dr. David Smith Lytle.**

Besides his involvement in the Punjabi metrical psalms, Lytle was involved in helping run a small lithographic press, a school for boys in Sialkot city area, and in serving as a pastor for a local congregation. In the minutes of the United Presbyterian General Assembly in 1896, Lytle is listed as a minister in Sialkot.[5] The work of Scripture translation in the language of a common man was very much on the heart of Lytle, and he had the privilege of making arrangements for the preparation of the Punjabi New Testament in Persian character.[6] After serving in the mission field for about nineteen years, Lytle passed away due to dysentery in 1899, at the age of fifty-two.[7] This suggests that the 1892 edition was prepared under his supervision as the head of the committee for the Punjabi Psalter. Moreover, it may be asserted that he largely contributed from 1892–1899 in preparing the 1908 edition of the Punjabi Psalms. However, his passing away in 1899 indicates that from

5. UPCUSA, *Minutes of the Thirty-Seventh General Assembly*.
6. Stewart, *Life*, 302.
7. PCUSA Archives, 6705.

1900 to 1908 someone else took over the chairmanship responsibilities. It is likely that the project of translating psalms in Punjabi verse was then led by Miss Mary Jane Campbell, as Emma Dean Anderson mentions that Miss Campbell worked with Lytle in preparing the 1892 edition of the Punjabi Psalms.[8]

## 2. MISS MARY JANE CAMPBELL

Mary Jane Campbell of Monmouth, Illinois, arrived in India early in 1885. First studying the Urdu language for a year; she moved on to study the Punjabi, Persian, and Hindi languages in Sialkot and Gujranwala. After which she had the honor to be chosen as the first young lady to work among the village people in Zafarwal, a town near Sialkot. This was indeed special in a male-dominant society, as living and serving in the countryside was certainly a difficult task for a single lady. It was no less than a real challenge for a young lady to move freely and serve effectively among the villagers. Even today after over a century, it would be a huge challenge for a young single woman to live by herself and work in the countryside in rural Punjab, as it would create serious cultural issues. Nevertheless, the confidence shown by her seniors speaks of the gifts and capabilities that they saw in Miss Campbell.

Mary Jane Campbell was gifted in languages and made speedy progress in language learning. After a year of her arrival in India she said: "By the end of 1886 I was able to speak the sweet Punjabi tongue in a fairly satisfactory manner. Friends used to say I had even learned the gestures used by the women."[9] William Anderson writes of Miss Campbell: "Going to the field while only a girl and having unusual linguistic ability, she mastered the Punjabi language."[10] Mary Jane Campbell was responsible for the publishing of 1892 trial version of the Psalms in Punjabi and had zealously been involved in teaching them to school girls and Christians in Zafarwal.[11] She was also part of the Zenana (Women) Missionary Society of the United Presbyterian Church in India, in which she served as a correspondence secretary.[12] She was awarded the highest civil award of the British government in India, called *Kaisar-i-Hind* (Emperor of India), in recognition of her

8. Anderson and Campbell, *Shadow*, 114.
9. Anderson and Campbell, *Shadow*, 48.
10. Anderson, introduction to Campbell, *Power*, 7.
11. PCUSA Archives, letter dated August 6, 1892, from Rachel Martin.
12. PCUSA Archives, letter dated February 23, 1891, from Mary Jane Campbell.

efforts and services against the use of opium and alcohol in the country.[13] This imperial medal was given to individuals for their extraordinary services for society, and interestingly, Gandhi had also received this award. The award shows that she had a deep concern for the society and was actively involved in keeping the society safe from drugs.

Miss Campbell was an impressive speaker whose speeches made an impact on the listeners; they were stirring and remarkable.[14] Miss Campbell served in the mission field for forty-two long years, from 1884 to 1926. This suggests that she was involved in preparation of the Punjabi metrical psalms from its beginning to completion. She was a talented author and focused her writings on the women of India that include: *One Hundred Girls of India* (1899); *Daughters of India* (1908); and *The Power-House at Pathankot: What Some Girls of India Wrought by Prayer* (1918). Additionally, she translated Christian materials into the vernacular, such as "Punjabi *Ilm-i-Ilahi*" (The Punjabi Theology).[15]

**Miss Mary Jane Campbell.**

13. Anderson and Campbell, *Shadow*, 349.
14. *Tenth Anniversary Memorial*, 222.
15. Steward, *Life*, 306.

## 3. REV. DR. THOMAS FULTON CUMMINGS

In the previous chapter, Dr. Cummings has already been mentioned as a man of outstanding linguistic ability and a pioneer in introducing language-learning techniques and methods. He served in the mission field for nineteen years, from 1889 to 1907. The dates indicate that he was part of the Punjabi Psalms committee from its early stages, and that he actively took part in the preparation of 1892 and 1908 editions of the Punjabi Psalms. Cummings served in Pasrur, a town in Sialkot, where he experimented in the various methods of language learning, and baptized new believers.

In the minutes from the 1893 United Presbyterian General Assembly, Rev. Thomas Cummings is listed among the United Presbyterian ministers in Pasrur, Sialkot.[16] However, in the 1896 minutes, Cummings has been listed as a minister based in Gujranwala.[17] Later on he taught as a lecturer of phonetics at Union Theological Seminary (1918–1925) and Drew Theological Seminary (1918–1933) and as a visiting lecturer at the Canadian School of Missions in Toronto. Cummings was also author of a number of books that include: *Roman-Urdu Primer* (1905); *Panjabi Manual and Grammar: A Guide to the Colloquial Panjabi of the Northern Punjab* (1912); *How to Learn a Language: An Exposition of the Phonetic Inductive Method for Foreign Resident Language Students; A Direct, Practical, Scientific Way of Mastering Any Foreign Language* (1916), and *An Urdu Manual of the Phonetic, Inductive or Direct Method: Based on the Gospel of John, with a Progressive Introduction to the Construction of the Urdu Language* (1916).[18] He was regarded as a "Scholar-Saint" and "linguist missionary."[19] In recognition of Rev. Cummings immense services, Miss Anderson writes that his "books on the teaching of Urdu and Punjabi have helped so many missionaries to be more efficient as linguists."[20]

## 4. MARTIN SISTERS, HENRIETTA COWDEN, AND WILLIAM MCKELVEY

Miss M. Henrietta Cowden, Mrs William M. McKelvey, Miss Mary Rachel Martin, and her sister Miss Emma Josephine Martin helped particularly

---

16. UPCUSA, *Minutes of the Thirty-Fifth General Assembly*, 427.
17. UPCUSA, *Minutes of the Thirty-Eighth General Assembly*, 221.
18. These books were published by the Sialkot Mission of the United Presbyterian Church of North America from Gujranwala.
19. PCUSA Archives, 6554.
20. Anderson and Campbell, *Shadow*, 128.

in the musical arrangements of the Punjabi metrical psalms. The above-mentioned women served in the mission field in India from 1905–1937, 1902–1927, 1890–1935, and 1896–1931, respectively, and the former passed away while in service. Although the record shows that Miss Mary Rachel Martin was already in the mission field while the 1892 edition of the Punjabi Psalms was being worked on, her participation in preparing this edition seems rather limited. First, Stewart comments that the notations in the 1892 edition were mainly prepared by David Smith Lytle.[21] And second, Emma Dean Anderson comments that Miss Mary Rachel Martin got involved at later stages of the Psalms project.[22] Nevertheless, all of the above-mentioned women were involved in preparing Western notations for a rather extensive edition of the Punjabi Psalms that was published from Benares in 1908.

Not much is known about these lady musicians who worked day and night in preparing Western notations for the Punjabi metrical psalms. Miss Mary Rachel Martin was of a rather calm and gentle character, very much gifted and skilled in music. Writing of her involvement in the Punjabi metrical psalms, Emma Dean Anderson mentions: "She secured an elderly Punjabi musician and hour after hour for months she listened while he played on his sattar—seven stringed instrument—and she picked out the notes and put them in place so they could be sung by Westerners."[23] Writing of her sister Rachel Martin, Miss Josephine Martin asserts that the Psalms in Punjabi is "one of her monuments."[24] Miss Emma Josephine Martin had been involved in education; she became in charge of a girls' school in Pathankot when Miss Mary Jane Campbell was given a new assignment. For a short while she also taught at Kinnaird College for Women, a renowned educational institution in Lahore. While Rachel Martin "proofread the music," Josephine Martin "proofread the words" for the Punjabi *Zaburs*.[25] The two sisters Mary Rachel Martin and Emma Josephine Martin were the daughters of Samuel Martin, who helped with the Urdu metrical psalms, and their childhood was spent in Sialkot.[26] Mrs. McKelvey was the wife of Rev. William McKelvey, and had served in the Lyallpur district (the present-day city of Faisalabad, in Pakistan). Miss Mary Henrietta Cowden had also served in the Lyallpur district.[27] After serving in India, she went to Egypt to con-

---

21. Stewart, *Life*, 304.
22. Anderson and Campbell, *Shadow*, 114.
23. Anderson and Campbell, *Shadow*, 114.
24. Martin, *Father*, 47.
25. Ballantyne, "Samuel Martin," 7.
26. UPCNA, *Annual Report*, 117.
27. UPCNA, *Handbook*, 134.

tinue serving with the United Presbyterian Mission. On the application for appointment as a missionary with the United Presbyterian Mission, she writes that she can lead in singing and plays a little piano. Henrietta Cowden was motivated to serve in India, when Miss Emma Dean Anderson spoke about the Christian work in India at her church.[28]

The task given to these women was very challenging and time consuming. It is principally due to the differences between the Eastern and Western musical systems, and it can be assumed that these women must have spent considerable time understanding the way local music works. As mentioned earlier, in contrast to Western music, Indian music is not written, it was nevertheless crucial to write down musical notations for the Punjabi metrical psalms for two reasons. The first, already mentioned by Emma Dean Anderson, was that the Western missionaries could also sing these psalms.[29] It was necessary as they were leading local congregations and were involved in evangelizing from place to place. Thus, it was expected of them not only to be able to sing and play these psalms but also to teach them to the locals wherever they went. The second reason is that, since Indian music is not written, it was very easy for these psalms to be sung to a totally different tune or with great variation. Such free movement in Indian music is often done by people according to their own inclination.[30] Thus, it was necessary to preserve the tunes of the Punjabi Psalter in a written musical form. It obviously did not help the locals as the Western musical notation was totally alien to them. On the other hand, it helped the missionaries in maintaining and teaching the set melodies of these Punjabi psalms in their respective fields.

## 5. REV. DR. IMAM-UD-DIN SHAHBAZ (CA. 1844–1921)

### 5.1. Conversion and Baptism

> *The greatest and the most lasting change was made in the area of music when the Rev. Imam-ud-Din Shahbaz translated the Psalms into metrical Punjabi and set them to Punjabi tunes . . . adding to the depth and appeal of Christian faith.*[31]

The story of the Punjabi Psalter is incomplete without mentioning Rev. Dr. Imam-ud-Din Shahbaz, a poet, teacher, theologian, pastor, and translator.

28. PCUSA Archives, 6562.
29. Anderson and Campbell, *Shadow*, 114.
30. Jairazbhoy, *Rāgs*, 124.
31. Webster, *Social History*, 188.

John Newton, a foremost missionary in the Punjab region, who produced a Punjabi grammar book (1851) and the Punjabi New Testament (1868), earnestly sought God to raise "bright jewels" for Christ within the land of India.[32] At the completion of the fiftieth year of the Presbyterian Mission work in India, he longed to see "far greater results" in the coming days. Dr. Shahbaz, a key person responsible for the preparation of psalms into the Punjabi language, can truly be regarded as a genuine response by God to Newton's prayer. His name, Imam-ud-Din, meaning "leader" of the "faith," truly reflects his life.[33] It is imperative to mention that, as a general practice in the Indian subcontinent, it is customary for poets to give themselves a pen name which eventually becomes their identity. Writing of the Christian poets of the Urdu language, Qurban mentions that Rev. Imam-ud-Din chose the noun "Shahbaz" as his pen name, which means "the royal falcon," its synonym "Shaheen" is also well used.[34] The title, beyond doubt, speaks of his profound vision and enthusiastic traits. The national poet of Pakistan—namely, Sir Dr. Mohammad Iqbal (1877–1938), born in Sialkot—also made frequent use of the falcon metaphor in his poetry, which became his identity as a poet.

32. Newton, *Presbyterian Mission*, 149.
33. Hayyim, *Farhang*, 140, 889.
34. Qurban, *Shuara*, 73.

Rev. Dr. Imam-ud-Din Shahbaz.

Imam-ud-Din Shahbaz was born to Muslim parents around 1844 in Zafarwal, a town in the east of Sialkot. Rev. Young writes that Dr. Shahbaz first came across the Christian message at the age of ten, took much interest after listening to the preaching done by the missionaries, and was baptized by Rev. Robert Clark in 1866 in Amritsar.[35] His conversion and baptism were a result of the labor of the Church Missionary Society (CMS).[36] Two questions arise here: first, who led him to Christ; and second, why did his baptism take place in Amritsar? Although a concrete answer to the former is difficult, a couple of things give indications in this regard. It is possible that Dr. Shahbaz met someone like Rev. Thomas Henry Fitzpatrick, who traveled from town to town and guided the inquirers concerning the Christian faith.

This is suggested by a couple of examples, the first being a man named Mian Paulus, who was the landlord of Narowal, a town in the south of Zafarwal, and who was guided by Rev. Fitzpatrick concerning the Christian faith. Later on, Mian Paulus came with Rev. Fitzpatrick to Amritsar so that

35. Young, *Sialkot*, 3.
36. Gordon, *India*, 433.

he could be baptized there. Similarly, Shamaun, a resident of a village near Amritsar, was led by Rev. Fitzpatrick to be baptized in Amritsar.[37] The CMS work was started in Narowal in 1859, the area was famous among missionary circles for having the highest number of conversions from Islamic backgrounds.[38]

One may pause for a moment and wonder why these new converts were being taken to Amritsar for baptism. This may involve a number of reasons, including the high security risks to the new converts. However, the work of the Church Missionary Society was concentrated in Amritsar, the new converts were baptized and guided to the Christian faith there, and the work was also known as the Amritsar Mission.[39] Rev. Robert Clark and Rev. Thomas Fitzpatrick were not only the pioneer Christian missionaries to Amritsar but also the first from the Church of England to serve and evangelize among the non-Christians in Punjab. Dr. Shahbaz was baptized by Rev. Robert Clark, a graduate of the Trinity College Cambridge, "the venerable missionary of Amritsar" as he was called by Dr. Gordon.[40] It may well be possible that Rev. Imam-ud-Din Shahbaz himself decided to come to Amritsar to be baptized. In this regard, it is worth mentioning the great Anglican scholar and apologist of the Indian subcontinent Rev. Dr. Imad-ud-Din Lahiz, a convert and former preacher of the famous "royal mosque in Agra," India, who was also baptized by Robert Clark in the same year,[41] writes: "I went myself to Umritsar, and received baptism from the Rev. R. Clark, of the Church of England; and the chief reason why I went to be baptized by him was, that he was the first Missionary who had sent me the message of the Lord by letter to Lahore, and I therefore thought it right to be baptized by him; and, besides this, I thought much of his devotedness and zeal."[42]

The reason for Dr. Shahbaz's conversion is noteworthy. He was moved by the attitudes of the missionaries who did not react to all the disgrace, disrespect, mocking, and insulting that was done to them by the crowds. Being inspired by this, he decided to acquire the word of God, and as a result of the diligent study of God's word he became a determined inquirer for the truth. For Dr. Shahbaz the inspiration was the demonstration of Christian character and attitude toward the opponents. The phrase "actions speak louder

37. Clark, *Account, Society*, 36.
38. Anderson and Campbell, *Shadow*, 147.
39. Clark, *Account*, 36.
40. Gordon, *India*, 439.
41. Powell, "Faith," 230.
42. Satthianadhan, *Indian Christians*, 175.

than words" proved correct in his case. He was much disturbed regarding the final judgment, and talking on this topic to a wandering Muslim saint he was greatly disappointed by the following answer: "Son, my hairs are white, but I'm sorry to say I haven't so far begun to think about death."[43] The fear of the final judgment was also an integral reason in the conversion of Dr. Shahbaz's contemporaries, as they could not find a satisfying answer to this issue from their religious leaders. In this regard, Imad-ud-Din Lahiz's experience is worth mentioning: "All the time my heart was pierced as a thorn with the words, 'every mortal must necessary go to hell; it is obligatory on God to send all men once to hell, and afterwards He may pardon whom He will.'"[44]

The major work among the depressed class in Zafarwal, the hometown of Dr. Shahbaz, was done between 1882 and 1887, where there was more than one mission station, and the work among women was especially focused upon by Miss Mary Jane Campbell after her appointment in the area.[45] However, prior to that Dr. Gordon writes that every effort to evangelize in Zafarwal was faced with great opposition, and since there was not even one Christian, the city was not given much attention in terms of evangelistic activities.[46] The height of opposition shown toward the Christian message speaks of the immense difficulties and hardships that one had to face in becoming a follower of Christ. It was in such difficult conditions that Rev. Imam-ud-Din decided to become a Christian. The difficulties that new converts, especially those from non-depressed classes, had to go through in those days are noteworthy. In this regard, words of Stewart are worth noting: "Persons of any age, or of either sex, who succeed in running the initial gauntlet and entering the Christian fold, there is the almost inevitable loss of property, parents, husband or wife, children, friends and everything else which men hold dear. The new convert must begin life over again."[47] The decision to follow Christ involved great opposition and sufferings, but Rev. Imam-ud-Din was willing to receive baptism at any cost. Writing of what happened to a new convert after baptism in those days, Stewart mentions:

> Especially when he received Christian baptism—from that very hour his neighbours, of whatever creed, began to hate him with a malignant hatred, and his own near relatives became his bitterest enemies. This hatred was shown by refusing to give him food or water, forbidding persons to sell anything to him, turning him out

---

43. Young, *Sialkot*, 3.
44. Parker, *Children*, 105.
45. Anderson, *Shadow*, 43–47.
46. Gordon, *India*, 431.
47. Stewart, *Life*, 231.

*of house and home, depriving him of his just share of his father's property, setting his wife and children against him, cutting him off from all communication with them, raising a mob against him, beating him, threatening his life, shutting him up without food in a dark room, conveying him away in the night to parts unknown, administering poison, and other similar treatment. If any one felt inclined to speak a word in favour of the persecuted convert, he well knew that by so doing he would expose himself to similar contumely.*[48]

The baptism of converts from Muslim backgrounds has always been viewed by their community members as final confirmation of leaving one's religion to become a follower of Christ. In the majority of cases, these converts are faced with increased opposition after they have been baptized.[49] Nevertheless, the forerunner of the faith remained committed and persistent as a true disciple of Christ.

## 5.2. Teaching and Evangelistic Work with Church Missionary Society

After his baptism in Amritsar, Rev. Shahbaz got involved in evangelistic work with the Church Missionary Society. He had a great zeal to share the Christian message to many others who still had not heard it. In this regard, Rev. Robert Clark mentions Rev. Imam-ud-Din among the list of eight notable converts who had been trained at the Amritsar Mission School to carry on the proclamation and teaching of the Christian faith.[50] It was resolved at the conference held in 1875 that "Imam-u-din, of Umritsur, be appointed catechist, first grade, on a salary of thirty rupees." Moreover, Rev. Imam-ud-Din had the gift of teaching, and as a teacher he taught at schools affiliated with the Church Missionary Society in Amritsar, where the society had a number of schools.[51] Dr. Shahbaz took part in evangelistic and teaching activities with the Church Missionary Society from 1866 to 1880.[52]

Besides teaching and evangelizing, Rev. Imam-ud-Din had a special interest in poetry. It was his tremendous gift of poetry that led him to get involved with the translation of the psalms into Urdu and Punjabi. Rev.

---

48. Stewart, *Life*, 179.
49. Braswell, *Islam*, 154.
50. Clark, *Account*, 38.
51. Clark, *Account*, 32.
52. CMS Archives, minutes of the thirteenth General Conference of Church Missionaries, held in Punjab in 1875.

Shahbaz was creative and rather keen on experimenting innovative things in the field of poetry. In 1880 the United Presbyterian Mission organized a poetry competition so that a suitable person could be selected for the translation of psalms into Urdu, and Rev. Shahbaz was declared the winner. The competition was announced in a weekly Persian-Urdu magazine called *Nur Afshan* (The Spreading Light).[53] It was published from Ludhiana by the American Mission Press; the magazine played a vital role in encouraging and motivating the native Christians. His achievement as winner of poetry competitions speak of his immense talents.

## 5.3. Work in Gurdaspur and Translation of the Urdu Metrical Psalms

Rev. Shahbaz was assigned by the Church Missionary Society to take up his new responsibilities with the United Presbyterian Mission for the translation of Psalms. This transition took place in July 1880, and Rev. Shahbaz came to Gurdaspur (a city in the present-day Indian Punjab), where during the early stages of the Urdu translation of Psalms he worked with Andrew Gordon, the man in charge of the Psalms project. Moreover, he took part in evangelistic activities in Gurdaspur along with Dr. Gordon, who initiated the work in Gurdaspur in 1872 and resided there until his return to the States in 1885.[54] This indicates that in Gurdaspur Rev. Imam-ud-Din was involved in the translation of psalms into Urdu between 1880 and 1885. It is possible that after Gordon's return to the States, Rev. Shahbaz moved to Scot Garh, near Sialkot, where Samuel Martin was based, so that he could carry on the work on the Urdu Psalter.

It is interesting to note that Rev. Imam-ud-Din has been referred to as "Rev. Shahbaz of Gurdaspur."[55] This may well be due to the fact that his journey of Psalms was started from Gurdaspur. However, the records of the United Presbyterian Church reveal some helpful information in this regard. Today, Zafarwal, the birthplace of Dr. Shahbaz, falls within the limits of Narowal district, which is part of the province of Punjab in Pakistan. However, before the partition in 1947, Zafarwal was part of the presbytery of Gurdaspur district, which is part of the present-day state of Punjab in India, and thus by some writers he is referred to as someone who originally

---

53. Joint Committee, *Christian Literature*, 210.
54. Gordon, *India*, 433.
55. Singh and Barrier, *Punjab Past and Present*, 196.

belonged to Gurdaspur.⁵⁶ It is to be noted that in 1947 the region of Punjab was divided among Pakistan and India by the Radcliffe commission.⁵⁷

## 5.4. Work in Sialkot and Translation of the Punjabi Metrical Psalms

It was in Sialkot where Dr. Lytle, the head of the committee for the metrical translation of Punjabi Psalms, was based and where Rev. Imam-ud-Din spent the longest period of his life in translating the Psalter and serving the Lord. While working on Psalms, he was ordained by the United Presbyterian Church in Sialkot, where he served for twenty years, from 1886 and 1906, at the First United Presbyterian Church. The complete translation of Urdu metrical psalms and the selection of psalms into Punjabi were published during his pastoral role in Sialkot. It is fascinating to find that on top of his pastoral responsibilities, he worked diligently on the translation of the Psalter. However, before the publication of the 1908 edition of the Punjabi Psalms from Benares, he was freed from the church work in 1906 so that he could fully concentrate on the translation of the Punjabi Psalms. In the minutes of the 1906 General Assembly of the United Presbyterian Church Rev. Imam-ud-Din Shahbaz has been listed among the native ministers in Sialkot.⁵⁸

It is significant to note that during the later stages of the Punjabi Psalms, Rev. Imam-ud-Din Shahbaz lost his sight. In this regard, the following account is noteworthy: "Often he would lie in his bed with his head completely covered while Babu Sadiq read to him. When once the stanza was formulated in the mind, he would dictate it back to Babu Sadiq." It is quite a powerful picture of deep pondering in putting the words into poetry; involving much patience, concentration, and memorization. In her personal letter to Frank Pressly, Henrietta Cowden calls Dr. Shahbaz a "modern Milton."⁵⁹ The 1909 annual report of the board of foreign missions records: "Appreciative mention should be made of the service rendered by the Rev. I D Shahbaz in making the metrical translation of the Psalms in Punjabi metre."⁶⁰ The words of Anna Milligan describe his last days: "There is Padri I. D. Shahbaz, the poet, grown old and blind, who put the Psalms into Punjabi verse and thus made them the most popular songs of the whole

---

56. UPCUSA, *Minutes of the Thirty-Fifth General Assembly*, 240.
57. Spate, "Punjab," 374.
58. UPCUSA, *Minutes of the Forty-Eighth General Assembly*, 820.
59. Pressly, "Zabur," 9.
60. UPCNA, *Annual Report* (1909), 216.

church of Christ in the Punjab." His abilities were further proved by the fact that as an acknowledgement of his work on the Punjabi Psalter, Rev. Imam-ud-Din was awarded the Doctor of Divinity degree which a man of that caliber truly deserved. In this regard, Anna Milligan writes: "Tarkio College honored herself in 1920 by conferring upon him the honorary title of D.D."[61] In 1921 Rev. Shahbaz passed away in Bhalwal, where the United Presbyterian Mission had several projects, including an evangelistic center, a boarding school for girls, and a hospital.[62]

Very little has been discovered about his family. While in Gurdaspur, his wife served as a vice president on the board of *Zenana* (Women) Missionary Society of the United Presbyterian Mission in India.[63] When the family moved to Sargodha, Mrs. Shahbaz did a great job running a dispensary at the hospital in Bhalwal and was a "most successful Bible woman." His son, Joseph Shahbaz, a committed Christian and "spiritual leader," was an officer in one of the Christian battalions of the British army in India.[64]

On March 13, 2017, I received an email from Dr. Shama Singh, who introduced herself as a maternal great-granddaughter of Dr. Shahbaz. She had read my article on the Punjabi *Zabur* published in 2014 in the *International Bulletin of Missionary Research*. I had plans to meet her in person in the state of Minnesota but had to cancel the visit due to family circumstances. According to her, Dr. Shahbaz had two sons and a daughter. In sharing about her grandmother named Rosa Bashir-ul-Nissa Sadiq (Dr. Shahbaz's daughter) she mentioned that her grandmother was well educated and knew Persian, English, Punjabi, and Urdu languages. She added: "When I learnt Urdu in College, she would write to me so I could be more fluent." The great-granddaughter of Dr. Shahbaz went to be with the Lord in May 2018. I regret not having the opportunity to hear the memories she had heard about Dr. Shahbaz from her grandmother. I'm so grateful that Dr. Shama Singh took the time to share info regarding the family of Dr. Shahbaz and some invaluable materials she had received from her grandmother in relation to Dr. Shahbaz.

## 5.5. Visionary and Inspirational Man

Rev. Imam-ud-Din was a visionary man. After taking charge as a minister in 1886, he raised thirty rupees for the United Presbyterian Foreign Mission

---

61. Milligan, *Facts*, 227.
62. Anderson and Campbell, *Shadow*, 280.
63. PCUSA Archives, letter dated February 23, 1891, from Mary Jane Campbell.
64. UPCUSA, *Triennial Report*, 172.

Board so that the money could be used in other parts of the world in mission activities.[65] It was indeed a step of faith and a heart for missions that led Rev. Shahbaz to raise funds for other mission fields. Understanding that a majority of the people came from rather poor backgrounds, probably did not have resources to help others, and were instead dependent on others for their own help looks significant. It was the mission-minded Rev. Shahbaz who motivated his congregation and raised funds for the work of God in foreign lands. In a way, this example sets a challenge before the Christian church in the Indian subcontinent concerning missions, which seems to have disappeared from the church in that part of the world, partly due to the lack of financial resources. Nevertheless, Rev. Imam-ud-Din, being in similar circumstances, managed to challenge his fellow brothers and sisters and was successful in the mission cause. At the United Presbyterian Punjab Synod conference held in Lyallpur (present-day city of Faisalabad, in Pakistan) on March 25, 1902, he spoke on resources for the spiritual growth of Christians, particularly in relation to creating self-supporting churches.[66]

Rev. Shahbaz was not simply involved in teaching and preaching but his life made an impact on those around him. Someone whose conversion was initiated by the living Christian testimony continued to reflect that Christian character through his own life. In this regard, Miss Anderson writes: "Rev. Imam-ud-Din Shahbaz, D.D., who, while not a teacher in either of these institutions, had great influence over many of the students. He was pastor of the congregation which was attended by many students in the early days."[67] The Christian Training Institute (CTI) and the theological seminary were considered the two vital institutions of the United Presbyterian Mission. Rev. Shahbaz was neither a teacher at the theological seminary where students were trained for the service of God, nor was he involved in teaching at the Christian Training Institute. Nevertheless, he was popular among students at both institutions and had an impact on them.

Rev. Shahbaz worked hard and diligently on the work he was assigned to. Describing his faithfulness and commitment to his work, his supervisor Dr. Gordon writes that Dr. Shahbaz was an "industrious, earnest and efficient" person.[68] Such an admiring comment is self-explanatory to demonstrate his interest in work and the high standards that he set for this "most

---

65. Stewart, *Life*, 315.
66. PCUSA Archives, 53/3.
67. Anderson and Campbell, *Shadow*, 113.
68. Gordon, *India*, 433.

commendable" work.⁶⁹ The words of Emma Dean Anderson compliment the work of Rev. Shahbaz:

> *I wonder sometimes if the songs of David ever sounded sweeter in Hebrew tongue sung in the hills of Judea and in the great temple in Jerusalem than they do in the plains and hills and the humble mud churches in the villages of the Punjab on the day of worship.*⁷⁰

The various phases of the life of Dr. Shahbaz speak of his passion for Psalms and love for the Word of God. Whether it was a transition from one Christian mission to another and working under the leadership of a new person, or continuously moving from one place to another with a whole shift of roles and responsibilities, nothing prevented him from proclaiming the Christian message. Wherever he went, he remained faithful and passionate in teaching and preaching the Word of God. The translation of the Punjabi Psalter was not merely an academic work, and it is momentous to see the grace and favor of God in the preparation of these psalms from the commencement of the work to its completion. When Dr. Shahbaz lost his sight while the work on Psalms was still in progress, it did not stop the translation process, and he was still proficient to form the words into poetry. One can say without doubt that this is indeed a manifestation of God's grace and wisdom that helped Dr. Imam-ud-Din to carry on the work to its completion. The events that took place in the life of Dr. Shahbaz while translating these psalms make the story of the Punjabi Psalter outstanding and even more wonderful.

## 5.6. Punjabi Zabur and the Indian Subcontinent

It is noteworthy that no other language in the Indian subcontinent (it may well be the only one in Asia) has the honor of having the entire book of Psalms in versified form that has been used for Christian worship.⁷¹ Punjabi is unique in that sense, and therefore the luminous and "remarkable" work of Dr. Shahbaz can truly be regarded as a precious gift to the Punjabi Christian community in the Indian subcontinent.⁷² Massey asserts that the contributions of Dr. Shahbaz are in fact for the whole of the Indian church.⁷³

---

69. Victor, "Punjabi," 39.
70. Anderson and Campbell, *Shadow*, 114–15.
71. Loh, "Music," 570.
72. Das Jain, "Panjabi," 554.
73. Massey, "Punjabi," 574.

It is important to mention that for several reasons the relations between India and Pakistan have always been strained. Due to the tense relationships like everyone else, the ordinary Christians in both countries do not have opportunities to come together. As a result, Punjabi Christians living in the two countries are unaware that the Punjabi Psalms are equally loved and cherished on either side of the border. This may be surprising and of particular interest to Christians in Pakistan who often assume that the Punjabi Psalms are only sung in their country. This may well be the same on the other side of the border. However, it is fascinating to find that the Punjabi Psalms are used among the Punjabi congregations in India with immense enthusiasm.[74] In this regard, Vidyasagar writes:

> *The best example is the translation of the Psalms into Punjabi by the Rev. Imam-uddin Shahbaz, which are still in use in most of the northern parts in India as far as Delhi and Uttar Pradesh. In some parts of the North West India, the worship service does not start unless the Zaboors (Psalms) are sung. Since they are composed in the popular forms of classic ragas, they can be used in whole of the northern region.*[75]

The picture of a rural service in the Indian Punjab portrayed by Campbell looks so identical to a rural service in the Pakistani Punjab that it is impossible to differentiate:

> *The opening song is a zabur or Psalm, to a fine old Punjab tune. "I was glad when they said, come let us go to the House of the Lord." The traditional final hymn is sung, "Rahega nan sada thikar" (The name of Christ will remain forever! It will remain as long as the sun remains . . . and all men will receive grace from His name).*[76]

Campbell continues that "even ten years ago the service in the courtyard would have consisted entirely on Psalms" and that these psalms are sung with great eagerness and enthusiasm by everyone.[77] Likewise, the use of similar instruments being used for worship and the singing of Punjabi psalms at the beginning and at the end shows that it is no different than a Christian service in the rural areas of Punjab in Pakistan.[78] The Punjabi Psalms were published in the Gurumukhi script in 1930.[79]

74. Timothy, "Catholicism," 75.
75. Dogar, *Community*, 22.
76. Campbell, "Church," 165.
77. Campbell, "Church," 205.
78. Caleb, "Punjabi," 122.
79. Dogar, "Psalms," 576.

The South Asian Punjabi Christian diaspora living in the Western world continue to make use of the *Zabur* in their communal worship. St. Andrew's Church Ilford (London), Calvary Chapel Norbury (London), Punjabi Masihi Church (Surrey, BC), Cornerstone Asian Church (Mississauga, ON), and Trinity International Christian Church (Philadelphia) are some examples of the diaspora churches that sing the Punjabi *Zabur* with great enthusiasm.

Fr. Inayat Bernard (rector of the Sacred Heart Cathedral in Lahore) stated that in 2016 he had the opportunity to visit the North Indian churches along with other priests under the leadership of Archbishop Sebastian Francis Shaw (Roman Catholic Archbishop of Lahore). He shared that in the cities of Amritsar, Jalandhar, Agra, and Delhi the *Zabur* in Punjabi were sung after the same tunes as used among the churches in Pakistan, and that there was no difference in the melodies at all. Rev. Fr. Inayat Bernard added that he very much enjoyed singing the *Zabur* during this visit.[80]

The work of Dr. Shahbaz has been mentioned in the publications of both Christian and non-Christian academic institutions in the Punjab state and elsewhere in India, including the Punjabi University in Patiala and the Christian Institute for the Study of Religion and Society in Bangalore. The Christian writings in Pakistan could have done more in focusing particularly on the Punjabi Psalms. On the other hand, the non-Christian academic circles in Pakistan hardly refer to the Punjabi Psalms, not even as Punjabi poetry, in their publications. John O'Brien writes concerning the exclusion of any mention of the Punjabi Psalms in Pakistani academia: "One can only wonder if an unacknowledged prejudice is at work in the failure to include any excerpts from it in anthologies of Punjab poetry."[81] It is appreciative that Rev. Shahbaz was given a mention in a Pakistani English newspaper by Muhammad Miraj in his article on the history of Narowal.[82] Sarwat Ali mentioned Dr. Shahbaz and his work in an article that focused on the church music in Pakistan.[83] A poet and writer, Khalid Mahmood, dedicated a few pages on Dr. Shahbaz in his book *Aai Purayy Di Waa* (The East Wind Comes).[84] Despite much effort, I was not able to acquire a copy of this book.

---

80. The "Rev. Dr. Imam-ud-Din Shahbaz Award" event, organized by the Christian Talent Society, was held at Alhamra Arts Council in Lahore, March 24, 2017; see https://www.youtube.com/watch?v=gO44d4vkjYM.

81. O'Brien, *Identity*, 567.

82. Muhammad Hassan Miraj, "The Poet and Kartar," *Dawn*, November 12, 2012, http://dawn.com/2012/11/12/the-poet-and-kartar.

83. Sarwat Ali, "Faith in Music," *TNS*, December 18, 2016, https://www.thenews.com.pk/tns/detail/562315-faith-music.

84. Jalil, "Nain Sukh's Short Stories Collection Launched," *Dawn*, November 27, 2017, https://www.dawn.com/news/1373160.

## 5.7. Poetic Features of the Punjabi Psalms

As Punjabi poetry developed it has been primarily influenced by Urdu and Persian poetry. Some great Urdu and Persian poetry has been written by Punjabi speakers, including the national poet of Pakistan, Dr. Mohammed Iqbal. As mentioned earlier, Dr. Shahbaz was well acquainted with the Persian and Urdu languages. Prior to the versified Psalms in Punjabi, he did a metrical translation of the Psalms in Urdu and wrote Christian odes in Urdu. In investigating the poetic features of the Punjabi Psalms, it is essential to mention that in essence the poetry of these psalms reflect the patterns and styles of Urdu and Persian poetry. The meter, rhyme, and refrain are the integral elements of Urdu and Persian poetry, and they all have been employed well in the poetic rendering of the Psalms in Punjabi.[85]

Meter is a rhythmic component in which a poetic piece of work is sung on a regular syllable and rhythm. The stanzas in the metrical translation of the Psalms in Punjabi are structured in a manner that shows consistency and equality in terms of length and rhythm. Rhyme refers to the use of identity or similar sounding words in poetry. The Punjabi Psalms used a variety of rhyme schemes, except for a few quatrains and an octave; these psalms are formed in couplets or *dohras* as they are called in Punjabi.[86] The recurrence of words at intervals is known as a refrain or "chorus" in poetry. The refrain is a vital poetical feature of the Punjabi Psalms. In the majority of these psalms, the refrain is mentioned as a chorus. Among the Pakistani churches, psalms are often identified and remembered by their chorus instead of their numerical number. Although the majority of the Punjabi psalms have a two-line refrain or chorus, some are of a single line, and some have no chorus, in which case the first stanza or a part of it serves as refrain.[87] The single-line chorus does not always occur at the opening of a stanza, it appears at the end of each stanza in a few psalms.[88]

### *Ghazal*

*Ghazal* is the most famous and standard literary form of Urdu poetry, having characteristics of meter, rhyme, and refrain.[89] In terms of length, a *ghazal*

---

85. Pritchett, *Poetry*, 71.

86. Singh, *Panjabi Dictionary*, 329.

87. E.g., Pss 23, 24 (part 2), 31 (part 1), 49, 51 (part 3), 63, 90 (part 2), and 94 (part 2) are of single line chorus whereas Pss 1, 4, 6, 7, and 9 (part 2) are without a refrain.

88. Pss 18 (parts 1 and 3), 92 (part 1), 95 (part 1), 101 (part 1), 119 (part 10).

89. Jafri, "Urdu Ghazal," 1395.

may have as few as five couplets and as many as fifteen couplets. An average *ghazal* consists of seven couplets and usually does not go beyond twelve couplets. A *ghazal* opens with a two-line rhyming couplet, and the ending of a second line in each subsequent couplet rhymes with the opening couplet.[90] Some of the Punjabi psalms are structured after the *ghazal* pattern, exhibiting a rhyme scheme of AA, BA, CA, DA and so on. Some of the examples include Psalms 16 (part 2), 20 (part 1), 22 (parts 1 and 3), 31 (part 4), 46, 84, 100, 103 (part 1), and 126.[91] Love is the soul of a *ghazal*, and love for the divine is demonstrated through some Punjabi psalms in the form of a *ghazal*.[92]

## *Masnavi*

*Masnavi* is a genre of Urdu and Persian poetry in which both lines of a couplet rhyme together. This type of poetry was common among the Persian mystic writers such as Jami and Rumi. Thus, *Masnavi* poetry exhibits the divine love and divine majestic beauty. A vast majority of the Punjabi psalms are formed in the *Masnavi* style that demonstrate rhyme pattern of AA, BB, CC, DD and so on. A few examples include Psalms 1, 2, 4, 5–6, 9, 15, 16 (part 1), and 22 (part 4).[93]

## *Qita*

In Urdu and Persian poetry, a quatrain may be a *rubai* (AABA) or a *qita* (ABCB) depending on the rhyme scheme.[94] A small number of Punjabi psalms are in four-line verse or quatrain, and they enjoy different rhyme patterns.[95] For example, an ABAB in Psalm 18 (part 5) and an AAAB pattern in Psalm 71 (part 3).[96] The *qita* may be observed in the third part of Psalm 10, the second part of Psalm 17, and the seventh part of Psalm 18, where

---

90. Kanda, *Ghazal*, 2–3.

91. These may be found, respectively, on pp. 12, 18, 19–20, 26–27, 46, 71–72, 85, 89–90, and 110 in the 57th ed. of the Sialkot Convention Hymn Book.

92. Kanda, *Ghazal*, 6.

93. These may be found, respectively, on pp. 3, 5–6, 7, 8–9, 10, 11, 12, and 21 in the 57th ed. of the Sialkot Convention Hymn Book.

94. Lewis, "Rubai," 1228.

95. Pss 9–10, 17–18, 25–26, 40, 55–56, 71, 81, 148.

96. These may be found, respectively, on pp. 145, 43, and 178 in the 1908 ed. of the Punjabi Psalms.

the second line of each quatrain rhymes with the fourth line.⁹⁷ Therefore, Psalms 10, 17, and 18 demonstrate ABCB structure after the form of a *qita*.⁹⁸

### *Chaupai*

*Chaupai* is a poetic component of *bhakti* or singing for devotional purpose in India. A *Chaupai*, literally meaning "four feet," is a four-line verse or a quatrain that has a fixed rhyme pattern of AABB.⁹⁹ Psalm 55 (part 3) is an example of a Punjabi psalm that is formed after a *bhakti* form of *chaupai*, having an AABB structure.¹⁰⁰

### *Musamman*

An eight-line poem in Urdu is called a *musamman*.¹⁰¹ A double quatrain, or a *musamman*, is only used in the Punjabi translation of Psalm 145, part 2. It has a total of four octaves or double quatrains. In this psalm, the second and the fourth lines repeat the same refrain, and the first and the third lines rhyme. The fifth, sixth, and the seventh lines rhyme, whereas the last line repeats the same refrain as occurred in the second and the fourth lines. This psalm shows an ABABCCCB pattern.¹⁰²

## 5.8. Poetic Themes of Dr. Shahbaz's Urdu Poetry

### *Assurance of Salvation*

As mentioned earlier, the fear of the judgment day and hell were key in the conversion of Dr. Shahbaz. The assurance of salvation through Christ therefore reflected in his poetry. For example, the following couplets express his deep sense of confidence in salvation through Christ that expels the fear of grave and death:

*Jo shaks Masih munaji ka hai muqir*
*Dar us ko phir kahan raha munkar nakir ka*

---

97. Kanda, *Rubaiyat*, 4.

98. These may be found, respectively, on pp. 20, 33, and 45 in the 1908 ed. of the Punjabi Psalms.

99. Lochtefeld, *Hinduism*, 146.

100. This may be found on p. 145 in the 1908 ed. of the Punjabi Psalms.

101. Hassan, *Akbarabadi*, 72.

102. It may be found on pp. 124–25 in 57th ed. of the Sialkot Convention Hymn Book.

> *Na qabar ki na mot ki parva hai usay*
> *Daman hai pakra jis ne meray dastgir ka*[103]

It may be noted that *munqir* and *nakir* mentioned in the first couplet are the two angels, who according to the Islamic belief investigates the deceased in the grave, and the future fate of the deceased is dependent on this investigation.[104] Dr. Shahbaz does a beautiful contrastive word play by using the word *muqir*, meaning the one who "confesses, acknowledges," and here it refers to the person who professes Christ, against the angel *nakir*, who asks questions to determine one's future fate. In the second couplet he continues that such a person does not even care about *qabar* and *mot*, meaning "grave" and "death," respectively, since he is clinging to Christ, whom he referred to here as *dastgir*, meaning "a helper, a protector and a guardian." His confidence and assurance in Christ is further shown in the following couplet:

> *Falak pe shahbaz apna ghar hai masih apna hai shahzada*
> *Ba-fazal-e-aizad hu ik member masihion ki anjuman ka*[105]

In this couplet, Dr. Shahbaz expresses an utmost assurance in Christ that his *ghar*, "house," is in fact in *falak*, "heaven," where *Masih*, "Christ," is the ultimate *Shahzada*, "prince." He is delighted by the fact that through the saving *fazal*, "grace," of *Aizad*, "God," he is now a member of the *anjuman*, "assembly" of Christians. This speaks of his concrete assurance that he is indeed going to heaven to be with Christ.

### Forgiveness of Sins

The theme of forgiveness from sins and new identity in Christ is evident in the poetry of Dr. Shahbaz. He is thankful that his sins are forgiven. For example, the following couplets show his deep gratitude:

> *Hazar shukar ay masih payare ajab hai reham tera mujh par*
> *Ke tujh pe iman laay asi hua hai poda tere chaman ka*
> *Jo bar-e-asian tha meray sir pe utar gaya tujh ko dekhte hi*
> *Sara-e-fani hai dar-e-dunya hai shoq dil mai ab us watan ka*[106]

---

103. These couplets are taken from the *Masihi Ghazal* (Christian ode) written by Dr. Shahbaz. The central point of this couplet is that anyone who professes Christ is not scared of death and the judgment that follows.

104. Zanaty, *Terms*, 161.

105. This couplet is taken from another *Masihi Ghazal* (Christian ode) written by Dr. Shahbaz.

106. These couplets are taken from *Masihi Ghazal* (Christian ode), by Dr. Shahbaz.

The abundance of his gratefulness may be seen in the phrase "*hazar shukar*," meaning "thanks" "a thousand" times, as he wonders at the amazing *reham*, "mercy," of his beloved Christ given to him. Dr. Shahbaz uses the imagery of *poda*, "a plant," that belongs to *chaman*, a "garden," to express his association with Christ. He identifies himself as *asi*, "a sinner, a disobedient," who by acquiring *iman*, "faith," in Christ is now forgiven. In the second couplet, he continues to stress *bar-e-asian*, the "load, burden" of "sin, transgression," that he once was carrying with him but that has now been removed. He does not desire *dar-e-dunya*, the "possessing" of this "world," as he sees it is as *sara-e-fani*, a "mortal" "caravansary," that is no more than a "temporary home of travelers." He has a great *shoq*, "interest, pleasure," in an immortal *watan*, "home, dwelling."

## Life With and Without Christ

Dr. Shahbaz brings confession of his previous sinful condition, and focuses on life with and without Christ in his poetry. For example, the following couplet describes this:

> *Meri khatain thi had se bahir tha bojh sir pe hazar man ka*
> *Mai mir-e-majlis tha asion mai gunhagaro ki anjuman ka*

This couplet is part of the same piece of poetry that has been discussed above; however, there is a clear contrast between the two. In the previous couplets, he speaks of his new identity in Christ and calls himself a member of the assembly of Christians, but in this couplet, he talks about his past sinful condition and life without Christ. Nevertheless, the use of terms and vocabulary in these couplets is somewhat similar. He confesses his *khatain*, "wrong actions," through the phrase *had se bahir*, meaning that they were "beyond limits." He feels it to the point where he says that he was carrying *bojh*, a "load, weight," of *hazar man*, one thousand "*maund*" (one *maund* is equal to eighty pounds or forty seers) of wrong doings, on his head. Moreover, he calls himself *mir-e-majlis*, a "president, chief of ceremonies," among the *anjuman*, "assembly, company," of sinners.

## Struggle with Sin and Call to Repentance

The ongoing struggle of dealing with sin may be observed in the poetry of Dr. Shahbaz:

> *Ya masih kis se kahoon tere siwa raz apna?*
> *Shoq-e-asian se nahi rehta hai dil baz apna*

> *Khinchay khinchay liay jata hai gunahon ki taraf*
> *Hay kesa hai ye dil mafsada pardaz apna*[107]

In these couplets he expresses his helplessness to deal with sin as he addresses Christ, the only person with whom he can share the *raz*, "secret," of his heart. He ponders his heart before Christ by telling him that his *dil*, "heart," does not keep *baz*, "abstain," from *shoq-e-asian*, the "desire" of sin. Lamenting on the sinful nature of his heart that pulls him toward sin, he takes *hay*, "a deep sigh." He describes his heart by the phrase *mafsada pardaz*, meaning the "manager" of "malfeasant" and evil. However, in the same ode he sees Christ as his ultimate hope:

> *Tera hamdard siwa uskay koi aur nahi*
> *Phenk de pesh-e-masih bojh tu shahbaz apna*

Dr. Shahbaz reminds himself that there is no other *hamdard*, "sympathetic," than Christ. In the end, he is convinced that he better repent and throw his *bojh*, "burden," *pesh-e-masih*, "before" "Christ." Likewise, he extends an invitation of repentance in another ode:

> *Gunah se ae thakay mando masiha pas ajao*
> *Siwa uskay tumhara nahi aur koi thikana hai*[108]

Based on Matthew 11:28, this couplet calls those weary of *gunah*, "sin," to come to *masiha*, "Christ." Dr. Shahbaz explains to such people that they have no other *thikana*, "permanent place," than Christ. He invites his audience to respond to his call to repentance.

In sum, the role of gifted linguists like Miss Mary Jane Campbell, Rev. Dr. Thomas Fulton Cummings, and Rev. Dr. David Smith Lytle in the making of Punjabi Psalms is remarkable. Likewise, the talented musicians like Miss Mary Rachel Martin, Miss Josephine Martin, Miss Henrietta Cowden, and Mrs. William McKelvey had an important role in the preparation of these psalms. Rev. Dr. Imam-ud-Din Shahbaz played a vital part as poet and translator, and he can unequivocally be regarded the hero in the story of the Punjabi *Zabur*. The outstanding work of the aforementioned contributors to the Psalms in Punjabi can truly be regarded as a precious gift to the Punjabi Christian community in the Indian subcontinent and across the globe.

---

107. *Masihi Git*, 72. These couplets are taken from Dr. Shahbaz's Christian ode that has been suggested in the Christian Hymn Book with Melodies to be used for repentance during Lent.

108. *Masihi Git*, 176. These couplets are taken from Dr. Shahbaz's second Christian ode in the Christian Hymn Book with Melodies.

# III

# The Punjabi Psalms

*Causes for Their Success and Delayed Preparation*

THIS CHAPTER ENDEAVORS TO explore the key factors behind the spread of the Punjabi Psalms, discussing the reasons for which these psalms rapidly became popular among the ordinary people. Moving from there, the focus is drawn on elements that hindered the preparation and delayed the making of the Punjabi Psalms. Finally, the variety of ways in which the Punjabi Psalms are used by the Punjabi Christians are discussed in this chapter.

## 1. KEY FACTORS BEHIND THE SPREAD AND SUCCESS OF THE PUNJABI ZABUR

### 1. 1. Mother-Tongue and Indigenous Music

Bassnett mentions that "language is a heart within the body of culture."[1] This proves absolutely true in the case of the Punjabi Psalms. Through language, man does not only communicate with his fellow men but also with God. The decision to use the mother tongue in translation of these psalms was certainly the most important factor behind the acceptability and use of the Punjabi Psalms among the ordinary people. It is vital to remember that,

---

1. Bassnett, *Translation*, 14.

prior to the availability of Psalms in Punjabi; they were first translated into the Urdu language, which did not attract the ordinary people, whereas when translated into Punjabi the result was of great appreciation from the natives. Punjabi was the language that was much cherished by the ordinary people in Punjab, as they named it *Mithi Zuban*, "a sweet tongue," and moreover, it was "the language of their childhood, their mothers and their homes."[2] In other words, an attempt was made to impose Urdu on the ordinary people in Punjab for whom it was no less than a foreign language.

At first, they were being deprived of singing in their heart language and music which alone could express their innermost emotions and gratitude before the Almighty. However, when they had the privilege to worship God in their native language and music, this is what happened: "In two or three places the hearers were so interested that they demanded the singing should be continued the whole night, . . . and in the case of some, the tears running down their cheeks have testified to the deep interest of their hearts."[3] Writing of the Psalms in Punjabi, Mary Jane Campbell asserts: "These have been set to the popular tunes of the Punjabi, and take wonderfully well with the people, who do love their own music and their own mother tongue."[4] These psalms began to make a deep impact on the life of ordinary Punjabi Christians as they became "an integral part" of their everyday lives, even the children knew "large portions of these psalms by heart" and the sweet sounds of the Punjabi Psalms could be heard "day and night."[5]

There has been no mention of how well the singing of Urdu metrical psalms to Western melodies was received particularly by the Christians in Punjab. As mentioned in the previous chapters, from the trend of using Urdu with Western melodies in Christian worship by different denominations it can be asserted that these psalms may well have been used in churches. Having said that, it needs to be mentioned that most of these were probably only used by the Western missionaries and by those who were comfortable with Urdu. However, the ordinary Punjabi Christians did not respond to the established form of Christian worship of that time, as the Western melodies seemed strange and unfamiliar to them. Instead they were enthusiastic when they had the opportunity to worship in their own mother tongue, using their own melodies and music, and as a result these psalms "became instantly popular."[6] In other words, they followed that which came from

---

2. Stewart, *Life*, 86.
3. Murdoch, *Manual*, 194.
4. PCUSA Archives, letter dated June 11, 1892, from Mary Jane Campbell.
5. Steer, *Good News*, 330.
6. Cox, *Imperial*, 149.

their hearts and wishes; the sort of worship style they adopted was in their origin and blood. It only became possible when it was realized that "the people of India are fond of their music" and that "music has an attractive power for the natives of the Panjab," the ordinary Punjabi Christians loved and enjoyed their music.[7] As mentioned in the previous chapters, the first publication of a selection of Punjabi psalms was in 1892 and by that time the ordinary people were beginning to make efforts to have the Christian songs in their own language and melodies. John Murdoch writes in this regard: "The music is gaining ground. In different parts of the country, apparently without any communication, a movement has taken place in its favour."[8] It shows that the simple villagers had a spontaneous response to their own music. Needless to say, the selection of psalms in Punjabi must have played an integral role in inspiring and motivating people in other parts of India. It is to be remembered that in 1895 the committee for the Punjabi Psalms was reactivated and was asked to translate the entire Psalter into Punjabi set to local melodies. It was the overwhelming response from the ordinary Punjabi Christians toward the selections of the Punjabi Psalms that made them a hit.

It would be helpful to briefly explore the *ragas* or musical system on which these psalms were set. *Ragas* are melody modes that have a capacity to communicate a unique feeling.[9] Moreover, "there are hundreds of ragas each expressing a different world of feeling and thought" with which people in the Western world are not normally familiar.[10] The theme, settings, and emotional status of the psalmist were kept in mind before deciding on any particular *raga*. For example, Psalm 121 ("I lift up my eyes to the hills") is sung to *pahari*, "of or belonging to the hilly, mountainous," *raga*, since it can best express the background environment and the feelings of the psalmist in that psalm. Similarly, Psalm 24 ("King of glory") is sung to *darbari*, "of or belonging to the court, courtier," *raga*, that is regarded as the most majestic *raga*.[11] This particular *raga* was composed by a well-known musician of Emperor Akbar's court and is considered to be a royal *raga*.[12] It is interesting to understand how melodies were chosen to best express both the contents and the emotions found in the psalms. It is worth noting that many Indian *ragas* are associated with Hindu deities and are sung at particular times and

---

7. Youngson, *Panjab*, 215.
8. Murdoch, *Manual*, 335.
9. Shahid, *Classical*, 9.
10. Sengupta, *Musicology*, 101.
11. Sharma, *Music*, 161.
12. Manon, *Music*, 75.

seasons.¹³ For example, *Malkaunsa raga* is sung in the cold season at Vallabhite temples in the morning hours, and *Megha raga* is sung in the rainy season.¹⁴ However, the Punjabi Psalms are not bound to be sung during a specific time of the day or season. It may be asserted that in selecting *ragas* for the Punjabi psalms, the focus was put on conveying emotions of the psalmist and the content through these *ragas*, rather than on specifying the psalms to be used at certain times of the day. As mentioned in the previous chapters, *Radha Kishan* was the key person in suggesting a particular *raga* for the psalms. Nonetheless, the responsibility for making the ultimate decision lay with Dr. Shahbaz.

As the psalms were put to local melodies, they are suited to be played on traditional Indian musical instruments. *Tabla*, an uneven pair of small, tuned, hand-played drums, and harmonium, whose "hand-operated bellows" are maintained by the left hand and the keyboard by the right, are the two most used instruments among churches in the Indian subcontinent.¹⁵ It is also a remarkable fact that the harmonium was first used in India for church worship. Few people are aware of the fact that it was actually introduced in India by the missionaries.¹⁶ As a general practice, in the Indian subcontinent people enter barefoot and sit on the floor at places of worship, the same is true for Christian worship.¹⁷ This is especially helpful in playing the aforementioned instruments, as they are designed to be played while sitting on the floor.

Other commonly used instruments for Christian worship are *dholak* "double-headed cylindrical or barrel drums" and the tambourine. In the Indian subcontinent, the above-mentioned instruments are not only used in Churches but also in Hindu and Sikh religious places.¹⁸ In the Punjabi churches, *chimta*, a "percussion instrument" made of large iron tongs, is particularly used in rural areas. In fact, it is a cultural symbol of the Punjab; hence it is used in Indian and Pakistani Punjab alike. The Sikhs in Punjab also use it for their devotional worship.¹⁹

---

13. Shah, *Culture*, 98.
14. Moorthy, *Raga*, 89.
15. Farrell, "Harmonium (India)," 307.
16. Brockschmidt, *Instrument*, 18.
17. Anderson and Campbell, "Africa and Asia," 117.
18. Thielemann, *Religious Music*, 25.
19. Sharma, *Heritage*, 174.

**Musical instruments used for Christian worship in the Indian subcontinent**

The Punjabi Psalms are a model of contextualization where scriptural truths were presented to the ordinary people within their own culture and context. They were put with local melodies into a language which brought to them the message of God with spontaneity and ease. When Christians in Punjab were given the liberty to use natural ways to praise God, they developed innovative and indigenous "forms of Christianity."[20]

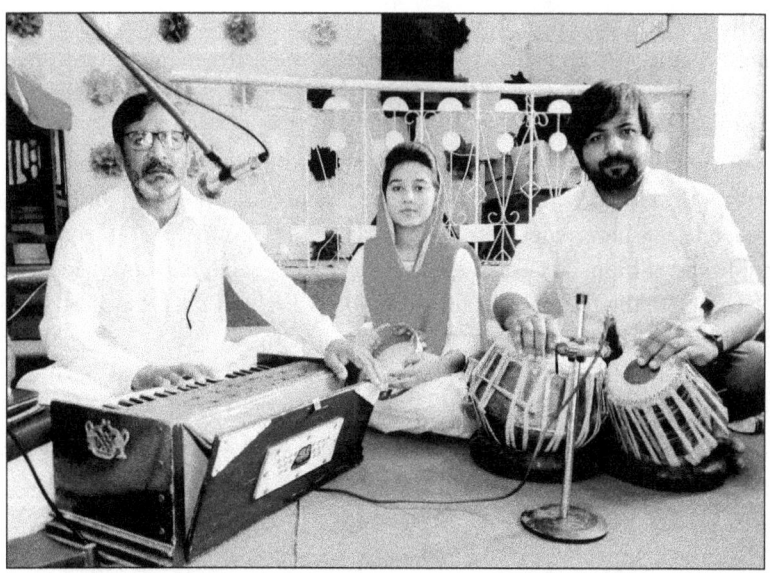

**Worship on Sunday morning at a local church in Pakistan**

20. Cox, "Lefroy," 67.

## 1.2. The Sialkot Convention

The profound relationship between the Punjabi Psalter and the Sialkot Convention is noteworthy as the two cannot be separated from each other. The Sialkot Convention is an annual Christian gathering that takes place in the month of September in Sialkot and is counted as the oldest and most eminent Christian meeting in Pakistan. Even before the partition in 1947, it was a renowned Christian meeting in the Indian subcontinent. The first Sialkot Convention was held in 1904; the Punjabi Psalms were first introduced at the second annual Sialkot Convention, where two thousand copies of the Punjabi Psalms were sold.[21] The records of the United Presbyterian Mission indicate that the Sialkot Convention was arranged in 1904 to commemorate the "semi-centennial anniversary" of the United Presbyterian work in India.[22] The Sialkot Convention is often compared to the Keswick Convention in the United Kingdom and is called "the Keswick of India."[23] In 2010, I had the opportunity to attend the Keswick Convention. The comparison between the Sialkot and Keswick Convention is justified, as the spiritual environment and fellowship of believers from across the country gathered under tents look very similar to the Sialkot Convention.

The book currently used among Pakistani churches that contains the Punjabi Psalter is known as *Sialkot Convention Geet Ki Kitab* (Sialkot Convention Hymn Book). The book was named after the annual Sialkot Convention where the Punjabi Psalms were widely used by ordinary Christians and became well-known.[24] The first part of the Sialkot Convention Hymn Book includes a selection of the metrical Punjabi psalms, whereas the latter part contains old and new Christian songs.

Editions of this book are published from time to time. In August 2019, the sixtieth edition was published, which is so far the latest edition available. As new songs become popular, they become part of the newly published edition. It is worth mentioning that the Sialkot Convention takes place under the tents at a place called *Bara Pathar* (Twelve Stones) in Sialkot. Here a hall is named after Rev. Dr. Imam-ud-Din Shahbaz, known as the "I. D. Shahbaz Hall," which was built in 1925.[25] It has been used as a residential building for the boys studying at the Christian Training Institute (CTI), whereas each September it is used as free accommodation

---

21. Young, *Sialkot*, 4.
22. UPCUSA, *Minutes of the Forty-Seventh General Assembly*, 316.
23. Anderson and Campbell, *Shadow*, 155.
24. Christopher, "Sialkot," 628.
25. UPCUSA, *Triennial Report*, 190.

for those who come from distant places to attend the convention. The CTI graduates who later went on to serve with various Christian missions in India were interestingly called "Psalm singing" pastors.[26]

**I. D. Shahbaz Hall in Sialkot**

The great spiritual revival in Sialkot was so powerful that at the second annual convention in 1905 "the chairman came down from his seat and declared the meeting to be in the hands of God's Spirit."[27] The accounts that describe the depth of revivals in Sialkot are captivating. A mission report on the Sialkot Convention in 1905 states: "Someone announced the 30th Psalm. It was sung throughout. . . . The 148th Psalm will long be remembered as the convention song. It was sung by day and by night."[28] The minutes of the 1906 General Assembly of the United Presbyterian Church say of the Sialkot Convention held from August 25 to September 3, 1905: "It has been a deep seated revival" which resulted in "the conviction of sin, cleansing of life, and joy in the Holy Spirit."[29]

26. Anderson and Campbell, *Shadow*, 110.
27. Carre, *Hyde*, 19.
28. Anderson and Watson, *North*, 258–60.
29. UPCUSA, *Minutes of the Forty-Eighth General Assembly*, 579.

The schoolgirls from various places who learned these psalms from Miss Henrietta Cowden came to sing and teach these psalms at large gatherings such as the Sialkot Convention, as Miss Cowden was given the responsibility to teach these psalms at all Christian schools for girls in the area. The United Presbyterian Mission had girls' schools in Sialkot, Pasrur, Gujranwala, Sargodha, Sangla Hill, Rawalpindi, Jhelum, Martinpur, Abbottabad (all-in present-day Pakistan), Dhariwal, and Pathankot (Indian part of Punjab).[30] Moreover, people from different places gathered in Sialkot for these meetings. They learned and sang the Punjabi Psalms and later on used them for Christian worship in their hometowns. The Christian gatherings at Sialkot have played an integral role in the spiritual growth of the Punjabi Christians and even to this day the Sialkot Convention is attended by various Christian denominations from all over the country.

The massive spiritual revival that began in Punjab at the commencement of the Sialkot Convention under the leadership of John Nelson Hyde (also regarded as "the apostle of prayer"), and the use of the Punjabi Psalter in those meetings, cannot be seen as a mere coincidence or "an unsought breeze from heaven" but rather as God working in that particular era in a specific place among specific people.[31] Roger Hedlund regards the Punjabi Psalms and the Sialkot Convention as the two major factors responsible for "conversions" and Christian maturity in the Punjab region.[32]

---

30. Anderson and Campbell, *Shadow*, 77–86.
31. Mcgaw, *Hyde*, 23.
32. Hedlund, "Pakistan," 719.

The annual Sialkot Convention takes place in the CTI premises

## 1.3. The Content of the Psalms

The spiritual depth and comfort found in the book of Psalms brought real hope to the depressed classes, who were being oppressed by those of the better social classes and were regarded as the "depraved poor" and the "illiterate menials."[33] The songs of justice and hope were relevant to their own conditions as they faced immense discrimination by society; they were treated badly and were seen as "untouchables."[34] For the outcast Punjabi Christians "it was not their poverty" that they disliked "but their slavery."[35] The Punjabi Christians were called the "sweepers and scavengers" of the Punjab.[36] They were unaccepted and unwelcomed by others due to the work they were involved in, as it was considered to be filthy and dirty.[37]

---

33. Massey, *Panjab*, 12.
34. Anderson and Campbell, *Shadow*, 53.
35. Madras, "Movement," 445.
36. Cox, *Imperial*, 120.
37. Perkins, "Caste," 305.

Consequently, the Punjabi Christians faced immense disdain from society. The following excerpt explains their condition:

> *These were outcastes who lived in the outskirts of the village, having no social contact with the upper castes in society except for working for them. They were imposed upon to do as part of their social religious duty all the filthy and loathsome jobs like sweeping and cleaning of houses, drains, sewage, cleaning cow-sheds, carrying cow-dung, animal carcasses and even human excreta. These impositions made them objects of public contempt, humiliation, discrimination and brutality of the kind that suppressed or eliminated the environment and opportunities necessary for human growth and development. People in power could therefore relegate them in society to the status of slaves.*[38]

However, these outcastes and rejected ones were greatly encouraged and touched by the psalms that spoke of restoration and not losing trust and hope in all situations. The depressed Punjabi Christians warmly welcomed the songs that spoke of protection and release from oppressors, as they themselves were not respected and "recognized" by society, the doors for equal work opportunities and education were shut down on them.[39] They experienced "dignity and love" through the singing of faith.[40] The content of the psalms, their message of deliverance, hope, and security in God, played a vital role in the spread of these psalms among the oppressed Punjabi Christians.

### 1.4. The Cooperation between the Mission Agencies

Another significant factor in the making of the Punjabi Psalter was the role of the various mission agencies, without whose contributions and cooperation the preparation and usage of the Punjabi Psalms would not have been possible. The part played by the United Presbyterian church remains absolutely vital in this regard. Nevertheless, the enormous level of cooperation and actions taken by the Church Missionary Society in this matter were crucial and significant. It is an interesting reality as discussed in the previous chapter, that Dr. Shahbaz served with the Church Missionary Society as an evangelist and teacher before he started working with the United Presbyterian Mission. It would not have been possible for Dr. Shahbaz to

---

38. Doger, "Community," 3.
39. Gordon, *India*, 173–74.
40. Adeney, *Poor*, 51.

work with the United Presbyterian mission without him being first released by the Church Missionary Society. It is a first-class example of cooperation and partnership between mission agencies, following the realization that the greatest need was for personnel exchange for Christian work.

This collaboration shown by the different mission agencies was the result of the Punjab Missionary Conference that was held in Lahore in 1863 in which the need and value of partnership between different Christian denominations in the Punjab was given much stress. The participants agreed that it was imperative to work together for the unity, stability, and strength of the native church of India.[41] The Church Missionary Society and the United Presbyterian Mission in Punjab had good working relations, and Dr. Shahbaz was not the first person who was generously transferred by CMS to the United Presbyterian Mission. There was a convert named Aziz-ul-Haq, who, like Dr. Shahbaz, was baptized by Rev. Robert Clark of CMS, received training for Christian service at the CMS institutions, and later on served with the United Presbyterian Mission.[42] The words of the Rev. Robert Clark are worth noting in this regard:

> *God's grace is not confined to any one Church or people . . . and we have seen also that converts of the Church of England are not better Christians than those of other Churches. . . . The strong bond in India between the United Presbyterian Mission and the Church Missionary Society was demonstrated by the fact that the invitation for CMS to work in Punjab was sent through Rev. John Newton of the United Presbyterian Mission at the request of an anonymous person who donated a large sum of money for CMS to begin its work in India.*[43]

The CMS work in Amritsar was established in 1852, and in 1867 a similar invitation was made by the Presbyterian Mission for CMS to work in Lahore.[44]

The *Masihi Git Ki Kitab* (Christian Hymn Book) published in Roman script from Agra by the CMS Industrial Press in 1914 included forty Punjabi psalms. The preface of this hymn book mentions: "We are also thankful to the Synod of the American Presbyterian Church for granting the permission to include eleven hymns from their book *Zabur o Git* [Psalms and Hymns] and forty Psalms from their book *Panjabi Zaboor* [Punjabi Psalms] for the

---

41. Newton, "Church," 309.
42. Gordon, *India*, 439.
43. Clark, *Account*, 4.
44. Salmon, *Punjab*, 20.

Punjabi congregations."[45] A letter dated May 7, 1913, sent from Lahore by the secretary of the British and Foreign Bible Society (Punjab Auxiliary) to the Bible Society office in London, concerning Scriptures in the Punjabi language states: "There is an edition of some of the Psalms in metrical version which are very widely used not only by the congregations connected with the United Presbyterian but also by the C.M.S. This edition seems most popular."[46] The Baptist Missionary Society also contributed toward the usage of these psalms among the locals by including a selection of the Punjabi psalms in their songbook in 1913 so that they could be used for Christian worship in their congregations.

The contributions to the making of the Punjabi Psalter made by various Christian missions are often not heard or remain unknown. Generally, people can be heard giving credit to one Christian denomination over the other, or overemphasizing the contributions made by one particular denomination. In order to appreciate the Punjabi Psalms to their full extent, it is vital to realize the depth of cooperation and understanding that different Christian denominations in the region of Punjab demonstrated for the Christian work. In Pakistan's present-day context, where the individual denominational achievements appear to be given much more significance than a combined strategical effort made by all denominations, united efforts and cooperation becomes much needed. The absence of a combined effort leads to further division and lack of collaboration between different denominations, which is unhealthy for the growth of the church. The church needs to learn to accept, appreciate, fully embrace, and rejoice in what the Lord is doing in and through each denomination. In this regard, prayers need to be made for God to revive the hearts and minds of Christian leadership of all denominations in Pakistan. If the church in Pakistan wants to effectively reach out to the lost and shine for Christ in a land where they live as a small minority, it is not possible until and unless the church as a whole has a combined vision. It will help to create a positive attitude, mutual respect, deeper appreciation, and a genuine spirit to win souls for Christ and his kingdom.

---

45. *Masihi Git*, 1; translation mine.
46. BFBS Archives, 468.

# The Punjabi Psalms

## 2. FACTORS DELAYING THE PREPARATION OF THE PUNJABI ZABUR

### 2.1. The Issue of Language and Class

It is now essential to look at the reasons that delayed the availability of Psalms in Punjabi and due to which the Western missionaries had divided thoughts on this subject. Stewart draws attention to this crucial issue when he writes: "Those interested in the work oscillated between the adoption of Eastern and Western meters."[47] Why were some reluctant to have Psalms translated into the Punjabi language set to Eastern tunes? In this regard, the *Indian Year-Book* mentions:

> In most Missions in India the attempt has been made to introduce English tunes in public worship. Missionaries in general are not acquainted with native music; they think European music much superior, and it has no heathenish associations connected with it.[48]

One factor for the delay in preparation of the Punjabi Psalms in local melodies was to do with favoring Western-style music by the Western mission agencies in general, although some members of the same mission seemed to disagree with that notion. Was it merely an issue of musical preference or was there something more to it? It seems that the issue was not solely about the style of melodies but of the language to which these tunes would be set. To understand this, it is important to look at the context of the church before the massive numbers of converts from the underprivileged class, who spoke Punjabi, became Christians and joined the Christian church in the north of India.

It is to be remembered that the Psalms were first translated into Urdu, or Hindustani as it was then called. It was the language that had been used by the churches in north India in their services; the floods of hymn books in Urdu were produced during the late nineteenth century in north India by various Christian missions. It was the language that the missionaries would normally study first upon their arrival in the north of India.[49] Urdu was considered to be a language of communication among the literates and those of the better social class, although it was not more than a foreign language to many ordinary people in the Punjab, especially the common countrymen and women. In this regard Christopher Harding writes concerning Urdu: "It was regarded as a dead language; many villagers did not even recognize the

---

47. Stewart, *Life*, 303.
48. Murdoch, *Indian Year-Book for 1861*, 236.
49. Cox, *Imperial*, 111.

sound of it, and assumed the missionaries were speaking English."[50] Since Urdu was the dominant language in the church, it is not hard to assume that it suited only a particular class of people with specific language criteria.

The substantial conversion of people from the depressed classes in the Indian subcontinent is generally referred to as "mass movement" or "group movement"; and in Punjab it originated from Sialkot particularly during the period 1870–1891 with the conversion of a man named Ditt.[51] There was an "amazing growth," and the impact of these massive conversions can be seen by the fact that the numbers of Christians in the Punjab increased from less than four thousand to approximately five hundred thousand.[52] However, from a tiny and dominantly literate class of people, it turned the church in Punjab into a huge and illiterate group of the unprivileged class.[53] In discussing the preparation of the metrical psalms, the divided thoughts among the missionaries, as indicated by Stewart, makes one think that some preferred to see the continuation of Urdu in the church while others insisted that Punjabi should be used instead. Nevertheless, in spite of the debate on this issue the committee was asked to translate the Psalter into Urdu. As a result, only the educated class and the Western missionaries could sing these psalms, whereas the majority of the ordinary people were left out, as they could neither read nor understand them.

Urdu was used by the literate class and had been an established language in the church, as it was regarded as the official language of the whole of north India, whereas newly converted Christians from the depressed class spoke Punjabi.[54] Urdu was the language in which a vast majority of Western missionaries in the north of India would preach.[55] Therefore for some it was no less than a nightmare to introduce Punjabi, the language of the depressed class, to be used in the church, especially in the presence of an educated class who had been using Urdu in the church. For example, one key missionary leader commented that Punjabi, the language of the first convert Ditt, was not fit for the church.[56]

It was feared that with the whole shift of language in the church, those of the higher class and literates would feel embarrassed and uneasy to adjust in the church setting. This must have been a difficult situation for the

---

50. Harding, *Punjab*, 94.
51. Pickett, *Movement*, 21.
52. Godfrey, *Outcastes*, 34.
53. Campbell, "Church," 150.
54. Murdoch, *Manual*, 62.
55. Mackenzie, *Mission*, 143.
56. Cox, *Imperial*, 120.

Western missionaries to keep side by side the two distinctive groups both in terms of language and social class. The problems that began as a result of the two distinct groups coming together can be seen by the fact that every effort was made to ensure that those of the higher social classes "would sit at the front of the church so that they would use the communion implements first, before they become polluted" by those belonging to the depressed classes.[57] The whole issue of class and language use hindered in the making of metrical psalms in Punjabi.

## 2.2. Mission Strategy

The second factor in delaying the translation of Psalms into the language of the ordinary people was to do with the mission strategy in the area. The pioneer missionary in Sialkot, Gordon, summarizes his thirty years of labor in the Punjab: "I began with my eye upon the large towns and cities, but have been led from them to the country villages. I began with the educated classes and people of good social position, but ended among the poor and the lowly."[58]

The mission agencies in India were not ready for these instant and massive conversions among the depressed classes, as it all seemed strange to them, and many of them were reluctant to take necessary steps to provide care for the floods of these poor people who were beginning to join the Christian church.[59] As a result, those who saw it more significant to evangelize among the literates and the higher social class felt that inquirers and converts from the higher class should not be lost at the cost of illiterate converts of the depressed classes whose numbers were much more than those of the literate and high social class. It is interesting to note that right from the beginning the strategy of the mission agencies in India was to concentrate on the literate and the higher social class; it was felt that they could influence others and could make a huge difference in the society, and therefore it was more essential to focus on these people in order to see lasting and better results.[60] One thing was clear: it was not God's strategy.

However, some missionaries, acknowledging and sensing the direction in which God was leading them and looking at the massive conversions among the depressed class, recognized the crucial need for translating Psalms into Punjabi for the ordinary people so that they could also praise

---

57. Massey, *Panjab*, 18.
58. Gordon, *India*, 447.
59. Cox, *Enterprise*, 211.
60. Cox, *Imperial*, 116.

God in their own language and music. Berner writes that the "great people movements in northwest India overturned the assumption most missions had held that winning the upper classes was a better strategy than attempting to win the lower."[61] The mission agencies in north India were rather surprised to see the unexpected results; they planned a strategy to reach out "from the top down" and it happened to be "from the bottom up."[62] As a result, mission agencies struggled to accept the reality and to consider a change in the mission strategy.

### 2.3. Attitude toward Fellow Missionaries

The third factor had to do with the poor attitude of missionaries toward their fellow missionaries. Since in general the strategy taken by the Christian missions was to focus on the literate and higher social class, the new initiatives to work among the depressed classes were objected to both by the missionaries of the same mission and of others. In other words, those who wished to initiate the work among the underprivileged were faced with immense pressure and cruel comments.[63] Some missionaries were not happy about activities and efforts aimed at the depressed classes as they suspected them to be harmful in evangelizing among the better social class. In this regard Gordon writes: "A missionary remarked publicly, at a general Missionary Conference, that it was 'bad policy' to receive such low persons."[64] Such negligence toward people of lower classes and rivalry among members of different and the same mission agencies was a hindrance in initiating work on the Psalms in Punjabi.

### 2.4. Government Support

The fourth and the final factor in delaying the preparation of the Punjabi Psalms was to do with government support toward maintaining the superiority of Urdu as an academic language. Urdu was not only taught at educational institutions, it was used in the courts and had a literary language status.[65] Moreover, it was the "lingua franca" in the north of India.[66]

---

61. Berner, "Pakistan," 629.
62. Cox, *Imperial*, 116.
63. Anderson and Campbell, *Shadow*, 53.
64. Gordon, *India*, 178.
65. Ekbal, *India*, 119.
66. Everaert, *Urdu*, 258.

In this regard, Stewart writes, "the authorities of the province exalt Urdu at the expense of Punjabi and make the former the chief vehicle of education, native literature and civil administration."[67] As Punjabi was not an academic language, it lacked the support of those in governance and caused some to think that it was not worth spending time and money on producing something in this language that was unlikely to be used.

---

67. Stewart, *Life*, 268.

# IV

# The Present-Day Usage of the Punjabi Psalms

## 1. DEVOTIONAL USE

### 1.1. Personal and Communal Piety

THE PUNJABI PSALMS ARE used in a number of different ways in Pakistan. First of all, the Christians use them for their spiritual growth and the building up of their faith in both personal and communal expressions of devotion. In writing about the importance of Psalms in Christian life, Graham Kendrick asserts: "If we want Christians to take responsibility for their personal worship lives, I don't think that we can do it without equipping them to use the Psalms."[1] The versified psalms have played a central role in the theological development of the church in Pakistan.[2] In general, Punjabi Christians, especially the older generation, know a number of the Punjabi psalms by heart. The majority of the older generation has had no schooling, thus memorization of God's Word as translated in the Punjabi Psalms helps

---

1. Kendrick, "Worship," 29.
2. Kuttianiamattathil, "Contextual," 414.

in learning about God's truth.³ The older generation in particular may normally be observed singing these Punjabi psalms very early in the morning as they start the day in their various tasks. Quite often their choice of psalm reflects their inner state, what they have been going through in life, expressing their spiritual, mental, and emotional condition through the singing of psalms before God.

My father was very fond of the Punjabi *Zabur* and these psalms were very close to his heart. I had my brother's harmonium at home, and I used to play many of the psalms on it. It wasn't perfect, as I had learned the harmonium out of interest through self-practice. One day I saw my father being very depressed for some reason. He was quiet and sitting alone in the porch area that day. I took out the harmonium and started playing one of his favorite *Zabur*, Psalm 16. It attracted him like a magnet, he came inside the room where I was playing the harmonium, without saying a single word he sat on a chair and closed his eyes as I continued to play the *Zabur*. It was an indication that playing this psalm on harmonium was working like a medicine, so I started singing the *Zabur* as well. With his eyes closed, he was contemplating the words:

> *Keep me safe, my God,*
> *For in you I take refuge.*
> *I say to the Lord, "You are my Lord;*
> *Apart from you I have no good thing."*
> (Ps 16:1)

My father was pouring out his heart before the Lord while listening to the *Zabur* being sung and played on a harmonium. It was amazing to see how the Punjabi Psalms are means of the spiritual uplifting of the believers.

## 1.2. Persecution and Discrimination

Here it is important to briefly mention the status and challenges of Pakistani Christians. The present day Christians in Pakistan are a "struggling" community that is often looked down upon by the majority.⁴ The negative attitude toward the Punjabi Christians continues to this day as they face discrimination, many are forced to engaged in jobs that are considered to be menial and thus they experience rejection and alienation.⁵ In other words, the general attitude shown toward them does not seem to be

---

3. O'Brien, "Identity," 85.
4. Gabriel, *Citizens*, 64.
5. Walbridge, "Law," 123.

different that of the days of mass movement when these lower caste poor people became Christians.

It is sad that many people look at Christians in Pakistan as people who are born to do messy jobs that no one else is willing to perform. Even at the government level, from time to time the sweeper and latrine-cleaning jobs are advertised in such a way as to clearly indicate that only Christians can apply for such jobs.[6] It is open discrimination; it indicates that such a sick mentality toward the Christians is deeply rooted in society. It also demonstrates how one community perceives itself to be innately superior and views the other community to be innately filthy and without any dignity. The Christian sewage cleaners throughout the country put their lives to risk in order to keep the sewage lines clean and running. They are not provided with any safety kits, they are often seen publicly going down the pits, gutters, and manholes, drawing the human waste and garbage with buckets in their hands. There have been several incidents in which the sewage cleaners have lost their lives due to inhaling poisonous gases found in gutters and manholes. On one occasion, the doctor refused to touch an unconscious Christian sewage cleaner named Irfan Masih. The doctor was fasting, and he believed that touching the dirty body would break his fast. Sadly, Irfan Masih passed away as a result of the doctor's negligence and refusal to provide medical treatment.[7]

Today, they are still called by the old terms that centuries ago were used for the lower caste groups, and are rather troubling and insulting terms for the Christians in today's Pakistani society.[8] Most of all, Pakistani Christians have been particularly targeted since the 1980s under section 295 of the Pakistan penal code concerning the blasphemy law that is often regarded as the hanging sword on the innocent Christians in Pakistan.[9] Section 295 (B) is concerning the defiling of the Qur'an, for which the punishment is life imprisonment. Section 295 (C) is about the use of derogatory remarks about the prophet of Islam (by words, either spoken or written or by visible representation, or by any imputation, innuendo, or insinuation, directly or indirectly), for which the punishment is death penalty or imprisonment for life. Moreover, according to the human rights commissions of Pakistan report, worship places of Pakistani Christians remained under attack by the

---

6. Zia ur-Rehman and Maria Abi-Habib, "Sewer Cleaners Wanted in Pakistan," *New York Times*, May 4, 2020, https://www.nytimes.com/2020/05/04/world/asia/pakistan-christians-sweepers.html.

7. "Sewer Cleaner Dies," *Pakistan Today*, June 2, 2017, https://www.pakistantoday.com.pk/2017/06/02/sewer-cleaner-dies-as-fasting-doctor-refuses-to-touch-patient/.

8. O'Brien, "Identity," 78.

9. Ahmed, "Minorities," 92.

extremists. It is "just one aspect of the difficulties that Pakistan's Christian population faced on account of their religious belief. They also faced widespread discrimination."[10]

The Pakistani Christians find comfort and peace by singing these Punjabi psalms as they continue to face discrimination by society. The first trial edition of the Punjabi Psalms published in 1892 contained fifty-five psalms. Besides the psalms of praise and adoration, a good number of the psalms carried the message of comfort and peace. In writing of the choosing of Punjabi psalms by the Punjabi Christians in Pakistan, O'Brien writes: "The choice had much to do with the way they looked at a future full of challenges," the preference for certain psalms was due to their message of protection and help that corresponds to the "helplessness and danger of their precarious minority position."[11]

At present, many of the well-known psalms among the Punjabi congregations include the ones that "deal with suffering and patience" as the Christians in Pakistan are often the victims of the blasphemy law for which the punishment is the death penalty.[12] Suffering for Christ is something that is deeply rooted in the lives of believers in Pakistan who experience social alienation, hatred, and discrimination for their lower social status as well as for their faith in Christ. Worshipping God through the singing of the *Zabur* identifies the conditions of these oppressed people. The message of God's faithfulness brings peace and comfort to their broken hearts as they repeatedly sing the words:

> *As for me, I call to God,*
> *And the Lord saves me.*
> *Evening, morning and noon*
> *I cry out in distress,*
> *And he hears my voice.*
> *He rescues me unharmed*
> *From the battle waged against me,*
> *Even though many oppose me.*
> (Ps 55:16–18 NIV)

---

10. *Human Rights*, 105.
11. O'Brien, *Construction*, 568–69.
12. Kim, *Religion*, 189–90.

## 1.3. Hope in the Age of Covid-19 Pandemic

Many of the psalms sung by the Pakistani churches carry the message of protection, deliverance, restoration, refuge, and trust in the Lord.[13] Today in the age of Covid-19, they sing even more of the psalms of protection, refuge, and hope in God.[14] During the last few months, I have observed that many of the quotations from the Psalms have been included in emails that I received from Christian friends in general. It is not surprising, since Psalms expresses the faith we can put in God in uncertain times.

The psalms of hope and protection are sources of strength and confidence in God for the believers in Pakistan during the age of Covid-19. They enthusiastically sing Psalm 91 with great reliance upon the Lord in a country where they do not have free access to much-needed modern medical technology these days, some people have reportedly lost lives as they did not have access to ventilators. They happen to find themselves in a community-based culture, where there is no concept of social distancing. In fact, such an idea is against their cultural and social values, and they find it extremely difficult to follow it. In such circumstances, they wholeheartedly put their trust in the Lord for his protection and sing these words with full confidence:

> *If you say, "The Lord is my refuge,"*
> *And you make the Most High your dwelling,*
> *No harm will overtake you,*
> *No disaster will come near your tent.*
> *For he will command his angels concerning you*
> *To guard you in all your ways;*
> *They will lift you up in their hands,*
> *So that you will not strike your foot against a stone.*
> (Ps 91:9–12 NIV)

Psalm 91 is one of the core psalms that Pakistan Christians are singing and drawing strength from these days. A friend of mine told me that in the city of Lahore in Pakistan, some Christians have written the words of Psalm 91 on the doorposts as an expression of their faith and trust in God. In our family devotions, we have been singing this psalm so frequently these past few months that our five-year-old have memorized it in Punjabi and even our eighteen-months-old attempts to join us in singing.

---

13. E.g., Pss 11, 16, 18, 23, 31, 46, 91, 121.

14. These psalms are much loved among the Pakistani Christians today. The selection of psalms found in the Sialkot Convention Hymn Book contains a good number of such psalms—e.g., Pss 16, 18, 20, 23, 31, 40, 46, 62, 69, 91, 102, 119 (part 20), 121, 130, 141.

In talking to a pastor from Pakistan, I learned that during the lockdown relaxation in the month of May 2020 he had to conduct eight funerals. These members did not die of Covid-19 though. In any case, culturally and socially it is an expectation that the pastor as a spiritual leader and shepherd must be present in-person to say the final goodbye at both churches and at the graveyard. The funerals in that part of the world are very participatory and open to the public. As a general practice, a funeral is attended by a majority of the community members to show support to the grieving family. Thus, the pastor had no other option than to be physically present at the funerals. I was very much concerned for the pastor because he did not have access to the protective kit while conducting the funerals, as there were several others around him. I inquired of the pastor if he was not scared of this situation? He said that he was a little worried, but he cannot leave his congregants alone. He added that in these unprecedented times the *Zabur* is his source of spiritual power. In times where there are so much fear and an increased number of deaths being reported from all around the world, the believers in Pakistan contemplate the words from another psalm they have been singing in the age of Covid-19:

> *God is our refuge and strength,*
> *An ever-present help in trouble.*
> *Therefore we will not fear, though the earth give way*
> *And the mountains fall into the heart of the sea,*
> *Though its waters roar and foam*
> *And the mountains quake with their surging.*
> (Ps 46:1–2 NIV)

There has been a lot of charity work being done in Pakistan since the spread of Covid-19. It is commendable how so many individuals, groups, charities, and show biz and sports stars are traveling from place to place to provide necessary food supplies to the needy. However, it was heartbreaking to receive the news on various social media platforms that Christians in different areas were not given the help they needed in the Covid-19 pandemic. Several people were seen complaining that they were first being asked about their religious affiliation, and when they had informed about their Christian faith, they were being ignored and the food distributors refused to provide them with the much-needed food supplies.[15] Despite such treatment, the believers continue to trust the Lord for providing their physical needs in the age of Covid-19 by singing the words:

---

15. A report is available on the Red Zone with Sajid Ishaq YouTube channel, HumSub.TV, https://www.youtube.com/watch?v=HmVZhxtDTxo.

*The Lord is gracious and compassionate.*
*He provides food for those who fear him.*
(Ps 111:4–5 NIV)

*I lift up my eyes to the mountains—*
*Where does my help come from?*
*My help comes from the Lord,*
*The Maker of heaven and earth*
(Ps 121:1–2 NIV)

**A Christian family worshipping in the age of Covid-19 in Lahore, Pakistan**

## 1.4. Liturgical and Cultural Use

The Punjabi Psalms also play a vital role in the church liturgy. It would not be unjust to count the second part of Psalm 24 (vv. 7–10) as the most familiar Punjabi psalm in Pakistani churches. The level of popularity gained by this psalm has to do with it being the opening song at the church service. Another reason for its popularity has to do with the use of excessive repetitions in this psalm, which make it easier to remember.

It is worth noting that Psalm 24, with its theme of God's sovereignty was also sung "on the first day" of the week by Levites in the temple.[16] Other than Psalm 24, the first part of Psalm 122 is also used as an opening psalm. However, Psalm 122 is not as popular as Psalm 24. Moreover, Psalm 24 is sung on Palm Sunday. In majority of the Pakistani churches on Palm Sunday, believers sing this psalm while walking in streets around the church in procession, carrying the palm branches. In some places, the processions may last for minutes, whereas in other places it may continue for hours as the participants enthusiastically shout for joy.

A church procession singing Psalm 24 on Palm Sunday

With great enthusiasm, the believers sing the words in a procession:

> Lift up your heads, you gates;
> Lift them up, you ancient doors,
> That the King of glory may come in.
> Who is he, this King of glory?
> Who is he, this King of glory?
> The Lord Almighty—
> He is the King of glory.
> (Ps 24:78 NIV)

The Indian Pakistani Church in Phoenix can be seen in a video carrying the palm branches as they enter the church in a lively procession while singing the Psalm 24, it shows that this practice is followed by diaspora churches as well. In this video, a man rides on a symbolic plush donkey signifying Jesus' triumphant entry into Jerusalem.[17] In Pakistan, one of the

16. Danby, *Mishnah*, 589.
17. The 2018 Palm Sunday video is available on the Indian Pakistani Church Facebook

largest processions on Palm Sunday is observed by the Catholic community of Youhanabad in Lahore. In some processions, the shofar and conch shell horn are used too. The Sialkot Convention Hymn Book recommends that Psalm 24 could also be used at the taking of Holy Communion.[18] Nevertheless, its practical use contradicts the recommendation made, as it is hardly sung for the Holy Communion. The suggestion seems in line with the first part of this psalm (vv. 1–6) that talks about seeking God with a pure heart in his holy place.

The last part of Psalm 72 is normally sung at the end of a Punjabi church service. This psalm authored by King Solomon is sung with great reverence by believers, as the congregations utter the words:

> *May his name endure forever;*
> *May it continue as long as the sun.*
> (Ps 72:17 NIV)

However, the Sialkot Convention Hymn Book does not list it among the closing psalms.[19] It is one of the well-known psalms being used among the Punjabi churches. Another interesting feature associated with Psalm 72 is the church offering. As a general practice in Pakistani churches, the offering is taken at the end of the service. Therefore, often Psalm 72 is sung as the offering psalm. On the other hand, the Book of Common Prayer used within the Church of Pakistan, the largest Protestant denomination in Pakistan, proposes it be sung to the Day of Ascension.[20] Sometimes Psalm 23, "The Lord is my Shepherd, I lack nothing" (NIV), is also used as the closing hymn.

Psalm 20 is regularly sung at funerals both at church and at the graveyard to express grief and sorrow. As people mourn, they contemplate the words:

> *May the Lord answer you when you are in distress;*
> *May the name of the God of Jacob protect you.*
> *May he send you help from the sanctuary*
> *And grant you support from Zion.*
> (Ps 20:1–2 NIV)

However, according to the thematic categorization of the Sialkot Convention Hymn Book, Psalm 20 is a reminder of a prayer-answering God; it suggests that it should be sung as a praise song when prayer has been

---

page, https://www.facebook.com/promila.wilson/videos/2138298879530439.

18. *Sialkot*, 490.
19. *Sialkot*, 484.
20. Synod Church of Pakistan, *Dua-e-Aam Kalisia-e-Pakistan*, 116.

answered.[21] The reason for this suggestion seems to be based on vv. 6–9 of this psalm, which focuses on God's victorious power in answering his people when they call upon him. The Book of Common Prayer used in Anglican churches in Pakistan suggests that it be sung at the dedication of the church building.[22] The psalm makes frequent reference to the sanctuary and offerings (vv. 2, 3, 6), which appears to be the reason for this suggestion.

The second part of Psalm 45 (vv. 10–17) is commonly used at wedding ceremonies in the church, when the bride enters the church accompanied by her father. As the bride and her father slowly walk to make their way to the front seats along with the bride's friends, a beautiful environment is created through the words:

> *Listen, daughter, and pay careful attention:*
> *Forget your people and your father's house*
> *Let the king be enthralled by your beauty*
> *Honor him, for he is your lord.*
> (Ps 45:10–11 NIV)

This psalm is seen as a royal psalm that was used at royal weddings in biblical times.[23] In the Indian subcontinent on a wedding day, the bridegroom accompanied by friends, relatives and family members arrives at the bride's house with drums, clarinets, trumpets and big horns that play well-known Bollywood wedding songs and traditional folk Punjabi wedding melodies.[24] It is a way of celebration. The arrival of the bridegroom at the bride's house to take her with him is reminiscent of the parable of the ten virgins that we read about in the Gospel of Matthew chapter 25. When the bridegroom is seen by those awaiting him, they shout with great joy: "Here's the bridegroom! Come out to meet him!" (Matt 25:6).

The Punjabi wedding is a good reminder that Jesus the bridegroom is coming soon to take his bride the church, who is adorned for him. For my wedding, I randomly went to a traditional wedding band to inquire about their availability. The band asked where should they meet? I suggested that we should meet outside the church building. After discovering that I was a Christian, the band asked if I would like for some of the *Zabur* (psalms) to be played at my wedding? He added: "We can play *Rab Khudawand Badsha Hai* (Ps 24) and *Shukar Yahowa da hi karo* (Ps 136) or any other *Zabur* that you may be interested in." I was very surprised to hear this, knowing that I was

---

21. Sialkot, 488.
22. Synod Church of Pakistan, *Dua-e-Aam Kalisia-e-Pakistan*, 258.
23. Bellinger, *Psalms*, 114.
24. Addleton, *Reflections*, 157.

talking to a Muslim person. I asked him how did he know about the Punjabi *Zabur*? And where did he learn them? He replied that many of his customers come from the local Christian community, and some request them to play the Punjabi *Zabur* on weddings. To accommodate the needs of their customers and from a business point of view they decided to learn a number of psalms that they now play on Christian weddings. I told the band that as soon the couple comes out of the church building, they can start playing Psalm 24. I was glad for some of the Punjabi *Zabur* to be played on my wedding day along with some traditional Punjabi folk melodies that people love to enjoy in celebration, as the party move toward the bride's house. Having a traditional musical band at a wedding is a must in the Indian subcontinent. It is interesting to observe that Christians who do not prefer any other melodies to be played on the wedding day have the alternative option to play the beautiful melodies of the Punjabi Psalms. It is interesting to note an unusual way in which these psalms are occasionally used.

Psalm 127 is usually read and preached from at the birth of a child, when parents bring the child for the first time in the church. Moreover, this psalm is often sung when someone invites friends and family to their newly built home as a sign for asking God to bless the new house. Likewise, Psalm 127 is sung and preached at the birthday parties of children.

Although, some of the Punjabi psalms have a somewhat set place in church liturgy, the majority do not seem to have a fixed order in a church service. The preacher occasionally selects the psalms according to the topic. Often the worship leader or the person conducting the service selects the psalms randomly to have a good mixture of different genres of psalms. For a vast majority of the churches in Pakistan, it is not normal for the preacher to inform the worship leader or the person conducting the service about the topic in advance, and usually it is not expected. Consequently, a random selection of psalms is made before the preaching is done. However, at the end of the preaching, often a psalm or hymn is sung that correlates with the topic being preached.

## 2. CREATING UNITY AMONG DIFFERENT CHRISTIAN DENOMINATIONS

The singing of the Punjabi Psalms has been successful in creating unity among churches in Pakistan. The metrical version of the Punjabi Psalms can be heard and sung at any church or denomination in Pakistan.[25] In fact, all major and minor Protestant denominations, such as the Church of Pakistan

---

25. O'Brien, "Identity," 85.

(unification of Lutherans, Methodists, and Anglicans),[26] Baptists, Brethren, Presbyterians (United and Reformed), Pentecostals, and Charismatic make use of these psalms. Within the Roman Catholic Church these psalms are widely used as well. According to Fr. Rev. Inayat Bernard, in the Catholic churches every morning a psalm is sung or read, and a mass cannot be completed without the inclusion of a *Zabur*.

It indicates that when a member of a particular denomination attends the church service of a different denomination, he or she is not faced with difficulty, as he or she can take full part in worship through the singing of these psalms. It is even more helpful for the vast numbers of illiterate Christians in Pakistan, particularly the older generation, to make use of these psalms in their religious, social, and family gatherings. They all can sing these psalms on occasions of joy, celebration, sorrow, and grief. It is to be noted that among the Pakistani churches, psalms are often identified and remembered by their chorus instead of their numerical number. This makes things easier especially for those who could not read but know the *Zabur* by heart.

The Punjabi *Zabur* are a symbol of unity and harmony among different Christian denominations in Pakistan, and they continue to build up a strong bond within the diverse churches. The metrical Punjabi psalms are beyond denominational boundaries. This reinforces the need to give credit to the entire Christian community in Pakistan for equally contributing toward the use of *Zabur* in worship. The beautiful melodies of *Zabur* can be heard all over the country, as the phrase in Pakistan goes, "from Karachi to Khyber," meaning from east to west, from corner to corner, the *Zabur* are much cherished.

A closer look at the church in Pakistan shows layers of fractions within the body of Christ; there is much visible disunity and it is hard to find things on which the overall Christian community demonstrates agreement. If there is one thing that strongly brings forth the unity of the Christian community in Pakistan, it is unquestionably the singing of the Punjabi *Zabur* by all churches, and the place they have in Christian worship among all denominations throughout the country. To appreciate the Punjabi Psalms to their full extent, it is vital to realize the depth of cooperation.

In sum, the mother tongue and indigenous music, the Sialkot Convention, the content of the psalms, and collaboration of Christian agencies were key factors in the spread of the Punjabi Psalms. The practice of neglecting illiterate people from the lower social class, disagreement among missionaries concerning evangelistic strategy, and lack of interest in the

---

26. Barrett, *Christian*, 572.

Punjabi language from the government caused delay in their preparation. The Psalms in Punjabi are used for spiritual and devotional purposes, they play a vital role in liturgy and have interesting cultural aspects to their use in the community of believer. The believers sing them with great confidence in the face persecution, discrimination, and mistreatment that they experience, since suffering for Christ is an everyday reality for them. In the age of the Covid-19 pandemic, the Punjabi *Zabur* are the source of spiritual strength, as Christians express their faith and trust in God by singing the psalms of hope, protection, deliverance, restoration, and refuge. One can hear these beautiful psalms being used in moments of happiness and grief, both at a personal and communal level. According to Fr. Francis Tanveer, "The Psalms in our vernacular by great Dr. I. D. Shahbaz are a Divine revelation. The Psalms are a great uniting spiritual and binding force to all the believers." The *Zabur* serve as a unifying force since they are sung among all Christian denominations in Pakistan.

# V

# Missiological Aspects of the Psalms in an Islamic Context

A CAREFUL OBSERVATION OF the Psalms in Punjabi reveals that these psalms have a number of terms and expressions that may be regarded as Muslim-friendly or familiar to Islam. However, this particular aspect of the Punjabi Psalms has never been explored. The Muslim-friendly terms in the Punjabi Psalms causes one to ask a few interconnected questions: Do the Psalms have bridge-building components for a dialogue between Christians and Muslims in Pakistan? What makes the Psalms special for sharing them with Punjabi Muslims in the Pakistani Islamic context? Is the existing translation of the Psalms in Punjabi suitable for them? What culturally available form and style is fitting to make the Psalms more acceptable to the Punjabi Muslims? What are some of the challenges in sharing the Psalms with the Pakistani Punjabi Muslims?

These questions may well lead to unconstructive, argumentative debate. However, it is important to mention that this is not the intention here. The core purpose of this chapter is to identify elements in the Psalms that can play an integral part in bridging gaps between Christians and Muslims in Pakistan. Moreover, the endeavor is to investigate commonalities for sharing the Psalms with the Punjabi Muslim brethren. This is not to deny that significant theological differences exist between Pakistani Christians and Muslims. However, it is an attempt to highlight constructive indicators rather than drifting into confrontational debate. Investigating commonalities between diverse religious groups living side by side can be more productive than stressing differences between the two, and in the case of Pakistan it seems even more important.[1] The Pakistani Punjabi Christians and Muslims share linguistic and cultural commonalities. Highlighting further bridge-building factors through the Psalms may help in narrowing gaps in a country where Christians are in a minority. Less than 2 percent of the population of Pakistan is Christian, and "an overwhelming majority" of the population, 97 percent, is Muslim.[2] As a minority community, it is crucial for the Pakistani Christians to seek ways to enhance their understanding of their fellow Muslim brethren and vice versa.[3]

First, some of the Muslim-friendly terms in the Punjabi Psalms will be surveyed. The response of the Pakistani Christians to the use of Islamic terms will be discussed. Second, the viewpoint of Islam on the Psalms, including intertextuality in the Psalms and Qur'an, will be highlighted. Third, the constructive cultural markers in Pakistani Punjabi society will be studied. Fourth, the selective common themes in the Psalms will be looked at for presenting to the Muslim brethren, particularly the characteristics of God in the Psalms and the Qur'an. Finally, some of the challenges involved in presenting the Psalms to the Punjabi Muslims will be highlighted. The notion of poetic Psalms for bridge-building in Pakistan has never been investigated before. This chapter will attempt to draw attention to how, in particular, the poetic form of the Psalms in Punjabi seems fitting to bridge gaps between the Punjabi-speaking Christians and Muslims in the Pakistani Islamic context, and how the Psalms, in a culturally appropriate style, are pertinent for sharing with the Punjabi Muslim brethren.

## 1. MUSLIM BACKGROUND OF DR. SHAHBAZ

Given the Islamic background of Dr. Imam-ud-Din Shahbaz, the presence of Muslim-friendly terms in the Psalms comes as no surprise. In fact, it is important in considering the notion of appropriateness of his Punjabi translation for the Punjabi Muslims. In this regard, it is worth noting that in the process of translation, it is probable for a translator's own personality to

---

1. Rumalshah, "Challenges," 52.
2. Mohiuddin, *Pakistan*, 26.
3. Asimi, *Minority*, 123.

Missiological Aspects of the Psalms in an Islamic Context

be reflected in his or her translation.[4] A person's background, upbringing, attitudes, knowledge, and social context all play a role in the development of one's personality.[5] Dr. Shahbaz was himself from a Muslim background, being born and raised in an Islamic environment. As discussed in the previous chapters, his conversion makes it evident that he was well aware of Islamic doctrine. Likewise, his personal poetry contains a considerable amount of Islamic terminology. On the one hand, some of his poetry can be regarded as polemical. On the other hand, it indicates that such a style of writing was spontaneous for someone from an Islamic background. Therefore, as a translator it was natural for Dr. Shahbaz to bring in his past Islamic experience and knowledge to translating the Psalms. Consequently, the choice of words and expressions in the translation of metrical Punjabi psalms appear to be Muslim-friendly.

## 2. MUSLIM-FRIENDLY TERMS AND THE PUNJABI PSALMS

The existence of Muslim-friendly terminology is the first stepping-stone in thinking about sharing the Psalms to the Punjabi Muslims in Pakistan. It is important to mention that in Pakistan, the Christians tend to avoid using some of the vocabulary in everyday communication that is perceived to belong to Muslims alone. This appears to be a commonality in countries where Muslims and Christians live side by side, and where language, and particularly Arabic religious vocabulary, make a distinction between "religious communities."[6] In the Punjabi translation of Psalm 42, the noun *eid* meaning "festival" has been mentioned; a word commonly used by Muslims in Pakistan for their religious festivals.[7] In contrast, the majority of the Pakistani Christians abstain from using this word in reference to their religious festivals.

Although one struggles to find a clear explanation regarding the use and prevention of certain words within Pakistani Christian circles, it is not difficult to observe that Christians in Pakistan refrain from using certain vocabulary. Hence, words labeled as Muslim, specific to or associated with Islam, are likely to be excluded by the Christians. For instance, if a Pakistani Christian uses an Islamic expression for greetings, very often he is likely to

---

4. Wegner, *Translations*, 358.
5. Doyle, "Translation," 22.
6. Thomas, "Terminology," 103.
7. Hayyim, *Farhang*, 401.

face unappreciative comments from his fellow Christians.[8] It indicates that some Pakistani Christians are quite cautious about Islamic terms, whether used by their own people or by outsiders in connection to them. For example, the word *Isai*, meaning "Christian" or "a follower of Isa," is commonly used by Muslims in Pakistan in reference to the Christians; this word is derived from the word *Isa*, used in the Qur'an for Jesus. In 2005, a petition was filed in the Lahore High Court by a Pakistani Christian against the use of the word *Isai* for Christians. The petitioner argued that the word *Masihi*, meaning "of the Messiah, appertaining to Christ," should be used instead.[9] This is due to the argument that Jesus of the Bible is not *Isa* of the Qur'an, therefore the word *Isai* should not be used for Christians. The Christian representatives, when they are invited to speak on media, often stress that they be addressed as *Masihi* and not as *Isai*.[10] It simply points to the reaction that Pakistani Christians show toward the use of Islamic familiar terms and expressions in general.

Despite the arguments discussed above, one discovers that the sort of vocabulary understood by the majority of the Christians in Pakistan to be exclusively Islamic and avoided for that reason, in fact appears in the translation of the Punjabi Psalms. It would help to briefly look at some of the terms used by Dr. Shahbaz about which some Pakistani Christians have strong reservations, including *Allah*, *Allah Ta'ala*, and *Isa*. As well as this, there are terms in the Punjabi Psalms that one hardly hears used by the Pakistani Christians in everyday communication. These terms, rooted in Islamic traditions, include *Sunna*, *Fajar*, and *Khabis*. Moreover, a number of other words in the Punjabi Psalms may be added to the list of words that are normally perceived to be Islamic, including *Fatwa* (Ps 149), *Kufar* (Ps 74), *Umma* or *ummat* (Pss 28, 47, 56, 62, 72, 78, 81, 85, 95), *Subhan* (Ps 17), *Momin* (Pss 31, 81), Ibrahim (Ps 47), *Ghaffur* (Pss 7, 60), *Ghaffar* (Ps 41), *Rehman* (Pss 9, 17, 40, 48, 65, 78, 86, 119, 138), *Rahim* (Pss 18, 62, 75, 116, 145), *Illahi* (Pss 8, 71, 119), *Ya-Illahi* (Pss 19, 73, 105), *Al-Qadir* (Ps 22), and *Rab-ul-Alamin* (Ps 143).[11] All these words indicate the presence of Muslim-friendly terms in the Punjabi Psalms.

---

8. The Christians in Pakistan normally use the word *Salaam* (peace) for general greetings. The Islamic expression *Assalam-alaikum* (peace be on you) is not used by Christians in Pakistan. Its use by Christians is normally not appreciated by fellow Christians.

9. Gill, "Will Rebranding," *Tribune Express*, September 7, 2016.

10. The Anglican bishop of Karachi, Sadiq Daniel, stressed this point during a religious talk show called "Aalim Online" that was broadcast by the Geo TV channel on August 5, 2009.

11. These terms may be found in the 1908 ed. of the Punjabi Psalms on pp. 363; 189;

## Allah and Allah Ta'ala

Allah is the name for God in the Qur'an, where the "Supreme Being" is mentioned by this name.[12] In reference to God, the Muslims in Pakistan also use the Arabo-Persian term *Allah Ta'ala* meaning "the Exalted, the Most High (God)."[13] The term Allah *Ta'ala* has been used in the Punjabi translation of Psalm 12 (part 2, couplet 6); and the term *Allah* in Psalm 18 (part 4, couplet 20), Psalm 35 (part 1, couplet 5), and Psalm 106 (part 3, couplet 27).[14] However, none of these psalms may be found in editions of the Sialkot Convention Hymn Book currently used for worship in Pakistani churches. The term *Allah* also occurs in Psalm 37 (part 4) and is still present in the Sialkot Convention Hymn Book.[15] The reason for this is probably because this particular section of Psalm 37 became rather popular. Nonetheless, while singing, the Christian gospel singers tend to replace the term *Allah* with *Yahowa* (Yahweh). For example, the late Rev. Ernest Mall, a very popular gospel singer, in his audio recording of Psalm 37 in Punjabi, substitutes the term *Allah* with *Yahowa* (Yahweh).[16] As indicated in the previous chapters, nowhere in the 1892 edition of selected psalms and in the 1908 edition of the complete Punjabi Psalms has Dr. Shahbaz used the term *Yahowa* (Yahweh) in his translation. Instead, terms such as *Khudawand* (Pss 1:6; 2:6; 16:7; 20:1; 24:10; 47:2; 55:16; 78:4), *Khuda* (Pss 16:8; 22:27; 33:2; 34:7; 36:5; 40:1; 103:8; 139:1), and *Rabb* (Pss 9:7; 22:23; 27:7; 34:1; 107:2; 126:1; 136:1; 145:13), respectively, meaning "owner, possessor, master," "God, Lord," and "God, possessor, preserver," were being used.

The decision to use Yahweh literally in the Punjabi Psalms was made before the second edition was published in 1916. It was probably done to make the translation of these psalms correspond to the original Hebrew.[17] The term *Yahowa* (Yahweh) was printed in bold type in this edition, possibly to highlight the tetragrammaton YHWH or to show the difference in

---

75, 129, 147, 157, 181, 203, 210, 215 and 241; 35; 83 and 210; 128; 11 and 154; 118; 17, 35, 114, 130, 160, 203, 218, 301 and 339; 43, 158, 191, 293 and 352; 14, 180 and 307; 49, 186 and 270; 53 and 347, respectively.

12. Hughes, *Islam*, 141.

13. Platts, *Dictionary of Urdu*, 326.

14. These may be found on pp. 24, 42, 95, and 272, respectively, in the 1908 ed. of the complete Punjabi Psalms.

15. The term occurs in couplet 21 of Ps 37 and may be found on p. 105 in the 1908 ed. Only part 4 of Ps 37 is included in the Sialkot Convention Hymn Book, and may be found on p. 35 in the 2014 ed.

16. Recording available at https://www.youtube.com/watch?v=IXPW7UUW_-s.

17. *Desi Ragan*, 3.

comparison to the previous edition. To this day several subsequent editions of the Sialkot Convention Hymn Book have unintentionally followed that practice.[18] Interestingly, one is not to find the word *Yahowah* in Urdu dictionaries currently available.

The Pakistani Christians in general do not use *Allah* in reference to God, instead they use the Persian word *Khuda*.[19] However, some may be heard using the word *Allah* freely in natural conversations which show the influence of the Muslim population among whom these Christians work and reside. In relation to the use of some specific terms such as *Allah*, the situation in Pakistan seems to be somewhat different from Malaysia, where in past years strong objections were made by Muslims that Malay Christians should not be allowed to use the word *Allah*, and that it exclusively belongs to them.[20] As a result, Christian publications and Bibles were banned due to this controversy. However, the Christians in Malaysia insisted on continuing to use this term.[21] It is worth noting that besides Indonesia and Malaysia, the term *Allah* is commonly used for God by Christians in the "Arab world."[22]

## Isa

The term *Isa* is the name for Jesus in the Qur'an.[23] It occurs in the translation of Psalm 95 (part 1, couplet 1) in the 1908 edition of the Punjabi Psalms.[24] Interestingly, the term has been substituted by the pronoun *oho*, meaning "the same, the very one," in the Sialkot Convention Hymn Book used today.[25] It indicates a tendency to abstain from using Muslim-familiar terms. Instead of *Isa*, the Pakistani Christians use the word *Yasu* for Jesus. As mentioned earlier, this is due to the argument that Jesus of the Bible is not the same as *Isa* of the Qur'an, therefore Christians should avoid using it.

---

18. For example, the 39th ed. of the Sialkot Convention Hymn Book, published in 1994, has several psalms where Yahweh is written in bold type, such as Pss 2, 4, 15–20, 22, and 27.
19. Nazir-Ali, *Islam*, 157.
20. Riddell, "Islamization," 167.
21. Goh, *Southeast*, 55.
22. Riddell, "Entitled," 42.
23. Adamec, *Islam*, 168.
24. It may be found on p. 240 in the 1908 ed.
25. In the first stanza of Ps 95 (part 1) the phrase *Isa Chatan Hai* (*Isa* is the rock) as found in the 1908 ed. has been replaced by *Oho Chatan Hai* (the same is the rock) in the Sialkot Convention Hymn Book.

## Sunna

The "exemplary behavior of the Prophet" of Islam that later generations are to follow is generally regarded as *Sunna* or as *Sunnat* in Punjabi and Urdu.[26] It is also referred to as "tradition" of the Prophet of Islam. In Pakistan, the term is commonly used in its general sense, such as the practice of growing a beard.[27] However, particularly in rural parts of the Punjab region it frequently refers to the practice of circumcision.[28] The term *Sunnat* occurs in the Punjabi translation of Psalm 81 (part 1, couplet 3).[29] Here, *Sunnat* is used in the sense of an old practice and tradition in Israel, to celebrate the festival with exceeding joy and trumpets as had been commanded by God. Although Psalm 81 part 1 is included in the Sialkot Convention Hymn Book, one hardly hears this psalm being sung in churches. For this reason, it is very likely that this particular term in the Punjabi Psalms has not been noticed.

## Fajar

Muslims pray five times a day, and the prayer offered at dawn is called "*Salat-alfajr.*"[30] In Pakistan, it is usually known as *fajar ki namaz* or *namaz-e-fajar*, meaning "prayer of daybreak" or "early morning prayer," respectively. The Persian word *namaz*, meaning "prayer," is commonly used, rather than the Arabic word *Salat*.[31] The word *fajar* occurs in the Punjabi translation of Psalm 5 (part 1, couplet 2), Psalm 22 (part 1, couplet 2), Psalm 46 (part 1, couplet 5), and Psalm 130 (part 1, couplet 6).[32] These occurrences point to the psalmist's deep desire to rise up early in the morning to pray and praise the Almighty. The Pakistani Protestant Christians normally use the word *ibadat*, "religious service, worship," for a church service instead of *namaz*. On the other hand, I have heard my Catholic friends using both *ibadat* and *namaz* to refer to a church service.

---

26. Juynboll, "Sunna," 166.
27. Shirazi, "Facial Hair," 119.
28. Wikeley, *Musalmans*, 47.
29. It may be found on p. 209 in the 1908 ed. and on p. 67 in the 2014 ed. of the Sialkot Convention Hymn Book.
30. Böwering, "Prayer," 227.
31. Lalljee, *Islam*, 23.
32. These may be found on pp. 8, 57, 127, 329 in the 1908 ed. and on p. 46 in the 2014 ed. of the Sialkot Convention Hymn Book.

## Khabis

The word *Khabis* is mentioned in the Qur'an for wicked and evildoers—for example, *Sura Al-Maidah* 5:100.[33] Although the term indicates a "bad" and "malignant" person in general, within the Islamic context in Pakistan it also denotes "an unclean spirit"; an evil spirit from the family of jinn, that is masculine in gender and has "red eyes."[34] This term occurs in the translation of Psalms 145 (part 3, couplet 12) and 146 (part 1, couplet 13).[35] In the Punjabi Psalms, the term is used in reference to the wicked. However, the Islamic religio-cultural understanding of this term cannot be ignored.

## 3. QUR'AN, HADITH, INTERTEXTUALITY, AND THE PSALMS

The purpose of exploring some Muslim-friendly terms in the Punjabi *Zabur* is to draw attention to indicators in the *Zabur* that may be worth noting in sharing the beautiful Psalms with Muslim friends. After having surveyed some of these terms employed by Dr. Shahbaz in his poetic translation, it is now important to look at the positive attitude to the Psalms in the Qur'an and *hadith*. Moreover, it would help to point out the engagement that medieval Muslim scholars had with the Psalms.

## The Qur'anic View on the Psalms

Christians are regarded as *Ahl-e-Kitab*, or "people of the Book," by the Muslims.[36] Muslims believe that the Torah, the Psalms, and the Gospel were given by God, and at the same time the Christian Scriptures are often charged by them as being corrupted.[37] Having said that, it may be noted that there is confusion concerning the authenticity of the Bible which exists in the minds of some people, because parts of the Christian Scriptures are considered to have maintained the revelation from God while others have not.[38] Moreover, the Qur'an itself does not provide exact information on this issue, and there is disagreement among Islamic circles as to whether

---

33. Hughes, *Islam*, 262.
34. Shahi, *Religion*, 138.
35. It may be found on pp. 354 and 356 in the 1908 ed.
36. Waardenburg, "Period," 3.
37. Nigosian, *Islam*, 65.
38. Talib, *Brotherhood*, 60.

the so-called alteration is to do with the way Christian Scriptures are being explained in "speech," or in the written "text."[39] Regardless of this, it is particularly the New Testament that is frequently targeted.[40] The reason for this is, understandably, the difficulties arising from attempts to interpret the statements mentioned in the Qur'an concerning Jesus Christ, rather than that of the core teachings about him found in the New Testament.[41]

With regard to the Psalms, normally one does not hear specific and strong opposing statements made by Muslims. It might be that ordinary Muslims have no real idea about the actual content of the Psalms, or that the more learned ones do not find its teaching threatening to the Qur'an and for which reason negative comment is not made against them. Nevertheless, the Qur'an speaks highly of the Psalms. There are two places where the Qur'an explicitly mentions the Psalms as divine revelation bestowed upon David: *Sura Al-Nisa* (4:163) and *Sura Al-Isra* (17:54).[42] Moreover, several Qur'anic passages speak of the exceptional blessing bestowed upon David to praise and worship God:

> And we subjugated with David the mountains and the birds to glorify; and We were doers. (*Sura Al-Anbiya* 21:79)

> And We bestowed grace from Us on David, O mountains and birds, echo (the words of) praise with him. (*Sura Saba* 34:10)

> Truly We subjected the mountains with him, to extol glory at evening and sunrise. And the birds were mustered, every one turned to him (extolling). (*Sura Sad* 38:18–19)[43]

## Intertextuality between the Psalms and Qur'an

The Qur'an has more intertextuality and correspondence with the Psalms than the New Testament.[44] For example, the powerlessness of idols mentioned in *Sura Al-Araf* (7:195) carries much similarity with description of idols in Ps 115:4–7. The language of the Qur'an appears to be largely of "psalmic and psalmic like" literature, similar to that being used in Psalms

---

39. Nazir-Ali, *Neighbour*, 18–19.
40. Glassé, *Encyclopedia*, 72.
41. Nazir-Ali, *Christ*, 27.
42. Horovitz, "Zabur," 372.
43. Khatib, *Koran*, 563, 599.
44. Hassan, *Shajara*, 2.

121 and 145.[45] There is a remarkable parallel between Psalm 104 and *Sura An-Nahl*.[46] The way Qur'anic *suras* from the early Meccan period are structured shows similarity to the Psalms. There exists a broad resemblance between *Sura Ar-Rahman* and Psalm 136.[47] Apart from this, one can observe vast similarity in a prayer found in *Al-Shafia Al-Sajjaidya* also known as the "Psalms of the Household of Muhammad," with Psalm 139. The prayer is offered on the twentieth day of Ramadan upon which man's inability to hide from God is being focused.[48]

According to Shabbir Akhtar, "The Quran never quotes from the Bible except for a verse" taken from the book of Psalms.[49] It is recorded in *Sura Al-Anbiya* (21:105): "For we have written in the Psalms, after the Remembrance, the earth shall be the inheritance of my righteous servants" taken from Ps 37:29.[50] It indicates that in comparison to other books of the Bible, the Psalms are more favored by the Muslims. It is true that several biblical narratives have some parallels in the Qur'an.[51] However, the statement made by Akhtar establishes that the Psalms in particular are viewed by Muslims as being more in line with the Qur'an, and vice versa.

## The View of Hadith on the Psalms

The collection of the sayings and traditions of the prophet of Islam and his companions is constituted by the *hadith*.[52] Like the Qur'an, the *hadith* makes references to the Psalms as revealed by God to David. There are several *hadiths* that focus on David's fasting and prayer, and regard his fasting as ideal, best and superior.[53] Similar *hadiths* are reported in Sahih Muslim.[54] The *hadiths* acknowledges that David was blessed with an attractive voice and was gifted in music. In this connection, the following *hadiths* are worth noting:

---

45. Elkayam, *Similarities*, 112–13.
46. Lodahl, *Bible*, 59.
47. Neuwirth, "Qur'anic," 733, 739.
48. McGinnis, *Sacred*, 212.
49. Akhtar, *Secular*, 380.
50. Arberry, *Koran*, 332.
51. Gabriel, *Islam*, 81–84.
52. Leaman, "Hadith," 229.
53. E.g., *Sahih Al-Bukhari* 3:31:195–201; 4:55:629–31; 6:61:572; 8:73:155; 8:74:294.
54. E.g., *Sahih Al-Bukhari* 2:6:2587–88; 2:6:2592; 2:6:2595–99; 2:6:2602–3.

# Missiological Aspects of the Psalms in an Islamic Context

> Narrated Abu Huraira: The Prophet said, "The reciting of the Zabur (i.e., Psalms) was made easy for David. He used to order that his riding animals be saddled, and would finish reciting the Zabur before they were saddled." (Sahih Al-Bukhari 4:55:628)[55]

> Narrated Abu Huraira: The Prophet said, "The recitation of the Psalms (David's Quran) was made light and easy for David that he used to have his riding animal be saddled while he would finish the recitation before the servant had saddled it." (Sahih Al-Bukhari 6:60:237)[56]

> Narrated Abdullah bin Amr: Allah's Apostle said to me: The fasting of (the prophet) David who used to fast on alternate days. And the most beloved prayer to Allah was the prayer of David who used to sleep for (the first) half of the night and pray for 1/3 of it and (again) sleep for a sixth of it." (Sahih Al-Bukhari 4:55:631)[57]

> Narrated Abu Musa that the Prophet said to him, "O Abu Musa! You have been given one of the musical wind-instruments of the family of David." (Sahih Al-Bukhari 6:61:568)[58]

> Abu Burda narrated on the authority of Abu Musa that the Messenger of Allah (may peace be upon him) had said to Abu Musa: "If you were to see me, as I was listening to your recitation (of the Quran) yester night (you would have felt delighted). You are in fact endowed with a sweet voice like that of David himself." (Sahih Muslim 1:4:1735)[59]

## Muslim Apologists and the Psalms

On the one hand, the Christian Scriptures have been targeted for being corrupted, and on the other hand they have been used to prove the authenticity of the Qur'an, and principally that of the prophet of Islam. The ninth- and tenth-century Muslim writers and apologists such as Ibn Qutayba sought to

---

55. *Sahih Al-Bukhari*, vol. IV, 415–16.
56. *Sahih Al-Bukhari*, vol. VI, 202.
57. *Sahih Al-Bukhari*, vol. IV, 418. The same *hadith* is repeated in *Sahih Al-Bukhari* 2:21:231.
58. *Sahih Al-Bukhari*, vol. VI, 514.
59. *Sahih Muslim*, 380.

validate the prophethood of the prophet of Islam through the Psalms.[60] He referred to a number of psalms to support prophecies—for example, Psalm 149.[61] Ibn Rabban extensively refers to the Psalms in a similar manner. He argues that every word associated with praise (*Mahmud*) in the Psalms is used in connection with the name of the prophet of Islam. He stresses that the word for praise is derived from the Arabic root (h-m-d), which simply points to the prophet of Islam, Muhammad—for example, Ps 48:1–2.[62] It is worth noting that in the early stages of Islam the translation of the Psalms into the Arabic language was available.[63] Ibn Rabban comments that the Psalms contain very beautiful hymns and Al-Masudi asserts that the total number of psalms is one hundred fifty.[64] Both of these statements are in accordance with the general understanding Christians have with regard to the book of Psalms. Historically, the Psalms seem to have been used in a polemical manner by the eminent Muslim apologists. However, it indicates the eager engagement that the Muslim scholars have had with the Psalms. Such ample involvement demonstrates that the Psalms have been taken seriously and special focus has been placed on the Psalms by distinguished Muslim writers.

## 4. CULTURAL BRIDGE-BUILDING COMPONENTS AND THE ZABUR

### Folk and Mystic Punjabi Poetry

It is at this point important to highlight some cultural bridge-building factors that are favorable in considering the Psalms for Muslims in Pakistan. This includes a rich heritage of mystic and folk poetry in the Punjabi language. Pakistan is basically an oral culture and the Punjabi language in particular has a rich oral tradition.[65]

In general, poetry is much embraced in the Punjabi culture and a great amount of mystical literature in poetic form has been made available in this language since the seventeenth century.[66] Bulleh Shah (1680–1758) may be

---

60. Adang, *Writers*, 112.
61. Tomes, "Sing," 250.
62. Adang, "Medieval," 144.
63. Schippers, "Psalms," 317.
64. Adang, "Medieval," 125.
65. Malik, *Culture*, 174.
66. Kohli, "Sufism," 4208.

regarded as the most prominent name among the Punjabi mystic poets.⁶⁷ His poems about searching for the truth, finding true love, self-denial, rejection of religious rituals, and of "bookish learning" in seeking God are recited in the land of Punjab.⁶⁸ Likewise, the mystical poetry of Sultan Bahu that advocates a personal connection with the divine rather than chasing the established forms of religion is narrated in Punjab.⁶⁹ Besides this, there are well-known Punjabi folk tales that are often recited and dramatized in the region of Punjab. The romance story of *Hir-Ranjha*, versified by the mystic poet Waris Shah; *Sohni-Mahinwal*, by Fazal Shah; and *Mirza-Sahiban*, by Pilu are among the popular folklores. In the Punjab, these "tales, stories" in poetic form are told by professional storytellers and musicians who memorize them to sing in public. A *qissa* is arranged "paratactically" whereby events are presented in an orderly way.⁷⁰ Moreover, there is a Qur'anic version of the story of Joseph and Potiphar's wife known as *Yusuf-Zulaikha*, which has been composed by several poets and is performed in Punjabi. Originally it was written in Persian by the mystic poet Nur-ud-Din Jami.⁷¹

Apart from the vast amount of mystic material, a wide range of Punjabi poetry, such as the love poetry by the renowned poet Munir Niazi, is available in the Punjabi language.⁷² In modern times, a new trend in Punjabi poetry has been introduced by poets like Anwar Masood, whose humorous poetry is amusing and at the same time thought provoking. A number of his books contain poetry in Punjabi. His poems are in great demand at Punjabi *mushairas*, "meetings at which poets recite their poems," and are well liked among ordinary Punjabis. The rich mystic and cultural poetic material in the Punjabi language is esteemed by people in the Punjab, and is equally admired at "folk and elite" levels.⁷³ This is worth noting, as it is hard to find something that is equally embraced by both common and privileged groups in Pakistan, owing to the enormous class distinction and divide in social status between the two. Essentially, the book of Psalms is visibly poetic; it is a set of beautiful poems.⁷⁴ The Psalms as poetry make them very special in a culture where poetry is much loved and appreciated.

67. Hanif, *Sufis*, 57.
68. Asani, "Poetry," 582.
69. Elias, *Bahu*, 2.
70. Prtichett, "Qissa," 503.
71. Singh, "Punjabi," 446.
72. Samiuddin, *Encyclopaedic Dictionary*, 451.
73. Heston, "Punjab," 496.
74. Longman, *Psalms*, 90.

## Punjabi Siharfi and the Acrostic Psalms

Parallelism has been regarded as the "hallmark of the Hebrew poetry." This core poetic device has been used eminently and consistently in the Psalms.[75] However, another evident poetic feature in the Psalms is known as acrostic poetry. In an acrostic poem, "the lines or group of lines" commence "with a successive letter of the Hebrew alphabet"; acrostic characteristic in the Psalms may be observed in the poetry of Psalms 25, 34, 111–12, 119, and 145.[76]

The acrostic feature has also been employed by the Punjabi mystic poets. It is known as *siharfi* in Punjabi poetry. In particular, the poetic work of the mystic poet Sultan Bahu is full of acrostic traits, and to some extent the acrostic form is used by the mystic Bulleh Shah, as well.[77] Interestingly, vast amounts of acrostic poems appear in the Sikh sacred writings in the Devanagari Punjabi.[78] Thus, the acrostic serves as a common poetic device both in the Psalms and in Punjabi poetry.

## Mysticism and the Psalms

In general, mysticism refers to a "direct communication between man and God."[79] Sufism is widely practiced in Pakistan, as evident from the abundance of mystic material in the Punjabi language. In the Punjab, the *dervish* and *fakir* "ascetic groups" use *zikr* as a mean of devotion; it is performed in silence and in both a low and a loud voice. Normally in mysticism, chanting the names of God in a repetitive manner is referred to as *zikr*.[80] It is common in the Punjab to use *tasbih*, "a string or chaplet of beads," when reciting the names of God.[81]

The Psalms speak of a closer connection with the Almighty. Montefiore states that it is in the Psalms that one finds "the doctrine of the direct communion with God."[82] The Psalms express a deep craving and yearning for God. Psalm 42 brings out the strong desire to seek God diligently and with all sincerity. Psalm 63 employs similarity of expression to Psalm 42, where the soul is desperately thirsty to have a communion with the divine. Psalm 37 exhorts and extends an invitation to have personal experiences of

---

75. Schökel, *Poetics*, 48.
76. Walford, *Israel*, 114.
77. Puri, "Bulleh," 134.
78. Singh, *Faith and Philosophy*, 104.
79. Hughes, *Islam*, 426.
80. Sells, "Dhikar," 373.
81. Wikeley, *Punjabi*, 33.
82. Montefiore, "Mystic," 145.

the Almighty. Psalm 139 speaks beautifully of conducting self-examination in order to maintain a true connection with God. Moreover, Psalm 51 portrays a deep and heartfelt necessity for the soul to be reconciled with the Almighty. In Psalm 103, the soul contemplates the many benefits granted to it by God.

Franken asserts that the Hebrew words *hagah* (Pss 1:2; 63:7; 77:13; 143:5) and *shekha* (Ps 119:97; Ps 97) demonstrate the mystic nature of the Psalms.[83] The verb *hagah* denotes a pondering "upon God and His works."[84] Likewise, the noun *shekha* signifies "meditation and devotion."[85] The root word of this noun has the notion of reflecting silently and audibly, and meditating both "inwardly and outwardly."[86] Judah Ha-Levi draws attention to the Sufi idea of *dhawq*, "taste," to be in line with the psalmist's invitation to taste God, mentioned in Psalm 34:9.[87] The Punjabi Sufi poet Farid presents this idea in this way: "Sweets are candy and sugar, honey and the buffalo's milk; yea, sweet are all those, but sweeter by far is God."[88] Hammerle points to the significance of the heart focused on the Psalms for knowledge (Ps 37:31); the heart is central for spiritual understanding in Sufism.[89] The great Punjabi mystic poet Bulleh Shah asserts: "I saw my Lord with the Eye of the Heart," God cannot be seen with the "material eyes."[90] Bulleh Shah's following couplet is worth noting in this regard:

> *Tear down the mosque and the temple; break everything in sight*
> *But do not break a person's heart; it is there that God resides.*[91]

## Translations of the Qur'an in Punjabi

It is worth mentioning that unlike the Christian Scriptures in Persian Punjabi,[92] several translations of the complete Qur'an in Persian

---

83. Franken, *Mystical*, 1920.
84. Harris et al., *Theological Wordbook*, 205.
85. Brown et al., *Hebrew and English Lexicon*, 967.
86. Harris et al., *Theological Wordbook*, 875.
87. Lobel, *Sufi*, 91.
88. Hanfi, *Sufis*, 104. The commandments of God are sweeter than honey to the psalmist, Pss 19:10 and 119:103.
89. Hammerle, *Sufi*, 47.
90. Hanif, *Sufis*, 73.
91. Maini, *Asian*, 92. The Punjabi couplet: *Masjid dha de mandir dha de, dha de jo kuch dainda; Par kisi da dil na dhain, Rab dilan vich rehnda.*
92. Sadiq, "Translation," 91.

Punjabi have been made available, including Sharif Kunjahi's "Al-Quran Al-Karim,"[93] Maulana Hidayatullah's translation of the Qur'an,[94] and the most recent translation being done by Tauqir Amaan Khan.[95] A metrical translation of the Qur'an in Punjabi with commentary was done by Maulvi Muhammad Hussain which has been published in seven volumes.[96] Moreover, the Ahmadiya community translated selected verses of the Qur'an in Punjabi, on the occasion of their centennial celebration.[97] There are sociolinguistic issues relating to Punjabi as a language in Pakistan, and some of those issues are discussed in the next chapter. However, the availability of Muslim religious material in the Punjabi language, and particularly in poetic form, indicates that the Psalms as poetry have a larger scope than other books of the Bible and are ideal for sharing with the Punjabi Muslim brethren in Pakistan.

## 5. Form and Style

It is now vital to discuss the suitable form and style for presenting the Psalms to the Punjabi Muslims. The vast cultural and mystic poetic heritage in the Punjabi language leaves no doubt that poetry is the most appropriate form for sharing the Psalms with Punjabi Muslim brethren. However, it is important to ask the question whether the Psalms in Punjabi verse may be presented in musical form. In order to deal with this question, it would help to look at the view on music among Muslim brethren in Pakistan. One often hears the statements made by the strict Islamic circles in Pakistan that music is *haram*, forbidden in Islam. It is worth noting that the fundamentalists have given "death threats" to a well-known Pakistani pop singer, Salman Ahmed, who is said to have sung Qur'anic verses on his guitar.[98] These strict Islamic circles argue that the only lawful instrument for religious and celebratory purposes is a *daf*, "tambourine"; this understanding is drawn from the *hadiths* such as *Sahih-Al-Bukhari* 2:15:103 and 5:59:336.[99] According to the *Tribune Express*, from 2000–2011, over one hundred attacks have been

---

93. This translation is available at the Academy of the Punjab in North America website, http://www.apnaorg.com/quran/.

94. Hidayatullah, *Quran-e-Majid*.

95. International Quran News Agency website, https://iqna.ir/en/news/2305564/holy-quran-translated-into-punjabi-for-first-time.

96. Hussain, *Tafsir*, 1.

97. Amjad, *Quran Karim*, 1.

98. LeVine, "Metal," 213.

99. Morgan, *Islam*, 199.

made on musicians and music shops in Pakistan by fanatical groups.[100] A recent survey showed that 79 percent of urban Pakistanis think that "pop music is un-Islamic" and 66 percent of these people were "pop musicians themselves."[101] It indicates the contradiction between practicality and belief in the Pakistani Islamic society.

However, there is vast disagreement among Pakistani Muslims of different sects on the use and role of music for religious devotion. This is due to the seemingly "ambiguous" Qur'anic references (*Sura Saba* 34:10 and *Sura Luqman* 31:6) concerning music, and the vagueness of statements recorded in the *hadith* on this topic.[102] Moreover, the *hadith* makes the use of music more controversial and prohibitive than the Qur'an itself.[103]

Pakistan is dominantly a Sunni Muslim country adhering to the *hanafi* school of thought; approximately 80 percent of the population belong to the Sunni sect and 20 percent to the Shiite sect. Nevertheless, numerically, the *Barelvi* sect of Sunni Muslims is in the majority, particularly in the rural areas of the most populated province of Punjab in Pakistan, where more than half of the country's total population resides.[104] In other words, the majority of the Pakistani Punjabi Muslims follow the *Barelvi* sect.[105] Unlike the Deobandi sect of Sunni Muslims, the *Barelvis* in Pakistan, like many followers of the Shiite sect, favor mysticism and adhere to the practices of Sufism.[106] This includes the use of music, dance, and poetry for devotions, and regular visitations and celebrations at Sufi shrines.[107] Within the Punjabi Muslim context in Pakistan, the versified Psalms put to music are accessible to the vast majority. For those who do not favor music, the Psalms may simply be presented in versified form without music.

---

100. "Militant 'Drive against Vulgarity,'" *Express Tribune*, November 10, 2011, https://tribune.com.pk/story/289812/militant-drive-against-vulgarity-14-killed-120-injured-in-last-10-years/.

101. Nadeem F. Paracha, "Indo-Pak: A Survey," *Dawn*, April 18, 2013, https://www.dawn.com/news/803234.

102. Riddell, "Music," 434.

103. Racy, "Music," 181.

104. Alavi, "Muslim," 31.

105. Deobandis and Barelvis are the two main Sunni sects in Pakistan; the former is generally regarded as hard-line. These sects originated in the two Indian cities of Deoband and Bareli from pre-partitioned India in the nineteenth century.

106. Murphy, *Pakistan*, 24.

107. Fair, *Education*, 58.

### Qawali

The most widely used musical style for religious purposes in Pakistan is known as *Qawali*.[108] It is the Sufi style of group singing that is led by the main singer, who reinforces the themes of mystic poetry through repetition and refrain.[109] The listeners reflect on the words in a devotional manner as a means of making a connection with the divine. The *Qawali* performance is accompanied by musical instruments such as harmonium and *dholak*, and involves rhythmic clapping by the singers.[110] The musical instruments used for *Qawali* singing are the same as those used for Christian worship among Pakistani churches. A *Qawali* may have some Qur'anic and *hadith* elements in it; however, in essence, it tends to focus on praising God and having a genuine connection with him. It discourages strict orthodox forms to access God, for which reason some of the mystic *Qawalis* are also admired by non-Muslims.[111] It is worth noting that a leading Pakistani Islamic scholar and the head of Minhaj-al-Quran organization, Dr. Tahir-ul-Qadri, has a large following in Pakistan. He has been taking an active part in *Qawali* gatherings, and encouraging its use for devotional purposes.[112] The *Qawali* form is suitable for the musical psalms.

## 6. Common Themes

### Psalms of Praise

It is now imperative to discuss the appropriate psalmic themes for the Punjabi Muslim brethren in Pakistan. To begin with, it is useful to look for selective themes, due to the large size of the book of Psalms and the different genres found in it, such as praise, lament, kingship, and wisdom. In seeking the appropriateness of the Psalms for the Punjabi Muslims, it is helpful to think about the shared themes. In sharing the Scriptures with people of other faiths, it is always useful to commence with a shared knowledge that already exists in the minds of the target audience. This approach is regarded as moving from "known to unknown," or from "familiar to unfamiliar"

---

108. Qureshi, "Devotional," 111.
109. Qureshi, *Qawwali*, xiii.
110. Qureshi, "Pakistan," 1048.
111. Hyder, "Qawwali," 93.
112. Philippon, "Sufi," 119.

knowledge.¹¹³ Such a methodology is effective in communicating with the target audience and it paves the way for new and unfamiliar information.

The Psalms are "rich and variant in content." However, praise and worship of the Almighty is always the primary theme emphasized in the Psalms.[114] In other words, God is at the center of this book, as every thought of the psalmists revolves around him and nothing seems to be out of his control and divine knowledge. The Psalms portray God as omnipotent, omniscient, and supreme. In the same manner, the Qur'an describes God as all-powerful and all-knowing.[115] It mentions that man was created by God to worship him.[116] Some of the shared characteristics of God, with regard to the praise and worship of him as mentioned in both the Psalms and the Qur'an, aid in bridging gaps and in seeking the appropriateness of the Psalms for the Muslim brethren. In connection with the characteristics of God, the significance of the ninety-nine names of God is valuable. The attributes of God are also referred to as "the beautiful names of God."[117] Although it is possible to engage in a long discussion on similar characteristics of God in the Psalms and the Qur'an, it would help to look at a few attributes to show commonalities.

## AL-BARI AND AL-KHALIQ: GOD THE MAKER AND GOD THE CREATOR

The creation stimulates the psalmists to survey the beauty and creativity of God, displayed in the form of earth, heaven, seasons, sea, and mountains (Pss 8, 19, 89, 107, 135, 148). The uniqueness of God causes the psalmist to marvel and to exalt him and pronounce his supremacy (Pss 18, 135). The psalmist has a burning desire within his heart to praise God (Ps 108). The praise of God is undeniably an utmost duty of man and every creation.[118] Like the Psalms, several occurrences in the Qur'an describe God as the maker and creator of heaven and earth, and of all things.[119] In Islam, the

---

113. Luzbetak, "Contextual," 112.
114. Allen, *Psalms*, 72.
115. Peters, "Allah," 78.
116. Geaves, *Islam*, 2.
117. Malik, *Prism*, 194.
118. Brueggemann, *Praise*, 1.
119. E.g., chs. 6:14 and 102; 12:101; 13:16; 14:10; 15:86; 35:1; 38:81; 37:105; 39:46; 40:62.

kind and affectionate nature of God is expressed through the earth that he created for human beings.[120]

## AL-RAZIQ: GOD THE PROVIDER

The caring nature of God causes the psalmist to adore him, for his wonderful provision (Pss 14, 68, 111). The Psalms marvel at God because of his timely provision for his creation and for feeding the hungry (Pss 104, 107, 132). Likewise, the Qur'an depicts God as the one who provides for his creation.[121] It signifies that despite all wisdom, human beings are unable to supply everything, and thus rely on the "bounty" of God who sustains them.[122] *Sura Al-Baqarah* 2:255 highlights that God consistently meets the needs of his creation, he never fails in maintaining this world and does this without sleeping or slumbering.[123] This echoes the dependable characteristic of God mentioned in Psalm 121.

## AL-ḤAKIM: GOD THE JUDGE

The Psalms emphasize the practice of justice in society.[124] God is just (Pss 7, 87, 112) and therefore he desires justice (Pss 9, 11, 33, 106, 140). Wickedness and injustice are strongly opposed in all their forms in the Psalms (Ps 34). Furthermore, God stands in opposition to those who practice discrimination (Pss 14, 37, 82), whereas his favor remains with those who practice justice (Pss 103, 119, 146). The Psalms describe God as the defender of the "fatherless and the oppressed" (Ps 10:18 NIV). The psalmist cannot stand the "sustained injustice" he sees in society and appeals to the just God to intervene. In fact, the "cries of poor and oppressed" are quite strong in Psalms 2–89.[125] The attribute of God as judge is highlighted in the Qur'an, where he is regarded as the best judge, and people are commanded to practice justice.[126] The majority of the Qur'anic references concerning justice are in relation to the Day of Judgment.

---

120. Akhter, *Faith*, 58.
121. E.g., chs. 2:25, 60, 212; 3:37; 5:88, 114.
122. Turner, "Rizq," 552.
123. Zarabozo, *Islam*, 31.
124. Westermeyer, *Hymnody*, 29.
125. Tucker, "Psalms," 163.
126. E.g., chs. 2:113; 4:58; 5:1; 5:50; 7:87; 10:109; 40:20; 95:8.

However, Rahbar asserts that the theme of justice is so widespread in the Qur'an that "almost every third verse" in the Qur'an speaks about justice.[127] The Qur'an encourages everyone to practice justice regardless of their social status.[128] The shared theme of justice has even more significance in the Pakistani society where there is a deep cry for justice, but justice is hard to be found due to corruption in the system. True loyalty to God results in "justice" and he desires to see justice in practice.[129]

## AL-MALIK: GOD THE KING

The Psalms regard God as "King and judge of the world." Several Psalms portray God as king, including Psalms 24, 47, 93, 95, 96, 99, and 145.[130] The Qur'an describes God as *Al-Malik*, the king.[131] It may well be translated as "possessor, lord, or ruler" and is one of the characteristics of God to which the Qur'an frequently makes reference to.[132] The Qur'an talks about the supreme dominion of God, and refers to him as "the true king" (*Sura Taha* 20:114).[133]

## AL-REHMAN AND AL-RAHIM: GOD THE COMPASSIONATE AND THE MERCIFUL

Two of the attributes that occur together frequently in the Qur'an are *Al-Rahman*, "the merciful," and *Al-Rahim*, "the compassionate." They serve as an "introductory formula" by appearing at the beginning of each *sura*, except *Sura At-Taubah*.[134] These two attributes portray the merciful and compassionate character of God. Likewise, the Psalms also focus on the compassionate nature of God.

It is worth mentioning that formulaic devices do occur in the Psalms to highlight the merciful character of God. For example, the Hebrew phrase *Rakhum-Wekhanun*, meaning "compassionate" and "gracious," appears in Pss 86:15 and 103:8. It occurs in the reverse order as *Khanun-Werakhum*,

---

127. Rahbar, *Justice*, 225.
128. Ahmed, *Quran*, 182.
129. Leopold, *Psalms*, 77.
130. Limburg, *Psalms*, 16.
131. E.g., chs. 20:114; 23:116; 54:55; 59:23; 62:1.
132. Hughes, *Islam*, 312.
133. Marlow, "Kings," 91.
134. Böwering, "Attributes," 318.

"gracious" and "compassionate" in Pss 111:4 and 145:8. The adjective *Rakhum* occurs independently only in Ps 78:38, whereas the adjective *Khanun* does not occur separately in the Psalms. Moreover, another formulaic arrangement to demonstrate the merciful disposition of God appears in Ps 112:4, where the phrase *Khanun-Werakhum-WeSadiqim*, meaning compassionate, gracious, and righteous, is used.[135] The phrase *Al-Rehman Al-Rahim* shows a remarkable resemblance to the Hebrew phrase *Rakhum-Wekhanun*.

## Psalms of Lament

Besides the majority of the psalms of praise, there are many psalms of lament.[136] The psalms of lament have a vital place in Pakistani society, where mysticism is widely practiced. These psalms speak of separation from God, and seek "intimate connection" with the divine despite life's troubled experiences. The Punjabi mystic poetry of Shah Hussain is full of "wailings and lamentations caused by the pang of separation" from God.[137] Moreover, there is a plea for God's grace in the psalms of lament to deal with the inside struggle with sin. The notion that the grace of God is fundamental, and that God not only grants his grace to the spiritual man but equally to the sinful to "attain communion" with him, is evident in the poetry of Bulleh Shah. Addleton draws attention to the "images of Jesus" in Pakistani literature and that they are appealing to the Sufi poets.[138] In connection to the psalms of lament, the commonly used expression *Masiha*, "of the nature or disposition of Messiah," is worth considering. In a political and general sense this expression is used for someone who may deliver others from challenges; for example, the late Dr. Ruth Pfau is regarded as the *Masiha* of lepers in Pakistan.[139]

Likewise, recently the singer Jawad Ahmed used the expression *Masiha* of the nation for the medical personnel to pay them tribute in the age of Covid-19.[140] However, in poetry the term *Masiha* depicts a savior in the

---

135. Brown et al., *Hebrew and English Lexicon*, 933, 843, 337.

136. Jinkins, *Lament*, 77. Approximately 40 percent of psalms fall into the category of lament and they are mainly found in the first three books of the Psalms. The last two books have dominantly praise psalms.

137. Hanif, *Sufis*, 114.

138. Addleton, "Images," 96.

139. M. Waqar Bhatti, "Pakistani Mother-Teresa," *The News*, August 11, 2017, https://www.thenews.com.pk/print/222902-Pakistani-Mother-Teresa-struggling-to-eradicate-leprosy-dies.

140. "Jawad Ahmad Salutes Doctors, Paramedics and Nurses," *Daily Times*, March 27, 2020, https://dailytimes.com.pk/583612/jawad-ahmad-salutes-doctors-paramedics-and-nurses-for-fighting-against-coronavirus.

midst of troubles; it is embedded both in Christ-like healing power and his sufferings.[141] For example, as used in the second couplet of Javed Qureshi's ghazal (ode) *diyar-e-gair*.[142] *Masiha* as a familiar poetic term is useful for employing in the psalms of lament that cry out for deliverance and help. Moreover, this term is useful in considering the messianic psalms for the Punjabi Muslims in Pakistan. The psalms regarded as messianic or that "refer to Jesus Christ" are fewer in number.[143]

## 7. Challenges

### Imprecatory Psalms

It is now important to point out elements that bring challenges to bridge-building between Punjabi Christians and Muslims and in sharing of the Psalms with the Punjabi Muslims. The imprecatory psalms are one of the challenges; therefore, sensitivity in selecting the appropriate themes and genres from these psalms is of value. The "imprecatory psalms" request vengeance and severe punishment for enemies—for example, Psalms 7, 35, 58–59, 69, 83, 109, 137, and 139.[144]

Regardless of the debate over the actual meaning and function of the imprecatory psalms, there are major ethical issues involved when considering the practical use of these psalms in today's society.[145] Although the language of revenge for enemies, unbelievers, and infidels is familiar to readers of the Qur'an (e.g., *Sura An-Nisa* 4:76; *Sura Al-Anfal* 8:39; *Sura At-Taubah* 9:5), the imprecatory psalms do not seem fitting for sharing at an initial stage with the Punjabi Muslim brethren in Pakistan. There is a risk that the imprecatory psalms may be wrongly interpreted and understood as a justification for a holy war against enemies. Ibn Qutayba's interpretation on Ps 149:6–9 is an example worth noting: "Now, which is that nation whose swords are two-edged, if not the Arabs, and who is the one to wreak vengeance on the nations that do not worship Him, and who among the prophets is the one that was sent with the sword if not His Prophet."[146]

141. Faiz, *Poems*, 78.

142. The couplet means: I'm falling apart every moment, wish there is *Masiha* a problem-solver. This *ghazal* is available at https://www.youtube.com/watch?v=6ggrumH1Qko.

143. Travers, *Encountering*, 180. Messianic psalms include Pss 2, 16, 22, 40, 45, 68, 110, 118.

144. Laney, "Imprecatory," 30.

145. LeMon, "Psalter," 109.

146. Adang, *Muslim*, 271.

*Uncommon Themes*

### God as Father

Many of the attributes of God mentioned in the Psalms and the Qur'an are common and vital for bridge-building. However, apart from the many shared attributes, some distinctive attributes of God are mentioned in the Psalms. Special care and wisdom is needed in seeking to share uncommon themes with the majority community in Pakistan's context. In order to portray the caring and loving nature of God, Psalms 68 and 103 refer to God as father. The idea of intimate relationship with the divine is generally unfamiliar to the orthodox Muslims. Although attributes such as *Rehman* and *Rahim* depict the merciful character of God, and the Qur'an does go as far as to assert that God is nearer to man than his "jugular vein" (*Sura Qaf* 50:16 ), the idea of God presented in human terms and relationship is absent in the Qur'an.[147]

However, the notion of an intimate relationship with God is an inspiring one to devout followers of the Sufi traditions.[148] The Punjabi poets Bulleh Shah and Shah Hussain use a bride-bridegroom analogy to demonstrate union with God, and Farid employs a husband-wife metaphor to demonstrate personal relationship between God and man.[149]

### God as Redeemer

A few psalms present God as a "redeemer." This notion is conveyed through the Hebrew word *goel* that occurs in Psalms 19, 69, 72, 74, 77, 78, 103, 106, 107, and 119. The idea of God as redeemer is unfamiliar to the followers of Islam, as it does not appear in the Qur'an.[150]

### Holiness of God

The Psalms put much more stress on the righteousness and holiness of God than the Qur'an, although the Qur'an describes God as *Al-Quddus* "the Holy."[151] In comparison to only two occurrences in the Qur'an (*Sura*

---

147. Khan, *Humankind*, 221.
148. Ul Huda, *Sufi*, 59.
149. Hanif, *Sufis*, 68, 144, 107.
150. Ruthven, *Islam*, 32.
151. Khimjee, *Attributes*, 28.

Al-Hashr 59:23 and *Sura Al-Jumuah* 62:1) of references to God's holiness, several psalms highlight the holiness of God.[152]

## Freedom of Expression

"Most of Scripture speaks to us, the Psalms speak for us"; this statement from the fourth-century Christian leader Athanasius reveals the uniqueness of the Psalms.[153] The expressions of joy and sorrow, of hope and despair, of ecstasy and agony are deeply expressed in the Psalms.[154] The liberty to articulate human sentiment makes God accessible and personal in the Psalms.[155] Such a freedom to describe human emotion and experience before God is completely missing in the Qur'an, which presents him as more distant and transcendent.[156]

### *Terms Requiring Special Attention*

Another challenge involved in sharing the Psalms with the Muslim brethren in Pakistan is some of the terms used in the Psalms that require special attention—for example, Zion, the Temple, Israel, and Jerusalem. A literal translation of these terms may give the wrong impression to the Muslim brethren that the Psalms propagate Jewish interests or encourage Zionism. Such an impression hinders presenting a true picture of these psalms. Moreover, these terms have the tendency to somehow incite anti-Semitic sentiments and shut the door to the Psalms being acceptable. The translation of some terms in the Pakistani Islamic context present challenges. Such terms demand a great deal of care in presenting Psalms to the Muslims. This is not to say that these terms cannot be translated or should be avoided; in fact, no compromise must be made on such terms. Therefore, it becomes crucial to seek best translation practices as well as having a concrete knowledge of Islam and biblical theology, particularly as it relates to the Psalms. As a first step it may be helpful to survey how many of these terms had been treated by Dr. Shahbaz in a broader sense.

---

152. E.g., Pss 22:3; 33:21; 60:6; 89:18; 97:12; 99:3; 99:5; 99:9; 103:1; 106:47; 111:9; 145:21.
153. Godlingay, *Psalms*, 23.
154. Broyles, *Experience*, 187.
155. Goldingay, *Psalms*, 242.
156. Geaves, *Islam*, 39.

Moreover, investigating corresponding phrases are useful for terms that are absent in the target language. For example, in the case of Punjabi Muslims, the term *haikal* as a literal rendering of the Hebrew term (*hekal*) for the temple does not seem very helpful for the reader.[157] It is an unfamiliar word in Punjabi or Urdu by itself. The phrase *deo haikal* is the only phrase in which one hears this word. It is a combination of two Persian words, *deo*, meaning "demon, monster, giant, huge," and *haikal*, meaning "figure, stature, shape," indicating a big and massive person or object.[158]

## 7.1. The Blasphemy Law

The minority Christian community in Pakistan experiences a strong sense of insecurity and fear in a majority Islamic country.[159] Aside from the prejudiced attitude by the majority, to a greater degree, this anxiety is caused by the blasphemy law of which Pakistani Christians are often victims.[160] The blasphemy law concerns section 295-B and 295-C of the Pakistan penal code.[161] There have been several false blasphemy cases against Christians especially since 1986 that resulted in brutal killings and attacks on the wider Christian community. The devastating burning of 178 Christian houses in Joseph Colony Lahore (2013); blasphemy accusations against an eleven-year-old girl suffering from Down syndrome, Rimsha Masih (2012); the assassination of the federal minister for minorities, Shahbaz Bhatti (2011); and Asia Bibi, the mother of five children sentenced to death and being released in 2019 after spending ten years in solitary confinement for a crime that she did not commit, are some examples of Pakistani Christians being targeted under the blasphemy law.[162]

In the age of social media, there have been incidents in which young Christians have sadly been under the blasphemy accusations for simply sharing, liking, and commenting on Twitter and Facebook. Even a text

---

157. Adriani, "Translation," 9.

158. Platts, *Dictionary of Urdu*, 559, 1245. For example, the largest Urdu newspaper, *Jang*, in a report describes a 5.8-meter-long lamp in Lilla Torg square, Sweden, as *deo haikal* (http://jang.com.pk/jang/jul2013daily/09-07-2013/u1597.htm).

159. McClintock, "Pakistan," 344.

160. Riddell, "Suffering," 7.

161. Section 295 (B) is concerning the defiling of the Qur'an, for which the punishment is life imprisonment. Section 295 (C) is about the use of derogatory remarks about the prophet of Islam (by words, either spoken or written or by visible representation, or by any imputation, innuendo, or insinuation, directly or indirectly), for which the punishment is death penalty or imprisonment for life.

162. Marshall, *Persecuted*, 209.

message can put someone under the blasphemy charges. Patras Masih, a young Christian man, was allegedly accused of sharing a blasphemous image on Facebook; he denied the charges against him. Later, his cousin Sajid Masih jumped from the fourth level after he had been heavily beaten by the interrogators and was fighting for his life at the hospital. The Christian families in Patras Masih's area fled as an angry mob threatened to burn their houses.[163] Such an environment of terror prevents Pakistani Christians from engaging comprehensively in dialogue with the Muslim community.

## 7.2. Inferior Social Status

The marginal social status of the Pakistani Christians is another challenge in bridging the gap between Christians and Muslims in Pakistan. For example, Asia Bibi was regarded an untouchable by Muslim woman over a cup of water.[164] The Christian minority in the majority Muslim country do not have equal rights and are facing "economic discriminations and political suppression."[165] According to Walbridge, the Pakistani Christian community is largely "poor and illiterate," the majority of them do not participate in "intellectual dialogue" and regard Christianity as the "religion of heart and soul," rather than that of academics.[166] Nevertheless, on a daily basis the ordinary Pakistani Christians do engage in dialogues with their Muslim neighbors at various levels. With regard to the intellectual dialogue that Walbridge referred to, there may be not very many Pakistani Christians who are actively involved in Christian-Muslim dialogue.

A small Roman Catholic Goan community[167] in the southern city of Karachi is interestingly not strictly labeled inferior or discriminated against in comparison to their Punjabi Christian brethren. This may be primarily due to their disassociation from menial jobs, their distinct culture, absence of the untouchability stigma, their use of the English language, which carries power in the society, and apparently they are "economically better off."[168]

163. Asad Hashim, "Suspect in Lahore Blasphemy Case Fighting for His Life," *Aljazeera*, March 3, 2018, https://www.aljazeera.com/news/2018/03/suspect-lahore-blasphemy-case-fighting-life-180303085358736.html.

164. Sadiq, "Encounter," 366.

165. Strohmer, "Neighbors," 10.

166. Walbridge, *Pakistan*, 167–68.

167. Thomas, *Christians*, 239. The Goan community originally come from the Indian Port of Goa that was evangelized by the Franciscans and Jesuits after the port was taken over by the Portuguese in the sixteenth century, intermarriages then took place between Indians and Portuguese.

168. Moghal, "Minorities," 28.

For example, they run some of the best educational institutions all over the country, and have comparatively better education, jobs, opportunities, and social status.[169] All this helps to some extent in dialogue with Muslims in Pakistan's complex social setting. For example, Fr. Archie D'Souza may be seen actively involved in dialogue with the Muslim neighborhood.[170]

It is a dilemma that the "background stigma continues to haunt" the Punjabi Christians,[171] and inequality in Pakistan makes dialogue with Muslims appear unimportant and nonserious.[172] In other words, a superior social status leads to a solemn, concrete, and constructive dialogue; inferior social status ends up with uninterested discussion without producing results. Moreover, sometimes Muslim seekers find it difficult to embrace Christianity due to the inferior social status of the Punjabi Christians in Pakistan.[173] It is understandable due to social hierarchies; however, a genuine follower of Christ must be ready to pay the cost of discipleship in Pakistan's Islamic context. Although the Protestant circles have several initiatives for bridge-building,[174] and there appears to be more support for this at the governmental level in recent years than ever before,[175] the inferior social status of the Pakistani Punjabi Christians and the misuse of the blasphemy law against Christians in Pakistan bring challenges in interacting effectively and confidently with Muslim brethren.

In sum, it may be observed that Muslim-friendly terms have been employed by Dr. Shahbaz in his translation of the Punjabi Psalms. Nowadays, the Pakistani Christians in general have reservations over the use of some of those terms. There are number of factors in considering the Psalms in Punjabi as a means of bridging the gap in the Islamic context of Pakistan. The intertextuality between the Qur'an and the Psalms, the engagement of medieval Muslim scholars with the Psalms, the common attributes of God in the Qur'an and the Psalms, the parallel between Hebrew acrostic poetry and

169. "The Tireless Educators of Karachi," *Dawn*, June 12, 2012, http://beta.dawn.com/news/725937/the-tireless-educators-of-karachi.

170. Walbridge, *Christians*, 186.

171. Asimi, *Minority*, 120.

172. Henry, "Peace Building," 78.

173. Larson, *Islamic Ideology*, 176.

174. The Anglican diocese of Lahore has a forum for dialogue with Muslims neighbors called "Faith and Friendship"; the diocese of Peshawar in the North and the diocese of Raiwind in the Punjab have some similar programs. Moreover, the Christian Study Centre in Rawalpindi as an academic forum is an example of interreligious initiatives in Pakistan.

175. The Ministry of National Harmony was founded in 2011 by the government of Pakistan to promote dialogue between people of different faiths. Moreover, there is Pakistan Interfaith League for the same purpose.

Punjabi *Siharfi*, the love for poetry in the Pakistani culture, an abundance of mystic poetic literature in the Punjabi language, and mystic practices in the Pakistani society are significant markers for bridge-building. The *Qawali* style of devotional music is broadly used in Pakistan and appears to be fitting to set the Psalms to this music. The Psalms as poetry in the Islamic context of Pakistan have full potential for playing a vital role in bridge-building, and for sharing the beautiful poetry of the Psalms with Muslim brethren of all ethnic backgrounds in Pakistan who have a rich tradition of mysticism and love for poetry.

# VI

## The Sociolinguistic Circumstances Facing Pakistani Punjabi Christians

*Their Effect on the Punjabi Translation of the Scriptures and the Future of the Metrical Psalms*

One may ask why the possibility of revising the Punjabi Psalms has not been discussed? Would a revised metrical translation in contemporary Punjabi not sufficiently meet the needs of the modern-day Pakistani Punjabi Christians? What are the obstacles and challenges involved? All these questions are valid, but they are not easy to answer. Nevertheless, they are crucial and unavoidable questions that need to be discussed. One might assume that, since the Psalms in Punjabi are so much loved by the Pakistani Punjabi Christians, they must be using the Punjabi Bible for reading and preaching. The Pakistani Punjabi Christians must be proud of their language, otherwise they would not sing the psalms in this language for worship. Sadly, the reality is far different. Unfortunately, it is a complex issue that cannot be simply explained from the surface. The behavioral attitude toward the Punjabi language among the Punjabi-speaking churches in Pakistan has direct effects on the availability of Scripture in Punjabi and on the continuation of these psalms in the future. Although the issues may seem detached from each other, they are in fact closely interconnected, as they concern the same Punjabi language.

# The Sociolinguistic Circumstances Facing Pakistani Punjabi Christians

In order to helpfully address the questions above, one must look back at history to dig for factors that have influenced and led to the present attitude of the church in Pakistan in relation to the revision of Christian Scripture in languages used in Pakistani churches, namely Punjabi and Urdu. The Christian minorities in dominantly Islamic societies face unique challenges which must also be taken into account. The British and Foreign Bible Society's correspondence from 1910–1972 regarding the Punjabi New Testament greatly assists in making some concluding comments on this matter. The communication concerns the matter of revision of Christian Scripture in the language in which translation work had been initiated over a century ago. Therefore, it is indispensable in explaining the obstacles in the light of Scripture work done so far, primarily in the Punjabi language. This chapter will draw attention to the complications involved in the availability of Christian Scripture in the Punjabi language by first looking at the historical facts with regard to the preparation and revision of the Punjabi New Testament in Persian Script. Then moving to the present sociolinguistic situation in general and among the Punjabi-speaking churches in particular, the sort of effects they are likely to bring to the metrical translation of the Punjabi Psalms will be discussed.

## 1. LACK OF AWARENESS OF THE ISSUE AND CULTURAL NORMS

### 1.1. Low Literacy Rate

First, it is important to mention that, by and large the majority of the ordinary Pakistani Punjabi Christians are unaware of the existence of linguistic barriers in the Christian Scriptures that had been translated over a century ago, including the metrical translation of the Psalms into Punjabi. Due to a lack of awareness this issue is hardly talked about, which indicates that often Punjabi psalms are sung habitually, and linguistic barriers are simply being ignored without discussion.

There are at least three major reasons for this. First, large number of Pakistani Christians lives in rural Punjab,[1] and the illiteracy rate is higher among the Punjabi Christians in comparison to others.[2] Since the majority of the people cannot read for themselves, they are unable to see this problem. If such issues are discussed with simple rural Punjabi Christians, some, if not all, would be willing and open to give their honest opinion on

1. Malik, "Minorities," 11.
2. Carey, "Education," 160.

the problem of comprehension. However, due to the lack of literacy, the majority does not even bother to give a thought on this matter and seem satisfied with singing the Punjabi Psalms without fully understanding them. It would not be wrong to assert that even among the Punjabi Christian preachers and lay persons in Pakistan, only a handful may be aware of the linguistic barriers in Christian Scriptures that had been translated long ago.

## 1.2. Mindset toward Religious Matters

Second, the mindset toward major and minor religious matters as demonstrated by the Muslim community in the Pakistani society is worth mentioning in this regard. In general, attempts to raise questions on religious matters, particularly the ones that are normally considered to have been standardized, are often considered suspicious and are seen as a direct challenge to things that have already been defined.[3] Such attempts are strongly discouraged and opposed, and people of the same faith would not be hesitant to label such persons as skeptical. In other words, what has been going on for quite some time is not supposed to be questioned, not even for further clarifications or understanding. It is natural that when a community lives in that sort of environment it becomes affected in some respects by ideas of the majority, and to some extent such an attitude in religious matters seems to be influencing some Christian circles in Pakistan.[4] When it comes to religious issues, some are quick to show their strong reaction. Thus, to argue that the language used in Christian Scriptures is out of date is likely to be opposed.

## 1.3. Shame-Based Culture

Third, such an attitude needs to be understood in the light of shame-based cultures, like Pakistan, where exteriority exceeds far beyond interiority, and where honor is highly esteemed.[5] In other words, admitting the lack of knowledge on a matter is considered shameful and pretending to have knowledge of something when one really knows nothing results in bringing honor in society. People in shame-based cultures are concerned about

---

3. Ahmed, "Nationalism," 98. For instance, *fatwas* were issued against the governor of Punjab, Salman Taseer, just because he requested for a discussion on the misuse of blasphemy law in Pakistan; consequently, he was murdered by his own security guard in 2011.

4. Walbridge, *Christians*, 186.

5. Pattison, *Shame*, 54.

saving face in society, as they are very concerned with what others think about them.⁶ In relation to the Punjabi metrical psalms, therefore, people do not want to lose face before others by admitting that they actually do not understand what they sing. Consequently, the problem is ignored. It needs to be remembered that Pakistani society is shame-based, where people are confronted by other members of the society if they attempt to react differently than the superficial cultural norms that surround them.⁷

## 2. FEAR OF PRESSURE AND CRITICISM FROM THE MUSLIM COMMUNITY

### 2.1. Accusations of Bible Being Corrupted

Muslims in Pakistan make a common charge against their Christian fellow countrymen, namely that the Bible has been altered, and Christians have corrupted the Bible.⁸ For this very reason, they argue, the Bible is unreliable and cannot be trusted anymore. Generally, *Sura* 2:79 and *Sura* 5:13 are quoted in this regard:

> *Therefore woe be unto those who write the Scripture with their hands and then say, "This is from Allah," that they may purchase a small gain therewith. Woe unto them for that their hands have written, and woe unto them for that they earn thereby. (Sura 2:79)*

> *And because of their breaking their covenant, We have cursed them and made hard their hearts. They change words from their context and forget a part of that whereof they were admonished. Thou wilt not cease to discover treachery from all save a few of them. But bear with them and pardon them. Lo! Allah loveth the kindly. (Sura 5:17)*⁹

In accordance with Islamic traditions, when a child is born to Muslim parents in Pakistan the call of prayer is whispered in his ears.¹⁰ The claim of the Bible being altered is made so persistently that, as a jest, some say that the child is told that the Bible has been changed by the Christians.

---

6. Louie, *Honor*, 3.
7. Lefebvre, *Kinship*, 264.
8. Nazir-Ali, *Islam*, 47.
9. Pickthall, *Koran*, 14, 137.
10. Bennett, "Islam," 94.

In contrast to the West, where an abundance of translations of the Bible exist and where new translations and revised editions of the Bible continue to appear from time to time, such practices are not done in Pakistan.[11] In fact, it is rather discouraged and unwelcome. For example, the Protestant churches still use the 1843 translation of the Urdu Bible, which has not been much revised since its preparation.[12] Likewise, no new translation of the complete Bible in Urdu, the national language of Pakistan, has been done by the Protestants since the establishment of Pakistan.[13] One of the reasons that has led the Christian leadership to abstain from producing a new translation of the Bible in a major language is the pressure and criticism of the Muslim community in Pakistan, where frequent accusations are leveled at Christians regarding the alteration of the Bible. Having a new translation or revising the existing translation is considered to bring negative effects by some. It is feared that the availability of more than one translation may wrongly be used as an excuse against the authenticity of the Bible. The difference of words and expressions in more than one translation in the same language is thought to cause more trouble. In Pakistan, this seems to be a common concern of some of the Protestant church leaders. The late Rev. Dr. Ziai, a renowned Pakistani Bible scholar (also served as a translation officer with PBS from 1989–91), explained the issue as follows:

> *The church at large has been reluctant to agree to any change in the text, because of the traditional Islamic objection that change means corrupting the Bible, and also because of the resistance in the past by Christian leaders and congregations. Some church leadership in Pakistan has actually been promoting opposition among the people against the new Urdu and English translations. For the same reasons, other translations also have not been revised.*[14]

The above statement touches on some complex and interrelated issues: there is the pressure of the Muslim community, the opposition by the Pakistani Christian leadership, the propaganda against new translations in

---

11. Daniell, *Bible*, 769.

12. Culshaw, "Bible Translation," 68.

13. A new translation of the Bible in Urdu (*Kitab-e-Muqadas*, the Old and New Testament in Modern Urdu) was published in 2010 by the Geo Link Resource Consultants, a group of independent scholars. However, except for some individual use, this translation has not become popular among Pakistani churches. In fact, its circulation seems to be discouraged due to the Muslim-friendly terms that have been used in this translation. The translation is available on the Urdu Geo Version website for downloading (http://urdugeoversion.com/wordpress/).

14. Ziai, "Translators," 245.

established languages, and the uncertain future of revising the Christian Scripture in other languages in which the translation had been done at some point in the past. With regard to the objection made by the Muslim community, it seems that some Christian leadership in Pakistan assumes that by not touching the existing text of the Protestant Urdu Bible it is possible to avoid this issue.

## 2.2. Kitab-e-Muqadas and Kalam-e-Muqadas

There is an important question that needs to be asked: is only one translation of the Bible in Urdu available and being used among all churches in Pakistan? If this is the case, then the concern for protecting the text of the Protestant Urdu Bible and attempts to shut the mouths of opponents by having a single translation may be argued to some extent. However, in reality it is not the case, as the Roman Catholic Church uses a different translation of the Bible in Urdu, not to mention that, apart from the translation, the two versions of the Urdu Bibles differ in the number of books found in them. Therefore, one should accept the reality that two different texts of the Urdu Bible, namely *Kitab-e-Muqadas* (The Holy Book) and *Kalam-e-Muqadas* (The Holy Word), are available in Pakistan.[15] It is wrong to think that the Muslims in Pakistan only regard the Protestant denominations and the Urdu Bible used by them as the true representation of Christianity in Pakistan. Likewise, it would be wrong to assume that the Muslims are unaware of the existence of a different text of the Urdu Bible used by the Catholic Church.

Since two different translations of the Bible in the same language are already available and used in Pakistan, the concerns of some Protestant church leaders, illustrated by Dr. Aslam Ziai, do not sound convincing. Having said that, it must be remembered that the Christians living as minorities in Islamic-majority countries look for ways to respond to the objections made by their Muslim brothers, and this fact needs to be appreciated. At the same time, it should not be forgotten that the idea of the Bible being altered is so deeply rooted among the Muslim community in Pakistan that having one or several translations of the Bible in the same language would not make any difference. If someone has the intention of making false accusations regarding the alteration of the Bible, he can do so, since two different translations in Urdu, Protestant and Catholic versions, are already available.

15. The Protestant version of the Urdu Bible, called *Kitab-e-Muqadas*, is published by the Pakistan Bible Society. The Catholic version of the Urdu Bible, called *Kalam-e-Muqadas*, was first published in Rome by the Society of St. Paul in 1958.

Thus, one does not need to wait for a new or revised translation. In other words, it does not seem logical that Muslims are simply waiting for a revision or a new translation of the Bible in Urdu to use it as an excuse to blame Christians for corrupting the Bible.

It is worth mentioning that an ecumenical committee had been set up in 1968 to discuss a "common Bible in Urdu" for Protestants and Catholics.[16] Since then, several discussions for an ecumenical translation have had taken place from time to time, but do not produce results, as both parties fail to reach a mutual agreement.[17]

### 2.3. Attempts to Ban the Bible

Those who actively make accusations of corruption in the Bible go far beyond mere charges, even to the point of demanding a ban on the Bible. In June 2011 the *Jamiat Ulema-e-Islam* (JUI-S), a religious-political party, urged the Supreme Court of Pakistan to take action against the use of the Bible in Pakistan. It demanded a ban by arguing that some of its "insertions" are blasphemous, particularly regarding the lives of the prophets.[18] This demand was made in reaction to the threats of burning the Qur'an by Terry Jones in the United States, and no action was taken on this request by the Supreme Court in Pakistan. It does show, however, that having a new translation or revision of the existing one would not change the attitudes of people who intend to use propaganda against the Bible by all means.

### 2.4. Revised and New Translation

The question, then, is to what extent are Pakistani Christians benefitting from having no revision and no new translation of the Bible in languages used within the Punjabi church? It is absolutely vital that people understand

---

16. "Common Bible in Urdu Planned," *Catholic Herald*, December 20, 1968, http://archive-uat.catholicherald.co.uk/article/20th-december-1968/7/common-bible-in-urdu-planned.

17. Catholic bishop of Karachi, Evarist Pinto, expressed desire for a joint translation of the Urdu Bible at a Bible translation conference in Karachi in 2001. He mentioned that efforts in the past have not been successful due to disagreements. See "Catholic Bishop Calls on Translators for Ecumenical Urdu Bible," *UCANews*, updated March 20, 2001, https://www.ucanews.com/story-archive/?post_name=/2001/03/21/catholic-bishop-calls-on-translators-for-ecumenical-urdu-bible&post_id=18103.

18. Hudson Institute, "Call to Ban Bible under Pakistan's Elastic Blasphemy Laws," *Eurasia Review*, June 9, 2011, http://www.eurasiareview.com/09062011-call-to-ban-bible-under-pakistans-elastic-blasphemy-laws-oped/.

the Scripture while listening and reading for themselves, as language changes considerably within a short period of time. It means that what was meaningful and understandable to the people centuries ago is not necessarily comprehensible to the generations that follow. Keeping this in mind, it is crucial that necessary revision takes place from time to time in accordance with the needs of the people. It does not seem wise that the Christian church in Pakistan has to suffer due to fear of criticism and pressure of the Muslim community. Such an attitude does not seem to bring any good to the church in Pakistan; rather, it is a hurdle in allowing people to gain a clear understanding of the Word of God.

It is interesting to observe that the Catholic Church in Pakistan appears to be taking the lead in this regard. In contrast to the Protestant Church in Pakistan, the Roman Catholic Church prepared a new translation of the Bible in Urdu after the nation's independence. The translation, mainly done by Fr. Liberius Pieterse,[19] was initiated in 1954 and was published in 1958.[20] The Catholic Bible Commission Pakistan (CBCP) lists the "translating, updating and publishing of the Holy Bible in Urdu and other local languages" as its first objective.[21] CBCP revised the old Urdu translation, and provided simplified words to some difficult words in the tenth edition published in 2011. It shows that the Catholic leadership in Pakistan adopts a different approach—i.e., to update the Holy Bible from time to time, to consider the needs of their people, and ignoring any criticism from opponents.

This sets a model for the Protestant churches in Pakistan in prioritizing the needs of their people rather than being obsessed by the pressure and criticism of the Muslim majority. The following note in the introduction of the Protestant Urdu Bible is worth noting: "The history of the Urdu Bible testifies that revision of the translation took place after every twenty or twenty-five years, and that the work of its calligraphy and publication continued. But, from 1930 up till now no work has been done in this regard."[22] It indicates the necessity of revision. It raises the important question: Why for the last ninety years has the Protestant Urdu Bible not been revised and why has the practice of revision been discontinued?

19. Stacy, "Bible," 15.
20. Walbridge, "Christians," 117.
21. Catholic Bible Commission Pakistan website (http://cbcpakistan.org/).
22. Introduction to the Protestant Urdu Bible, *Kitab-e-Muqadas*, published by the Pakistan Bible Society, Lahore, 2008; translation mine.

## 3. PUNJABI NEW TESTAMENT IN PERSIAN SCRIPT

Having looked at external issues, it is appropriate to explore the internal issues within the Punjabi-speaking Christians regarding the preparation of Christian Scripture in their own mother tongue, Punjabi. The correspondence between the British and Foreign Bible Society (BFBS) in London and its Punjab auxiliary in Lahore sheds light on this matter. It is crucial to go through details found in this correspondence as it uncovers the elements whose effects may be observed in the Punjabi-speaking church in Pakistan to this day. The correspondence points to the obstacles that occurred in revision and elements that led to ceasing further translation work in Punjabi.

Here it is important to mention that there are two dialects of the Punjabi language. One spoken mainly in the Indian state of Punjab is known as the Eastern Punjabi. It has loan words from Sanskrit and is written in Gurumukhi script. The Punjabi spoken in the province of Punjab in Pakistan is normally referred to as Western Punjabi. It is written in Persian script and has loan words form Arabic and Persian. The translation of the Punjabi New Testament in Persian script was published by the BFBS in 1912. One thousand copies of the first edition were printed at Nol Kishore Printing Press through the Ghulam Qadir Masihi Printer in Lahore.[23] The second edition was published the following year in 1913 and the third edition was published in the year 1940.[24] The revised version was published in 1952; minor corrections were made in this version, mainly involving spelling, grammatical errors, and replacing of some awkward words.[25] The Punjabi New Testament in Persian Script faced a number of challenges before reaching the point of revision as well as initiating further translation work in Punjabi. Before discussing the present-day situation in the church in Pakistan in general, it is important to look at those challenges one by one.

### 3.1. The Attitude of the Preachers, Evangelists, and Lay People toward Their Mother Tongue

Going through the BFBS correspondence, it is clear that the major challenge in revising the Punjabi New Testament in Persian Script and its usage among the ordinary Punjabi people was to do with the general behavior of the Punjabi preachers, evangelists, and lay people. By and large, the attitude

---

23. *Injil Sharif.*

24. BFBS Archives, letter dated July 5, 1951, from Rev. Chandu Ray to Rev. Bradnock.

25. BFBS Archives, letter dated November 17, 1949, from Rev. Chandu Ray to members of the translation committee for Persian-Panjabi.

of the Punjabi church leaders was negative toward the use of their own mother tongue; the matter of revision, usage, and initiating further Scripture translation work in the Punjabi language was opposed by them.

Long before partition, the Urdu language was being used for the training of Punjabi church leaders, even at the village level, and all lecturing at theological seminaries was done in the same language.[26] In other words, Urdu became the language of theological training for Punjabi church leaders. As a result, Punjabi was looked down upon by the Punjabi leadership as it was not viewed as a language of the educated but of those belonging to an uneducated background. An important meeting for the revision of the New Testament in Punjabi was held on October 23, 1934, in Lahore. A vast representation of mission agencies working in Punjab was present at the aforementioned meeting. Several participants shared the concern that the major obstacle in the effective use of Scripture in Punjabi was the unhealthy attitude of the Punjabi church leaders including the preachers, evangelists, and lay persons toward the use of their mother tongue. These have been referred to as *manads* in general, meaning those who proclaim or preach.[27] The following comments, made by several participants at that meeting, explains the issue:

> *I find that all workers amongst the village congregations are much more inclined to use Urdu when reading than Panjabi. It may be because it is more educated to know Urdu.*
> —Miss A. C. Newton, Church of England Zenana Missionary Society, Batala

> *I feel that it would be much better if our pastors and manads used it. Since they have not to any extent done so in the past there is no hope that they will do so in the future.*
> —Miss K. Beattie, United Presbyterian, Sangla Hill

> *We ought to insist on it being used by manads.*
> —Mrs. A. C. J. Elwin, Church Missionary Society, Bannu

> *Personally I use a copy continually, but few of our pastors do so.*
> —Dr. Nesbitt, United Presbyterian, Sialkot City

> *A few of my pastors and manads use the Panjabi Testament.*
> —Rev. Paul A. Miller, United Presbyterian, Lyallpur

---

26. BFBS Archives, letter dated October 23, 1934, from Mr. Church (secretary Panjab auxiliary, Lahore) to Rev. Smith (secretary BFBS, London).

27. Platts, *Dictionary of Urdu*, 1070.

> *The Indian pastors as a rule seem to prefer to use the Urdu and make their own translation at time.*
> —Rev. J. C. Alter, United Presbyterian, Zafarwal

> *From a thirty years' experience I say without fear of contradiction that for the ordinary illiterate congregation in the villages you might as well read the Gospel in English as in Urdu; both languages would be equally unintelligible. The suggestion that the manads can read from the Urdu version and translate at sight does not appeal to me in the very least. There are three or possibly four or five men in the Panjab who can do this, but my painful experience is that many of our padris who attempt this make a very painful mess of it, their reading is not intelligent, and their translations are often very crude, and often, when they come to a difficult word, it is not translated at all and we get the word as it stands in Urdu or Persian, with the result that not a single person has been able to follow the lesson intelligently.*
> —Rev. Canon Hares, Church Missionary Society, Gojra

> *My experience so far has been that as we are taking more education, the Urdu knowing people are using English now, and those who know Punjabi are now using Urdu.*
> —Mrs. Samuel, United Presbyterian, Rawalpindi City

The correspondence shows that a minority of the Western missionaries made good use of the Punjabi New Testament in Persian script. They were the people who realized the value of Scripture in the mother tongue and encouraged others to use it:

> *I have found Grahame Bailey's New Testament in Persian Punjabi invaluable, and use my copy for district work. It seems as if it had only been of use for us missionaries from the West. I know that our Indian fellow workers use the Urdu Testament.*
> —Rev. Alexander, Church of Scotland, Jammu[28]

In contrast, the majority of the Western missionaries used Urdu rather than Punjabi, as Urdu was an established literary language in Punjab before partition, and it was natural for missionaries to be familiar with that language.[29] The words of Miss K. A. Hill explain:

---

28. BFBS Archives, minutes of the committee meeting for revision of the New Testament in Persian Panjabi held on October 23, 1934, at the Panjab Auxiliary of the British and Foreign Bible Society in Lahore.

29. Mir, *Punjab*, 12.

> *I think it would be most profitable if missionaries in village work use the Panjabi (Persian) New Testament. Manads and teachers would soon follow the example.*
> —Miss K. A. Hill, United Presbyterian, Sialkot

The familiarity with Urdu and its use by Western missionaries may well have to do with the language-learning policy of individual mission agencies in the Punjab. However, one should not forget the fact that it was the colonial era and the church leadership was in the hands of Western missionaries, whose majority used Urdu for preaching and teaching.[30] In other words, preaching in Urdu had already been standardized among the churches in Punjab during the colonial period. Consequently, local Punjabi church leaders followed their superiors and made use of Urdu for preaching among ordinary rural Punjabis. It indicates that the Punjabi Christian preachers regarded Urdu as the most appropriate language in which preaching could be done. Since people with authority in religious affairs used Urdu, the Punjabi church leaders naturally followed their pattern to gain respect and authority by preaching in the same language.

Sadly, the same attitude toward the use of Punjabi continued in the years to follow, as Punjabi church leaders gave preference to Urdu and avoided the use of Punjabi for teaching and preaching. For example, in 1937 the secretary of the Punjab auxiliary of the BFBS wrote in a letter that "pastors, catechists, etc. when reading the scriptures and teaching seem to prefer to take the Urdu version."[31] Unfortunately, this thinking continued to grow although the colonial period came to an end, and church leadership was very much transferred into the hands of local Punjabi Christians. In 1971, Mr. Gauhar Masih comprehensively addresses the same issue as follows:

> *The demand for Punjabi Scriptures is still very low and uncertain. The psychological barrier in the minds of the Clergy is quite strong. They unfortunately feel and quite incorrectly also that Punjabi is the language of uneducated and so very often on would find a Pastor struggling to translate Urdu into Punjabi while reading the Scripture lesson to the congregation and trying to preach in Urdu whereas a sermon by him in Punjabi would be better understood by the members of the congregation.*[32]

---

30. Cox, *Imperial*, 53.

31. BFBS Archives, letter dated February 17, 1937, from Mr. Church to Rev. Smith.

32. BFBS Archives, letter dated March 30, 1971, from Mr. Gauhar Masih to Rev. Wootton.

## 3.2. Education

The BFBS correspondence shows that, since education was not provided in the Punjabi language, there was little support for Scripture translation in this language. The majority did not favor Punjabi as education in Urdu was spreading.[33] It was heavily stressed at both government and church levels that education in Punjabi was not supported.[34] Thus, the objection that time and money should not be wasted on translation work in Punjabi continued to be used as an argument to abstain from having Scripture in that language. At the same time, a handful of people, such as Dr. Grierson, disagreed with the view that Punjabi would be displaced in favor of Urdu in the days to come.[35]

Despite the negative perceptions and objections, when the Punjabi New Testament in Persian script was first published in 1912, there was good demand for this book.[36] An advertisement was published in the local newspaper that said: "The Complete New Testament in Persian Punjabi: this long expected and much desired book is at length ready and the New Testament is available for the villagers of the Punjab in their mother tongue."[37] The fact that one thousand copies of the first edition were sold within a year indicates how warmly the New Testament in Punjabi was received.[38] It shows that the opposition against Scripture in Punjabi due to the inaccessibility of education in this language had overstated the case. However, such objections continued to be made, and for this reason the revision of the Punjabi New Testament faced long delays. Likewise, the work on the Old Testament had to be stopped as support was lacking.

## 3.3. Lack of Trained Personnel

Another challenge in revising the Punjabi New Testament in Persian Script was the lack of trained personnel who could undertake the revision. The BFBS correspondence suggests that the shortage of trained people to do the job was an obstacle in revision of the Punjabi New Testament, and it also

---

33. BFBS Archives, letter dated January 4, 1911, from Mr. Church to Rev. Kilgour referring to the comments on Punjabi by Mr. Grey, education secretary of North India.

34. BFBS Archives, letter dated February 17, 1937, from Mr. Church to Rev. Smith.

35. BFBS Archives, letter dated January 2, 1911, from Mr. Church to Rev. Kilgour, referring to the comments of Dr. Grieson, who prepared an extensive linguistic survey of India.

36. BFBS Archives, letter dated October 3, 1912, from Mr. Church to Dr. Kilgour.

37. BFBS Archives, literary notes of the Panjab auxiliary of BFBS, September 1912.

38. BFBS Archives, letter dated July 5, 1951, from Rev. Chandu Ray, Secretary Bible Society Panjab auxiliary to Rev. Bradnock, translation secretary BFBS.

hindered translation of the Old Testament. The work of the New Testament in Punjabi was supervised by Rev. Graham Bailey, while the final draft was checked by Rev. Brendon and Mr. Daud Singh.[39] Rev. Bailey did not do the translation himself, but it was done under his supervision mainly by his local Punjabi colleagues.

The New Testament was published in 1912, and the following year discussions were started on translating sections from the Old Testament. Rev. Bailey had departed to the United Kingdom by that time, and it was felt necessary to invite him to commence the Old Testament work in Punjabi, as indicated in the letter dated May 7, 1913, from the secretary of the Panjab auxiliary: "The New Testament edited by Mr. Bailey has been such a success that there was no doubt in the minds of the committee as to who should be invited to do further translation work in this language."[40] Although the book of Genesis was completed in 1915 by Rev. Bailey, he was unable to continue with the translation work in Punjabi.[41] The following year, Rev. John Newton revised Genesis.[42] After the death of Rev. Newton in 1918, who had been involved in working on the Old Testament for more than two years, the matter of translating Scripture in Punjabi remained largely silent from 1919–1933. No suitable person was found to work on translation,[43] although requests were continuously made to the BFBS by the Presbyterian mission to resume translation in Punjabi.[44] As a result, a temporary revision committee for the New Testament was formed in May 1934 that included some notable names, such as Rev. Barkat Ullah, A. Dungwreth, A. W. Gordon, Canon Hares, Rev. Labhu Mall, and H. F. Nesbitt. The major meeting of this revision committee took place on October 23, 1934, in Lahore, where representatives of several mission agencies in Punjab participated.[45]

However, no progress was made during the next four years, from 1935–1938, as the committee could not decide on the person who could do the job. In 1939 another important committee meeting took place in which it was decided that Rev. Labhu Mall and Mr. Joshua Fazal-ud-Din be approached to take up the revision work, the former to act as chairman of the revision committee.[46] After five years of the setting up of this revision

---

39. BFBS Archives, letter dated June 16, 1911, by Mr. Church to BFBS in London.
40. BFBS Archives, letter dated May 7, 1913.
41. BFBS Archives, minutes of the Panjab auxiliary, dated April 19, 1915.
42. BFBS Archives, letter dated February 16, 1916, from Mr. Church to Dr. Kilgour.
43. BFBS Archives, letter dated July 9, 1918.
44. BFBS Archives, letter dated December 3, 1923.
45. BFBS Archives, letter dated December 3, 1923.
46. BFBS Archives, letter dated February 13, 1940, by secretary Panjab auxiliary Mr. Church.

committee, no progress was made with regard to the work in Punjabi, as indicated by Rev. Krishnaswamy, secretary of the Panjab auxiliary of the BFBS, in a letter dated July 26, 1943.[47] The search for suitable personnel to revise the Punjabi New Testament and to initiate further Old Testament translation work continued. In 1947, Dr. Nesbitt and Rev. Jalal-ud-Din were recommended to help with the revision work.[48] Due to their unavailability, a new revision committee was formed under the headship of Dr. H. J. Stewart, which included Rev. Canon Jawahir Masih, Rev. C. B. Stuntz, Rev. J. D. Brown, Rev. K. L. Nasir, Rev. Paterson, Rev. A. Thakur Das, and Miss M. Sunder Singh.[49] Finally, the revision of the New Testament in Punjabi was done in 1951 by Dr. Harris J. Stewart, Mr. Feroze Khan Tarar, and Rev. Qadir Bakhsh. It was hoped that the Old Testament work would make similarly steady progress under the supervision of Rev. Stewart.[50] However, no further translation work was done in Punjabi after 1951. Rev. Stewart returned to the United States after serving in India for many years, while Rev. Qadir Bakhsh passed away and no national worker was found to replace him.[51]

During the next eighteen years, no meeting or discussion took place on Scripture translation in Punjabi. In 1970, Dr. Daskawie was proposed as a valuable person for future translation work in Punjabi, and the following year, Mr. Joshua Fazal-ud-Din was recommended for the same task, but no practical steps were taken.[52] Mr. Gauhar Masih explains the situation in his letter dated March 30, 1971:

> *One very great difficulty that I am experiencing these days is to find a suitable person to even do the revision so that if Punjabi scriptures are needed they could be printed immediately. Rev. Feroze Khan Tarrar unfortunately is not acceptable to a very large majority of the members of the General Committee. Mr. Joshua Fazal Din who has versified the New Testament in Punjabi would I think be not amenable to any suggestions by anybody if he does*

---

47. BFBS Archives, letter dated June 26, 1943, by secretary Panjab auxiliary Rev. Krishnaswamy.

48. BFBS Archives, minutes of the general committee meeting held April 16, 1947, in Lahore.

49. BFBS Archives, letter dated November 17, 1947, by secretary Bible Society Panjab auxiliary Mr. Chandu Ray.

50. BFBS Archives, letter dated July 31, 1951.

51. BFBS Archives, letter dated October 14, 1955, by secretary of the BFBS Panjab auxiliary Mr. Chandu Ray to Wilfred Bradnock of BFBS.

52. BFBS Archives, letter dated February 25, 1970, by secretary of the West Pakistan Bible Society Mr. Gauhar Masih to Rev. Wootton of BFBS.

# The Sociolinguistic Circumstances Facing Pakistani Punjabi Christians 121

*the revision. He feels and perhaps rightly there is no one better qualified than him.*[53]

It becomes evident through the BFBS correspondence that the lack of trained personnel hindered the task of Scripture translation in Punjabi. Although several revision committees were formed from 1913–1970, no solid step was taken to resume translation work in this language.

## 3.4. Insufficiency of Financial Resources

It can be gathered from the BFBS correspondence that, to some extent, the insufficiency of funds affected the overall translation work in Punjabi. Although it was not the major obstacle, plans and actions had to be delayed because of it. At the committee meeting for the revision of the New Testament in Punjabi held in 1934, those who suggested discontinuing publication or postponing the revision work did so due to the unavailability of funds. For example, Rev. A. Dungworth of Church Missionary Society Clarkabad stated that "while Bible society funds are low I do not think the expense of a revision would be justified." Miss H. Kidley of the Church of Scotland, Sialkot, asserted that "most of us feel that, under present financial difficulties, it would be best not to undertake the expense at present of revising and reprinting it." Likewise, Commissioner N. Muthiah of the Salvation Army Lahore mentioned that "if the society is in any way in need to conserve their funds, I would say the Persian Panjabi Testament might safely be left for a period at any rate."[54]

The correspondence also indicates that the Punjab auxiliary itself seemed unwilling and uninterested in making financial arrangements for this particular work. Instead, it wished for the mission agencies interested in the translation work to take up the financial responsibility for revising and resuming Scripture translation in Punjabi. Letter dated May 22, 1934, sent from Mr. W. H. L. Church, secretary of the Panjab auxiliary in Lahore, to Rev. Edwin Smith of BFBS in London, says: "It is hard for some of our friends to realise that the Bible society has not unlimited funds at its disposal. It is not always understood that revision work is undertaken in the interests of the churches and missions using the version; the Bible Society does not benefit by the undertaking."[55]

53. BFBS Archives, letter dated March 30, 1970.
54. BFBS Archives, minutes of the committee meeting for revision of the New Testament in Persian Panjabi held on October 23, 1934, at the Panjab Auxiliary of the British and Foreign Bible Society in Lahore.
55. BFBS Archives, letter dated May 22, 1934.

A decade after the aforementioned letter, similar remarks may be observed from minutes of the general committee meeting of the Panjab auxiliary held in Lahore on April 16, 1947. The secretary was asked to write a letter to the Board of Foreign Missions of the United Presbyterian Church of North America to request Dr. H. S. Nesbitt to help with regard to the revision of the Panjabi New Testament, and that "the Bible Society would be most grateful if he could come here with no financial obligation involving the Bible Society."[56] The correspondence seems to indicate that the Punjab auxiliary of BFBS itself was reluctant to take concrete steps in revising the translation work in Punjabi and was not convinced of producing any further work in this language. If the auxiliary was indeed interested in taking up the work in Punjabi, it would have given priority to this work by taking it seriously, would have arranged for the necessary funds, and would not have left things to the interested mission agencies to make the necessary arrangements.[57]

### 3.5. Scripture in Punjabi Affected by the Issue of Revising the Urdu Bible

The matter of revising the Bible in Urdu language had influenced translation work in other languages, as indicated by Dr. Aslam Ziai. The Scripture translation in Punjabi was directly affected in particular as shown in the BFBS correspondence. The translation work in Punjabi often had to be postponed as it was considered less important in comparison to Urdu.[58] In 1968–69, the idea of revising the Urdu Bible was strongly opposed. Due to the strong reaction against revising the Urdu Bible, the revision of Scripture in other languages was largely discouraged.[59] In this regard, it would be interesting to investigate if this has to do with Punjabi being the dominant language of the Christian community, and it may not necessarily be the case with other languages spoken in Pakistan.

---

56. BFBS Archives, letter dated April 16, 1947.

57. Letter dated December 18, 1934, sent from the editor superintendent BFBS in London to secretary auxiliary branch in Lahore, indicates that the BFBS London office had funds of one thousand rupees for the revision of the Punjabi New Testament in Persian Script. However, since the auxiliary branch showed reluctance in this matter, the plans for revision were postponed and the funds available for this work were not utilized.

58. BFBS Archives, letter dated February 22, 1924.

59. BFBS Archives, letter dated July 21, 1971, from Mr. Gauhar Masih to Rev. Wootton, acting translation consultant BFBS.

## 3.6. Special Interest Shown by the United Presbyterian Mission

The correspondence sent from the Punjab auxiliary in Lahore to the British and Foreign Bible Society office in London shows that the United Presbyterian mission was keen on having the Scripture in the Punjabi language. The mission showed great interest in this regard and made efforts to overcome hurdles by providing both financial and personnel support to revise the New Testament in Punjabi and to resume the Old Testament translation. In fact, the mission was eager to have the complete Bible in the Punjabi language, although it never happened.

The minutes of the Panjab auxiliary committee dated December 3, 1923, mention that "the committee considered a request from the United Presbyterian Mission for the translation of the Old Testament, or, for immediate purposes, Joshua, Judges and Proverbs. Resolved to ask the United Presbyterian Mission for further particulars, and for some information as to the need and likely demand for these books."[60] In another letter, the secretary of the Panjab auxiliary, Mr. W. H. L. Church, wrote to Rev. Edwin Smith of BFBS in London that "the United Presbyterian Mission is taking some steps to make more use of Musalmani Panjabi, so it is quite possible there may be an increased demand for the New Testament."[61] Mr. Chandu Ray, secretary of the Bible Society Panjab auxiliary, wrote to Rev. Bradnock of BFBS in London on October 22, 1951, that "for the last three years we have had free services of the Rev. Dr. Harris J. Stewart and his colleagues. Dr. Stewart received personal grants from America for his helpers, and so the Society had hardly any expenses, as I have already explained this to you in my letter of 18th August in connection with the Persian Panjabi translation."[62] It is noteworthy that Dr. Harris J. Stewart was a United Presbyterian missionary and, as indicated by Rev. Chandu Ray, Dr. Stewart's colleagues Rev. Qadir Bakhsh and Mr. Feroze Tarar, who revised the New Testament in Punjabi, were financially supported by his mission agency for the task of Scripture in Punjabi.[63] Besides financial and personnel support, the mission was attempting to initiate literacy in Punjabi.[64] This way the mission was hoping to tackle the objection that Scripture in Punjabi was not worth producing since education was not provided in this language.

---

60. BFBS Archives, letter dated December 3, 1923.
61. BFBS Archives, letter dated March 7, 1935.
62. BFBS Archives, letter dated October 22, 1951.
63. *United Presbyterian*, UPBFM, 46.
64. BFBS Archives, letter dated May 3, 1938.

The BFBS correspondence makes one wonder why the Presbyterian Mission in particular was keen in seeing the Scripture in Punjabi. The mission made every possible effort to overcome hurdles of finances, the training of personnel, and education in Punjabi. Why was it making all such efforts while others simply seemed reluctant in making any advancement in this regard? One could only think of the previous experience that the United Presbyterian Mission had with the translation of Psalms in Punjabi. One could only assume that the Presbyterian Mission was thrilled to see the fruits of producing Scripture in this language among the ordinary Punjabi Christians. They had seen the love and affection of the Punjabi Christians toward their mother tongue and it caused them to make efforts to see the Word of God in this language. The mission must have been firmly convinced that if the Psalms in poetical form can play a huge role in the spiritual development of the Punjabi Christians then how much more the availability of the Word of God in this language would do for them.

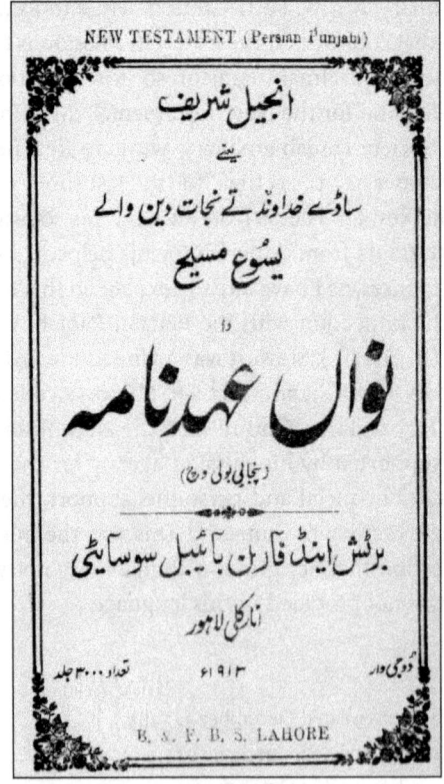

**Punjabi New Testament in Persian Script**

## 4. PRESENT-DAY SOCIOLINGUISTIC SITUATION

Looking at the correspondence spanning over a century on translation of Christian Scripture in the Punjabi language, one wonders what the present situation is with regard to the behavior toward Punjabi language among the Christians in Pakistan. Are things different from the past or have they not changed from what they were a hundred years ago?

The role and status of different languages has been a huge issue after the establishment of Pakistan, and it seems to be growing quite rapidly. In order to understand this, it would be helpful to look briefly at the present general linguistic situation in the country. English and Urdu are regarded as official languages of Pakistan; and are considered to be academic languages since they are used as mediums of instruction at educational institutions in Pakistan.[65] Punjabi is the mother tongue of more than half of the total population of Pakistan, numbering over one hundred million people.[66] In spite of that it is far behind from other provincial languages such as Sindhi, which has made considerable developments since the establishment of Pakistan, while Punjabi has not even gained the status of official language in the province of Punjab.[67] On the other hand, Urdu, which is only spoken by just over 7 percent as their first language, is the national language of Pakistan.[68] In other words, English and Urdu are used in domains of power, including the social, political, educational, and economic circles.[69] Punjabi is seen as a nonintellectual language and even Punjabis hesitate to use it in public, especially in the urban areas.

A survey done among the Punjabi students by Dr. Sabiha Mansoor reveals that the majority of Punjabi students display negative attitudes to Punjabi.[70] Dr. Rahman mentions that Punjabi parents in urban areas prefer "to teach Urdu and English to their children and consider these languages more sophisticated and cultured than Punjabi."[71] Such an attitude is connected with social status in the society. The knowledge of academic languages, Urdu and English, is understood to give better opportunities for employment, and they are associated with the elite in Pakistan.[72] On

---

65. Rahman, "Education," 252.
66. Bhatia, "Languages," 127.
67. Rahman, "Power," 30.
68. Rasool and Mansoor, "Contemporary Issues," 234.
69. Rahman, "Multilingualism," 88.
70. Mansoor, *Sociolinguistic*, 170.
71. Rahman, *Politics*, 208.
72. Rahman, "Urdu," 115.

the other hand, Punjabi is not the language of power domains.[73] It is often seen as a backward language that brings embarrassment to its speakers, and whose speakers are hurriedly labeled as village yokels and rustics by the educated class.[74]

Since Punjabi Christians are part of the same society, they have also been greatly affected by the current sociolinguistic situation in Pakistan. As a matter of fact, a large majority of Christians in Pakistan are from Punjabi-speaking backgrounds, except for a small number of Christians from Rajasthani-speaking backgrounds in rural Sindh, and the Goan Christians from the Konkani-speaking backgrounds in the urban Sindh.[75] It must be remembered that at the time of partition, the majority of Punjabi Christians had no education and the church was predominantly illiterate. The literacy rate among Punjabi Christians is still low and the majority of them reside in rural Punjab.[76] At the same time, many Punjabi Christians have now settled in big cities and towns. The negativity toward the use of their mother tongue by Punjabi Christians living in big cities seems to be increasing.

Karachi is the largest city of Pakistan, a city of more than twenty million people and predominantly Urdu speaking, thus the inhabitants of Karachi are rightly proud of their Urdu accent.[77] Some Punjabi Christians living in Karachi can be heard saying that school children should not be allowed to visit the province of Punjab for holidays or for any other reason, otherwise they would pick up the Punjabi accent. I have observed many young people in Karachi feeling so ashamed to converse in the Punjabi language, it is not that they do not understand Punjabi. The underlying reality is that they do not wish to give the impression of having anything to do with the Punjabi language, or even to acknowledge that this language is spoken by some in their households.

At any rate, the attitude of Punjabi Christians living in the big cities shows that they like to keep their children away from the influence of the Punjabi language. In urban areas in the province of Punjab, where many Punjabi Christians reside, the situation is no different. In cities like Lahore, Multan, Gujrat, Gujranwala, and Sialkot, I have observed a majority of the people introducing themselves to me in Urdu and then continuing long conversations in the same language. Why not converse in Punjabi instead? The reasons are the same as mentioned above. In rural areas in the province

---

73. Rahman, *Ideology*, 380.
74. Zaidi, "Sociolinguistics," 43.
75. Gabriel, *Citizens*, 21.
76. Carey, "Theological," 160.
77. Siddiqi, *Ethnicity*, 95.

of Punjab, where the majority of Punjabi Christians live, such an attitude does not appear to prevail. Part of the reason may be that the literacy rate among rural Punjabi Christians is low. Having said that, I have met children from my extended families living in rural Punjab, some of whom attempt to use more Urdu than Punjabi. I have seen their parents feeling proud listening to their children converse in Urdu, it somehow gives an educated feel to the family. It is to be noted that in rural areas people do not have enough resources to provide education to their children and the opportunities of receiving quality education does not exist in rural parts of Pakistan.[78] In any case, Punjabi may still be seen as a dominant language among rural Punjabi Christians, although, being influenced by urban Punjabi Christians, they do their best within their limited resources for their children to use Urdu.

One thing is clear, that the psychological barrier in the minds of Punjabi church leaders, and the general incorrect view that speaking Punjabi is the sign of the uneducated, is the continuation of ideas deeply rooted since the colonial era long before the establishment of Pakistan. The comments made by various individuals at the 1934 conference with regard to the revision of the Punjabi New Testament make it crystal clear that the use of Punjabi as a language in the Punjabi church was practically rejected by Punjabi church leaders. As far as the Punjabi Christian church in Pakistan is concerned, the present attitude toward Punjabi is a continuation of the mindset that may be traced back even before partition. Things have not changed since then, as Urdu is still the dominant language used in the Punjabi churches in Pakistan. Whether it is a small Punjabi-speaking church in a tiny village in the province of Punjab or a dominantly Punjabi-speaking background Christian church in the center of the largest city in Pakistan, the preaching is done in Urdu.[79] It is sad to observe that, in general, the only place where preachers use Punjabi during the sermon is when a joke is made or when the purpose is to make people laugh. In other words, it shows that the use of Punjabi in preaching is limited to fun alone and no serious preaching is done in that language. It makes one think, in fact, how much of the church preaching in Urdu is being understood by the believers who only speak and understand the Punjabi language, especially the older generation.

The mindset toward religious matters in the Pakistani society, shame-based culture, and illiteracy among the Pakistani Punjabi Christians are factors for the lack of awareness on the issue of linguistic barriers in the Punjabi *Zaburs*. The fear of pressure and criticism from the Muslim community, the accusations of Bible being corrupted, and attempts to ban the

---

78. Talbani, "Change," 140.
79. Cox, *Imperial*, 53.

Bible are some challenges in the Pakistani Islamic context for revising the Scripture. The historical documents concerning the Punjabi New Testament in Persian script makes it evident that the foremost obstacle in its preparation and use was to do with the poor attitude of the Punjabi preachers, evangelists and lay people toward their mother tongue.

The same unhealthy attitude toward Punjabi as a mother tongue has not changed among the dominantly Punjabi-speaking church in Pakistan. The negative attitude has resulted in a lack of interest in Scripture translation in the Punjabi language. It is crucial for the leadership to challenge the perception that speaking Punjabi brings shame and using Urdu brings authority, attention, and respect. It is a miserable aspect of society. If the singing of the Punjabi Psalms has contributed to the spiritual growth of the Punjabi church, then how much more the Scriptures in the same language would benefit the Pakistani church. Why do the Punjabi Christians in Pakistan work so hard to forget the language of their forefathers? Why do they fear to speak in the language of their parents? Why do they feel ashamed to teach the Punjabi language to their children? Does Punjabi deserve such poor treatment, the language we learned from our parents? It is the language in which we worship God through the singing of the *Zabur*. The negative attitude toward Punjabi as a language puts the use of Punjabi *Zaburs* at risk, a heritage of the Punjabi-speaking church.

# Conclusion

WORSHIP AMONG THE PAKISTANI churches cannot be envisaged without the singing of psalms. Psalms translated into the Punjabi language in versified form can unequivocally be regarded as the most accustomed, read, sung, recited, and memorized part of Scriptures by the body of Christ in Pakistan.[1] The story of the Punjabi Psalms is fascinating. Although it is factual that Pakistani believers take pleasure in singing the Punjabi Psalter, it is discouraging that they do not endeavor to uncover the fascinating history that lies behind them. It might have multifarious reasons, but a couple of them are observable. First, people apparently do not try and discover such history, and second, when something becomes habitual in society, it is often easy to neglect things and take the benefits for granted. The words of Rev. William Galbraith Young are noteworthy in this regard: "I am convinced that Asian Churches would gain much if they realized the riches of the Christian inheritance they have in a past of Asian Christianity. To so many, Christianity seems an importation from the West."[2] It was the metrical translation of Psalms in Urdu that paved the way for the metrical translation of Psalms into Punjabi. A vast majority of Punjabi Christians may find this surprising, as they are unaware of the existence of Urdu metrical psalms and one struggles to locate the whereabouts of the Urdu metrical psalms. Equally, the vast majority have not come across the 1892 edition of the selected Punjabi psalms, although some may have seen the 1908 edition of the Punjabi *Zaburs*. Both of these editions are rare as they are not easily accessible. Today, the Punjabi

---

1. Sadiq, "Imam-ud-Din Shahbaz," 36.
2. Young, *Church History*, vii.

Christians are being introduced to the Punjabi Psalms through the Sialkot Convention Hymn Book.

The Punjabi metrical psalms are a classic example of native Christian music that was composed by and is used to this day with enthusiasm by local people.[3] And in the words of Jeffrey Cox: "It is in Punjabi hymnody, rather than in bureaucratic creations of the missions, that one finds the fullest expression of indigenous Punjabi Christianity."[4] The work of Rev. Dr. Imam-ud-Din Shahbaz exhorts the Punjabi Christians in making genuine attempts to perceive these psalms as a precious heritage. There seems to be a lack of appreciation and recognition from the Punjabi Christians toward the outstanding contributions of Dr. Shahbaz. As Massey argues that Punjabi Christians and scholars alike seem to have ignored the input of Dr. Shahbaz toward the development of the Punjabi church, they appear to have failed in recognizing his immense contribution.[5]

In Pakistan, the Christian Talent Society organizes an annual "Padri Dr. Imam Din Shahbaz Award" event. In this annual event, leaders from both the Protestant and Catholic Church are invited to share their thoughts regarding the Punjabi *Zabur*, awards are distributed, the life and work of Dr. Shahbaz is remembered, and the beautiful *Zabur* are sung by individuals and choirs. According to Mr. Ilyas Masih (general secretary, Christian Talent Society), the vision of the society is to promote awareness concerning Dr. Shahbaz and his work on the Punjabi *Zabur*.[6]

Trinity International Christian Church in Philadelphia, led by Pastor Azhar Alam, organized an event on the "life and work of Dr. I D Shahbaz" in 2013, where I had the honor to speak. The well-attended event was joined by believers from different churches in Philadelphia. In the same year, I had the pleasure to speak at another event held in Philadelphia at the Presbyterian Church of Pakistan USA. In the UK, Calvary Chapel Norbury, led by Pastor Ilyas Mughal, organizes the annual *Sham-e-Mazamir* event to pay tribute to Dr. Shahbaz. In 2013, I had an opportunity to share about the life and work of Dr. Shahbaz at this event.[7] The efforts made by some to appreciate and celebrate the life and work of Dr. Imam-ud-Din Shahbaz is commendable.

---

3. Saleem, "Pakistan," 267.

4. Cox, *Imperial*, 148.

5. Massey, "Heritage," 32.

6. The ninth "Padri Dr. Imam-ud-Din Shahbaz Award" event, organized by the Christian Talent Society, was held at Alhamra Arts Council in Lahore, March 24, 2017; see https://www.youtube.com/watch?v=gO44d4vkjYM.

7. Calvary Chapel Norbury YouTube channel; the 2013 event video is available at https://www.youtube.com/watch?v=hoUoccUzo_I&t=1213s.

## Conclusion

However, it is like a drop in the ocean, and much more needs to be done in this regard.

Dr. Shahbaz made a lasting impact on people around him, whether it was as a poet, teacher, translator, or pastor. The loss of sight during the last stages of the Punjabi Psalter did not prevent Dr. Shahbaz from putting the psalms into verse; it indicates his incredible passion and commitment to his work. It is worth noting that glimpses of the key elements in the conversion of Dr. Imam-ud-Din are evident in his personal poetry. The poetic themes of Dr. Shahbaz's poetry include the assurance of salvation, forgiveness of sins, life with and without Christ, struggle with sin, and call to repentance. The poetical styles employed by Dr. Shahbaz in translating the Punjabi Psalms consist of Ghazal, *Masnavi*, *Qita*, *Chaupai*, and *Musamman*. The decision to use the mother tongue and indigenous music in preparation of the Psalms in Punjabi was key to making them a hit among the ordinary Punjabi Christians.

The Psalms in Punjabi are an excellent example of a "contextualized" form of Christian worship.[8] Consequently, it attracted ordinary people, as they felt that their spiritual needs were met through something that was produced in their language and in their style of music. The musical team was rather creative in putting the Psalms in Punjabi to local melodies and tunes. The early years of the annual Sialkot Convention were crucial in spreading and making the Punjabi Psalms popular. People who attended the Sialkot Convention would take with them the tunes they learned, in order to teach others in their respective villages and towns. The present-day Sialkot Convention Hymn Book that is used for worship among different denominations in Pakistan contains a good selection of the Psalms in Punjabi, and is the result of the annual Sialkot Convention where these psalms were repeatedly sung. The content of the Psalms attracted the oppressed and depressed people of lower castes, who embraced the message of hope, deliverance, protection, and justice in them. It was the cooperation of the various mission agencies in Punjab that made it possible for the Punjabi Christians to have it and to enjoy the beautiful book of Psalms in poetic form. Without such a cooperation it would not have been possible.

The plans to produce Psalms in Punjabi set to local tunes were faced with long delays due to the preference of higher social class over the lower social class and of preferring academic- and literate-status language over nonliterate- and backward-status language. The delay was furthered by the mission strategy of various mission agencies in the Punjab in general to reach out to the educated and better-off groups rather than the uneducated

---

8. Nazir-Ali, *Muslim-Christian Encounter*, 81.

and underprivileged groups. Moreover, the rivalry attitude within members of the same and different mission agencies and the partiality of the government support to a particular language in the Punjabi region caused delay in initiating the work on translating the metrical psalms in Punjabi.

Today the Punjabi Psalms are used widely among Punjabi-speaking churches in Pakistan. It would not be wrong to say that, within a Pakistani context, corporate worship within churches is considered incomplete if the Punjabi Psalms are excluded. Hence, they can be viewed as the heart of Christian worship in Pakistan. The Punjabi Psalms have made an unfathomable impact on the Christian church in Pakistan and have given her "an unrivalled familiarity" with the lovely book of Psalms.[9] These versified Psalms have played a central role in the theological development of the church in Pakistan. In general, Punjabi Christians, especially the older generation, know a number of the Punjabi psalms by heart. The majority of the older generation has had no schooling, thus memorization of God's Word as translated in the Punjabi Psalms helps in learning about God's truth. Bishop Michael Nazir-Ali, the former bishop of Rochester and Raiwind, regards these psalms as "the basis of the spirituality of the Pakistani church"; he remarks that "one thing that has really influenced me in thinking about God is the Psalms in Punjabi."[10] In the words of Arthur Victor: "These Zaburs have touched the deep chord in the hearts of the Punjabi Christians."[11]

The Pakistani Christians undergoing all kinds of discrimination and persecution express their deep inner feelings and faith through the singing of these psalms. Whether it is an occasion of celebration or of sorrow, the Psalms in Punjabi may be heard. The Christian community in Pakistan uses them in their religious and social gatherings. Regardless of denominational affiliations, the Psalms in Punjabi are used among all Christian churches in Pakistan. It has helped in creating unity and harmony among Christians of different denominations. When they get together for communal worship, they have one thing in common to sing and that is the metrical Punjabi psalms by which they can praise God. The Psalms in Punjabi are beyond denominational boundaries. They equally belong to the Presbyterians, Anglicans, Methodists, Baptists, Brethren, Pentecostals, Charismatics, Roman Catholics, and anyone else who uses them to worship God. It is fascinating to observe the variety of ways in which these psalms are being used in liturgical and cultural setting. However, the practical use of the Punjabi

---

9. O'Brien, *Construction*, 567.

10. M. Nazir-Ali, "The Good Fight," interview by Huw Spanner, *Third Way*, http://www.thirdwaymagazine.co.uk/editions/nov-2011-/high-profile/the-good-fight.aspx.

11. Victor, "Punjabi," 39.

Psalms indicates that these psalms are not always used according to their recommended usage. Similarly, the sensitivity in selecting particular psalms for specific occasions seems to be not fully appreciated.

The Muslim-friendly terms employed by Dr. Shahbaz in his Punjabi psalms draw attention to the notion of sharing psalms with the Muslims. Terms that are normally labeled as Muslim-specific and are not used by the Punjabi Christians today were made use of by Dr. Shahbaz in his translation, although such terms have since either been substituted, or psalms containing these terms are excluded from the Sialkot Convention Hymn Book. The number of constructive indicators discussed is encouraging when considering the Psalms as a means for bridging the gap in the Islamic context of Pakistan. The Qur'an views the psalms of David as revealed by God; the *hadith* speaks highly of the Psalms, and the engagement of medieval Muslim scholars with the Psalms shows the significance they saw in them. The intertextuality between the Qur'an and the Psalms is useful when looking at the Psalms as an agent for bridge-building. Here it is worth mentioning that theology of the Psalms is widespread both in the Old and New Testament, poetic Psalms for the Pakistani Punjabi Muslims has the advantage of introducing them to the wider biblical motifs.[12]

The embrace of and love for poetry in the Pakistani Punjabi culture is a significant marker. There exists an abundance of mystic poetic literature in the Punjabi language, and versified translations of the Qur'an being made available in Punjabi are positive indicators for presenting the Psalms in Punjabi verse. The parallel between Hebrew acrostic poetry and Punjabi *Siharfi* is useful. Although the Psalms contain a variety of themes, the God-centered language shows correspondence between the Psalms and the Qur'an. Nevertheless, sensitivity in selecting the themes and genres of Psalms to present is crucial when looking to share them with the Punjabi Muslims. In this regard, the common attributes of God in the Qur'an and the Psalms are significant, the beautiful names of God, known as the *Asma-ul-husna*, are vital in bridging the gaps.[13]

The mystic aspect of the Psalms and mystic practices in Pakistan are another important bridge-building factor. The spirituality in the Psalms is a valuable impetus that mystic followers may find motivating and appealing for their own spiritual strengthening. All that matters is to "enter through the right door."[14] The Psalms in poetic form appears to be fitting in an oral

---

12. Wenham, *Psalms*, 182. There are 121 psalms that have been directly cited or alluded to in the New Testament.

13. Samat, *Names*, 1.

14. Bütler, "Indigenization," 387.

culture where poetry is much embraced. In the Pakistani Islamic context, the Psalms may be put to music for the vast majority who see music as a means for devotion. The *Qawali* style of devotional music is broadly used in Pakistan, and seems fitting to set the Psalms to this music. It is worth noting that despite opposition to the use of music by strict Islamic circles, music in general is cherished in Pakistan; whether it is sociocultural or in religious gatherings of the millions of mystic followers.[15] The practical use of music in Pakistan is visible, from television and radio to public transport and wedding parties.[16]

In considering the notion of bridge-building through use of the Psalms, it is important to give special attention to some terms in the Psalms that are sensitive and may possibly incite anti-Semitic sentiments in an Islamic context. Some of these terms include Zion, the Temple, Jerusalem and Israel. A more literal translation of these terms may not be helpful for the Muslims, as it may wrongly give the impression of propaganda for Jewish nationalism. Seeking a more meaningful translation by keeping the religious, linguistic, and cultural issues in mind is vital to avoid any misunderstanding. Here it is important to mention that seeking alternatives for sensitive or challenging terms does not mean compromising at the cost of meaning in the original. Investigating substitutes for difficult, unfamiliar, and contentious terms helps in reducing misunderstanding.[17]

The employing of familiar language and expressions for the target audience is critical for effective communication. Some of the terms familiar to Islam employed by Dr. Shahbaz suit the Muslims, and although Pakistani Christians have reservations about the use of some of those terms, considering them in translating psalms for the Punjabi Muslims may possibly be helpful. The present form of the Punjabi Psalms does not seem quite ideal for the Pakistani Punjabi Muslims. Moreover, the inclusion of imprecatory psalms for the Muslims may not seem appropriate as a first step, for ethical issues and for any wrong understanding that may be extracted from these psalms as justification for a holy war.

It is worth mentioning that due to inferior social status, poverty, illiteracy, and the fearful environment in which the majority of Pakistani Christians have been living, there has not been much aspiration from the Pakistani Christians in general for dialogue. Due to the lack of confidence in people of other faith, some Pakistani Christian parents strongly advise their children not to mix with Muslims and avoid friendship with them. It

---

15. Wikeley, *Punjabi*, 155.
16. Qadeer, *Pakistan*, 246.
17. Spencer, "Musalmani," 165.

is understandable that they are protective and concerned for their children due to the fear of blasphemy. However, such restrictions result in negativity and struggles within these children, particularly when they grow up and step into the practical world, finding themselves surrounded by an overwhelming majority of Muslims. By and large, there does not seem to be a deeper desire among Pakistani Punjabi Christians to "understand the Muslim mind and to create as few stumbling-blocks as possible" for them.[18] In the Muslim-majority countries, the Christian minority seems not to show adequate interest in engaging in effective communication with their Muslim neighbors.[19] Lack of interest hinders greatly in having dialogue.

The cautious position of many Pakistani Christians regarding the use of Islamic-associated terms is understandably due to the theological differences that such terms carry.[20] However, to a large extent, such resistance may well be due to one's minority status in the society, where one wishes to be seen differently from the majority and strives to keep one's separate identity.[21] There appears to be a competitive spirit among the Christian minority, as some Pakistani Christians tend to demonstrate "religious intensity" in order to prove that they are far more devoted in following their religious duties than their Muslim neighbors. In the words of Walbridge: "It is a point of pride with many Pakistani Christians that they also fast and must undergo the same hardship as Muslims."[22]

It is one thing to maintain one's own individual identity in religious affairs, but it is another thing not to let it become a stumbling block in dialogue with people of other faiths. Many Pakistani Punjabi Christians think that "they first of all must show that they are different from the Pakistani Muslims."[23] The unnecessary effort for a distinct identity as a minority community ends up in drastic clash, immense struggle, and failure to integrate with the majority. As Fr. Bonnie Mendes asserts: "Emotionalism will not get us anywhere" in Pakistan.[24] There is no question that the ill-treatment that the Christian community receives from the Muslim community in Pakistan results in frustration and terror among the Pakistani Christians.[25] It seems that by suffering at the hands of the Muslims, some Pakistani Christians

18. Nazir-Ali, *Islam*, 157.
19. Glassman, "Muslim," 439.
20. Garlow, *Response*, 59.
21. Gabriel, *Citizens*, 97.
22. Walbridge, *Christians*, 187–88.
23. Bütler, "Dialogue," 329.
24. Mendes, "Challenges," 98.
25. Bütler, "Resurgence," 354.

have become hard-hearted toward them. However, such an unhealthy attitude cannot be justified, as it hinders in bridging the gap between the two. Highlighting the need for a transformation in attitude among the Pakistani Christians toward their Pakistani Muslim brethren, Asimi states:

> The ingrained Christian negativity towards Islam and Muslims is an internal poison which is eating up Christians. This poison must be extracted at all costs.... From Sunday pulpit sermons to local seminars and other communication means, Christians must be led to move toward the development of a positive and constructive attitude towards Islam and Muslims.[26]

Bishop Michael Nazir-Ali asserts: "I have for long argued for a program of interfaith dialogue and research sponsored by the government of Pakistan and its friends."[27] Despite the efforts made by the different church institutions and the government of Pakistan in recent years, the tolerance level of the majority group toward the minority groups does not seem to have improved; at the time of writing it is getting worse day by day. Consequently, the Christian minority continues to be the victim of social and religious discrimination. It may not be wrong to assert that some Pakistani Christian leaders struggle to engage in dialogue with a genuine and loving spirit. For example, a former Anglican bishop, gave a statement to form a Christian resistant group by the name of *Sipah-e-Masiha*, "Defenders of the Messiah," to protect the Christian community, arguing that there are *Sipah-e-Sahaba* and *Sipahe-Mohammad* militant groups in Pakistan to protect the rights of Sunni and Shiite Muslims, respectively.[28] Although the statement was given in frustration as a reaction to the consistent attacks on Christians and there was no seriousness in that statement, it indicates that even prominent Pakistani Christian leaders struggle to do meaningful dialogue. Despite the hardships and sufferings, exploring ways for bridge-building is crucial for the survival of the Christian community in the steadily intolerant culture of Pakistan. In the words of Bishop Michael Nazir-Ali: "In today's world, it is increasingly important that there should be dialogue between people of different faiths."[29]

The specific sociolinguistic factors facing the Pakistani Punjabi Christians affect the availability of Scripture in Punjabi, and any consideration for a revision of the Psalms in Punjabi within the Christian circles. It needs to

---

26. Asimi, *Minority*, 139–40.

27. Nazir-Ali, *Multiculturalism*, 98.

28. Jason Burke, "'Christian Taliban' Take Up Arms," *Independent*, February 11, 1999, http://www.independent.co.uk/news/christian-taliban-take-up-arms-1070113.html.

29. Nazir-Ali, *Convictiont*, 111.

be mentioned that there are peculiar challenges that arise when initiating a new translation or revision of the Christian Scriptures for Pakistani Christians; however, such challenges do not normally hinder producing Christian Scripture for the Muslim communities in Pakistan, especially if there has been little or no previous work. This applies to the Punjabi Psalms in poetic form for the Punjabi Muslims. Although here the focus is on Punjabi Muslims in Pakistan, the Saraiki-speaking Muslims in Southern Punjab and the Sindhi-speaking Muslims in rural Sindh have a rich tradition of mysticism and love for poetry, and the Psalms as poetry are equally fitting for these communities. The Psalms as poetry in the Islamic context of Pakistan have full potential for playing a vital role in bridge-building, and for sharing the beautiful poetry of the Psalms with the Muslim brethren.

The task of Bible translation, whether a completely new translation or revision of an existing one, cannot be adequately done without properly trained and qualified personnel.[30] In general, things in this regard are not very different from the past, as few Pakistani Christians may be found suitable and trained for the task of Scripture translation. The church does not seem to be making this important task a priority, although a few parachurch organizations have made efforts in training the mother-tongue translators, particularly from the minority language groups, to initiate Bible translation projects in Pakistan. As the church in Pakistan is predominantly Punjabi-speaking, it should not be difficult to find the right people to initiate a new translation in Punjabi or to revise the old version, if church leadership wished to do so. Compared to the predominantly illiterate Punjabi-speaking church before the partition, the Pakistani Punjabi Christians, particularly in the urban areas, are now eager for the new generation to receive education.[31] In a few cases, a total shift may be seen where children are educated to a considerable level whereas the parents did not have any opportunities for education. This fact is appreciative as the urge for education is beginning to grow for children among the illiterate parents, but this is not the case for the majority of Punjabi Christians in Pakistan.[32]

What has not changed is the attitude toward the use of Punjabi among the dominantly Punjabi-speaking church in Pakistan. Preaching and teaching continues to be in Urdu, while the training of church leaders continues to be done in Urdu, with some English. In comparison to the Pakistani Punjabi Christians, the Indian Punjabi Christians have the complete Punjabi Bible and they have every right to be proud of reading the Word of God in

---

30. Fry, "Translators," 430.
31. Walbridge, "Pakistan," 124.
32. Evans, "Faith," 178.

their own mother tongue.³³ The majority of Pakistani Punjabi Christians are even unaware of the existence of the Punjabi New Testament. Part of the reason is that it is not made available to the public, and as a result people have no knowledge of its existence. In fact, many Pakistani Punjabi Christians would be surprised to hear that the New Testament was translated in their mother tongue.

Why are Pakistani Punjabi church leaders so keen to use Urdu and avoid using their own mother tongue in public preaching, both in urban and rural parts of the country? It is evident that the use of Urdu brings respect and honor to the speaker, as it is used in the domains of power in Pakistan. The church leadership does not want to take the risk of being labeled as uneducated and uncultured by preaching in their mother tongue. It is assumed that people will not take them seriously, they will be made fun of and they will lose the respect of their audience. It is thought that the Punjabi language cannot give the respect that is desirable, but Urdu can. Nevertheless, it is obtained at the expense of creating a huge distance between the speaker and the listener. Both come from the same background and culture, and yet the preachers confusingly try to use a different language to communicate the Word of God. Apart from the propaganda against the availability of Christian Scripture in the Punjabi language in Pakistan by some, which Dr. Ziai and Mr. Gauhar indicated, it has often been suggested that, since people read the Urdu Bible they do not need a Punjabi Bible, and that if there is a Punjabi Bible then it will be difficult for people to read.

In actuality, Urdu and Punjabi in Pakistan are both written in the same Persian script, and for that reason it should be easier for someone from a Punjabi background to read Punjabi in Persian script when he or she is able to do the same in Urdu.³⁴ Having said that, it is equally true that it takes a little time to get used to something that one has never done before or have always been hesitant of doing. But the question is whether the ordinary Punjabi Christians have been approached to find out if they want the Bible in their language. Is it right to just assume that all Punjabi Christians in Pakistan are against having the Scripture in their mother tongue? It does not seem to be the case. For example, Joshua Fazal-ul-Din was a well-educated Punjabi Christian intellectual and an enthusiastic supporter of the Punjabi language in Pakistan.³⁵ In the 1960s, he translated the New Testament in Punjabi verse and wrote on the life of Christ in Punjabi prose.³⁶ As with the

---

33. Loehlin, "Gurmukhi," 66.
34. Munshi, "Indo-Aryan," 524.
35. Manav, "Joshua," 1868.
36. Munshi, "Indo-Aryan," 524.

Punjabi New Testament, Punjabi Christians in general are unaware of the existence of these works. Nevertheless, it indicates that Pakistani Punjabi Christians wish to see Scripture in Punjabi.

Individuals have been encouraging the use of Punjabi among the Punjabi-speaking churches. The comments of a local Punjabi pastor in Pakistan, regarding the issue of comprehension in preaching done in Urdu to the simple Punjabi villagers, who neither speak Urdu nor understand it, is interesting to note. He writes that after the preaching, the villagers can be heard telling the preacher: "Dear Pastor, the sermon was very good but I did not understand anything." According to this pastor who runs a Christian Punjabi fellowship, he has been regarded as a heretic by some church leaders because of his campaign for using Punjabi in preaching and for the use of Christian Scripture in Punjabi.[37] It indicates that when someone attempts to raise their voice for the use of Punjabi language in preaching, he is often turned down. At the same time, it shows that some people do feel the need for Christian Scripture in Punjabi and make attempts to draw attention to this matter regardless of the strong resistance.

The following extract from the Pakistan Bible Society website affirms the views of the aforementioned pastor, with regard to the Punjabi among Pakistani churches: "In our ecclesiastical context pastors, preachers and evangelists in most of the situations prefer to conduct worship services in Urdu. It does not bother them at all if people in the remote area with less or no education do not understand even a word."[38] The negative attitude has resulted in a lack of interest in Scripture translation in the Punjabi language. Millions of speakers of this language in Pakistan are still deprived of having the Bible written in Punjabi and being able to take pride in it. Summarily, it may be said that as far as the availability and use of Scripture in Punjabi is concerned, significant opposition from the Punjabi Christian leadership may be expected. A number of objections are expected to arise in order to discourage any move in that direction. A campaign against such efforts shall be expected as happened in the past. At the same time, it is crucial to bring attention to this matter.

One would agree with the notion that Pakistani Punjabi Christians should not be prohibited from being able to read the Word of God in their language, as this is their fundamental right. It is important that things are not assumed, and decisions are not made on assumptions. Practical steps

---

37. The article with the title "Great Deception with Millions of Pakistani Punjabi Christians" was published on the *Pakistan Christian Post* website, http://www.pakistanchristianpost.com/viewarticles.php?editorialid=1169, and on the Academy of the Punjab in North America website, http://www.apnaorg.com/articles/pastor-ilyas/.

38. Pakistan Bible Society website, http://pbs.org.pk/Publishing.php.

seem crucial to make the Word of God available to Punjabi Christians in Pakistan and then things can be analyzed accordingly. Dr. Graham Bailey, who supervised the Punjabi New Testament in Persian script, wrote letters to the revision committee for the New Testament saying that if the Old Testament in the Punjabi language is made available, it will be sold far more than other languages in the area in which the Old Testament has already been prepared.[39] One feels a strong need for the Word of God to be made available in Punjabi in both print and audio format. Recognizing its importance, Rev. Krishnaswamy wrote in his letter: "In the meanwhile the fact remains that the Panjabi is the native language of the people of the Panjab and that the scriptures need to be in that language so that it can appeal to the soul of the people."[40]

It is only through a change of attitude toward the Punjabi language from church leaders that Punjabi as a language may reach the place it deserves among the Punjabi-speaking churches in Pakistan. It is crucial for the leadership to challenge the perception that speaking Punjabi brings shame and using Urdu brings authority, attention, and respect. If the singing of the Punjabi Psalms has contributed to the spiritual growth of the Punjabi church, then how much more the Scriptures in the same language would benefit the Pakistani church. The Scripture in the mother tongue is crucial for the consistent growth of the church.[41]

There is not a straightforward answer to revising the existing metrical translation of the Psalms in Punjabi. On one hand, it may be asserted that since the Punjabi Psalms are regarded as heritage, it might not be a good idea to suggest changes in the poetry of these psalms. Changes may cause difficulties, particularly for the illiterate Punjabi Christians who make good use of these psalms and have learned many of them by heart. At the same time, it should be mentioned that some changes may be observed in the current poetry of the Punjabi Psalms found in the Sialkot Convention Hymn Book, compared to the 1892 and 1908 editions of the Punjabi Psalms. It may be argued that, especially keeping the illiterate Punjabi Christians in mind, it would be appropriate not to suggest further changes in the psalms currently being used and found in the Sialkot Convention Hymn Book. Having said that, it does not mean at all to ignore or undermine the linguistic barriers found in these psalms. They are critical to deal with, and the obstacles have been discussed in detail in the previous chapters.

---

39. BFBS Archives, letter dated November 17, 1939.
40. BFBS Archives, letter dated May 3, 1938.
41. Less, "Objective," 73.

Moreover, it may be noted that any new metrical translation of the Psalms to be used for worship among Pakistani Punjabi Christians may be appreciated but is unlikely to be used. For example, from time to time individuals may be seen composing and introducing new tunes for some of the Punjabi psalms. Such compositions are normally welcomed but their practical use in the corporate worship in churches never happens. It is understood that doing so causes difficulties for the majority of the people to adjust to the new tunes; people like the old melodies, and they feel at ease with the old tunes, as they are familiar with them. Thus, on the one hand it may be said that changes in the poetry of Punjabi psalms currently in use are not helpful. This may make things more complicated for the illiterate people. On the other hand, if the psalms that have been left out are to be included in the Sialkot Convention Hymn Book then it becomes crucial to do necessary revision.[42] Some of the old-fashioned Punjabi words may benefit from replacing, whose connotations are now rather offensive and inappropriate, although such words may not have had wrong connotations at the time they were first used in the translation.[43]

How does the current sociolinguistic situation among the Punjabi-speaking churches affect the Punjabi metrical psalms? It puts the use of Punjabi Psalms at risk. As a heritage of the Punjabi-speaking church, the Punjabi Psalms would be greatly affected in the future by this ongoing negative behavior toward Punjabi. One should not forget the reality that after all these psalms are in the language that is losing its place and acceptance in the eyes of its own speakers in a rapidly changing society. The Urban Punjabi church is already dominated by Urdu and the rural congregations are influenced by the standards and style set by the urban churches. These are alarming signs for the church in Pakistan. It may be hard to believe that one day the Punjabi Psalms may disappear from the Punjabi congregations or may not be valued as they had been in the past, yet the slow but constant risky changes in the Pakistani church cannot be denied. The practical steps from the Christians in Pakistan as individuals and community are decisive for the preservation of this heritage. More awareness among the Punjabi congregations about the history of these Punjabi psalms and the spiritual

---

42. It should not be forgotten that a selected number of psalms are found in the Sialkot Convention Hymn Book that is used for worship among the Punjabi churches in Pakistan. The book does not include the entire Punjabi Psalms as found in the 1908 complete edition of the psalms in Punjabi.

43. For example, the feminine noun is used in the sense of a widow in the 1908 ed. of the Punjabi Psalms in Pss 68:6; 78:72; 109:7; and 146:12. However, now it is commonly understood with reference to a woman of loose character, who may be involved in prostitution (Platts, *Dictionary of Urdu*, 600).

impact that they have made among the ordinary and illiterate people, especially during the early days of the Christian church in Punjab seem crucial. Besides, due to the negative behavior toward the mother tongue, the issues of identity and belonging as individuals and community are also at risk. Since language is linked to cultural identity, a rather negative attitude toward its use diminishes one's own cultural identity.[44]

Why should Punjabi be only restricted to worship? It can equally be used for preaching to the Punjabi Christians. It does not seem right for the Punjabi language to be reserved for only making jokes while preaching. One might argue that, despite the unavailability of the Bible in Punjabi, the continuation of the Punjabi Psalms will not be faced with any harm. However, one should not forget that this consistent shift, where day-by-day Punjabi as a language is becoming more restricted within the Punjabi church, has already started to bring unhealthy results. Particularly in the cities, the new generation feels ashamed and hesitant to sing the Punjabi Psalms. It is not that they dislike them but because they are in the language that is looked down upon both by the church and society in general.

It would be wrong to assert that Punjabi Psalms would lose their importance and use within the Punjabi-speaking churches in Pakistan in the near future. But it would be prudent to anticipate that if the negativity toward Punjabi among the Pakistani churches continues, it would not be surprising to see the use of Punjabi Psalms diminishing within the urban areas, and to see an increasing number of young people avoiding their use both in public and private devotions. As a matter of fact, it is basically the older generation who have kept the Punjabi Psalms going to this day. They are most likely to continue to do so as long as they live, as would many others who cannot read and for whom the Psalms in Punjabi are like a Bible. The availability of Scripture in Punjabi and support from the church leadership for its usage among the churches in Pakistan is indispensable to secure the future of the Punjabi Psalms for generations to come, as the two are interconnected. The reading and preaching of Scripture in Punjabi seem necessary in overcoming the increasing negative behavior toward Punjabi, the language in which these psalms are sung.

There are some important questions that need to be taken seriously: Why do the Punjabi Christians in Pakistan are working so hard to forget the language of their forefathers? Why do they fear to speak in the language of their parents? Why do they feel ashamed to teach the Punjabi language to their children? Does Punjabi deserve such poor treatment, the language we learned from our parents? It is the language in which we worship God

---

44. Nanda, *Anthropology*, 115.

# Conclusion

through the singing of the *Zabur*. The negative attitude toward Punjabi as a language puts the use of Punjabi *Zaburs* at risk, a heritage of the Punjabi Christian community across the globe.

I would like to briefly comment on the second volume that I plan to publish in the future with regard to the Punjabi *Zabur*. The next volume simply studies the linguistic and translational aspects of the Punjabi Psalter. It asks some significant questions, such as: Is the Punjabi translation of the *Zabur* in accordance to the original text of the Old Testament? This is an extremely vital and most relevant question in the present scenario of the church in Pakistan, and consequently requires appropriate care. It examines the *Zabur* in light of translation studies and surveys any linguistic barriers.

A few areas mentioned above for the future study on *Zabur*, is a small endeavor to appreciate the splendid work of Dr. Imam-ud-Din Shahbaz and to acknowledge his contributions in giving the beautiful Psalms to the Punjabi-speaking community worldwide, in their own language. There are of course many more characteristics of the Punjabi Psalter that need to be explored. The young Punjabi Christians have much before them to research and to help the church discover regarding their precious heritage, the Punjabi *Zabur*.

# Bibliography

Acharya, Vijay. "Bhajan." In *Encyclopaedia of Indian Literature*, edited by Amaresh Datta, 435–36. New Delhi: Sahitya, 1987.
Adamec, Ludwig. *Historical Dictionary of Islam*. Lanham: Scarecrow, 2009.
Adang, Camila. "Medieval Muslim Polemics against Jewish Scriptures." In *Perceptions of Other Religions: A Historical Survey*, edited by Jacques Waardenburg, 143–59. Oxford: Oxford University Press, 1999.
———. *Muslim Writers on Judaism and the Hebrew Bible: From Ibn Rabban to Ibn Hazm*. Leiden: Brill, 1996.
Addleton, Bettie. *The Day the Chicken Cackled: Reflections on a Life in Pakistan*. Bloomington, IN: CrossBooks, 2009.
Addleton, Jonathan. "Images of Jesus in the Literature of Pakistan." *Muslim World* 80 (1990) 96–106.
Adeney, Miriam. *God's Foreign Policy: Practical Ways to Help the World's Poor*. Vancouver: Regent, 1998.
Adriani, Nico. "Some Principles of Bible Translation." *Bible Translator* 14 (1963) 9–13.
Ahmed, Ishtiaq. "Religious Nationalism and Minorities in Pakistan: Constitutional and Legal Bases of Discrimination." In *The Politics of Religion in South and Southeast Asia*, edited by Ishtiaq Ahmed, 81–101. Abingdon, UK: Routledge, 2011.
Ahmed, Mahmood. *The Magnificence of the Quran*. Riyadh, Saudi Arabia: Maktaba, 2006.
Ahmed, Ziauddin. *Islam: Universal Religion*. Karachi, Pakistan: Royal, 1989.
Akhtar, Shabbir. *The Quran and the Secular Mind: A Philosophy of Mind*. Abingdon, UK: Routledge, 2008.
Akhter, Shamim. *Faith and Philosophy of Islam*. Delhi: Kalpaz, 2009.
Alavi, Hamza. "Ethnicity, Muslim Society and the Pakistan Ideology." In *Islamic Reassertion in Pakistan: The Application of Islamic Laws in a Modern State*, edited by Anita Weiss, 21–47. New York: Syracuse, 1986.
Allen, Ronald. *And I Will Praise Him: A Guide to Worship in the Psalms*. Grand Rapids: Kregel, 1992.
Amir, Saleem. "Being a Missionary in Pakistan." *Studia Missionalia* 55 (2006) 263–83.

Amjad, Yaqoob. *Quran Karim Dian Chunia Ayatan* [Selected verses of the Quran]. Rabwah, Pakistan: Nazrat Isha'at, 1989.
Anderson, Allan, and Edmond Tang. "Independency in Africa and Asia." In *Cambridge History of Christianity*, edited by Hugh McLeod, 9:107-30. Cambridge: Cambridge University Press, 2006.
Anderson, Emma, and May J. Campbell. *In the Shadow of the Himalayas: A Historical Narrative of the Missions of the United Presbyterian Church of North America as Conducted in the Punjab, India, 1855-1940*. Pittsburgh: UPBFM, 1942.
Anderson, William, and Charles R. Watson. *Far North in India: A Survey of the Mission Field and Work of the United Presbyterian Church in the Panjab*. Philadelphia: UPBFM, 1909.
Arberry, Arthur. *The Koran Interpreted*. Oxford: Oxford University Press, 1964.
Asani, Ali. "Birds in Islamic Mystical Poetry." In *A Communion of Subjects: Animals in Religion, Science & Ethics*, edited by P. Waldau et al., 170-78. Chichester, UK: Columbia, 2006.
———. "Sufi Folk Poetry." In *South Asian Folklore: An Encyclopaedia*, edited by M. Mills et al., 582-83. London: Routledge, 2003.
Asimi, A. D. *The Christian Minority in Pakistan: Problems and Prospects*. Winnipeg: Word, 2010.
Ballantyne, Agnes. "The Samuel Martin Family." *United Presbyterian* 6 (1955) 6-7.
Barrett, David, et al., eds. *World Christian Encyclopedia: A Comparative Survey of Churches and Religions in the Modern World*. New York: Oxford University Press, 2001.
Bassnett, Susan. *Translation Studies*. London: Routledge, 1991.
Bellinger, William. *Psalms: Reading and Studying the Book of Praises*. Peabody: Hendrickson, 1990.
Bennett, Clinton. "Islam." In *Rites of Passage*, edited by J. Holm et al., 90-112. London: Pinter, 1994.
Berner, Isle. "Pakistan." In *A Dictionary of Asian Christianity*, edited by Scott Sunquist, 628-31. Grand Rapids: Eerdmans, 2001.
Bhatia, Tej. "Major Regional Languages." In *Language in South Asia*, edited by B. Kachru et al., 121-31. Cambridge: Cambridge University Press, 2008.
———. "Punjabi." In *Concise Encyclopedia of Languages of the World*, edited by Keith Brown, 885-89. Oxford: Elsevier, 2009.
———. "Punjabi." In *International Encyclopedia of Linguistics*, edited by William Bright, 299-302. Oxford: Oxford University Press.
Bible Society Archives, Cambridge University Library. BFBS Archives: Panjabi, Feb 1909-Mar 1952 BSA/E3/3/468/1.
Bible Society Archives, Cambridge University Library. BFBS Archives: Panjabi, Mar 1952-Dec 1971 BSA/E3/3/468/2.
Böwering, Gerhard. "God and His Attributes." In *Encyclopaedia of the Qur'an*, edited by Jane D. McAuliffe, 316-31. Leiden: Brill, 2002.
———. "Prayer." In *Encyclopaedia of the Qur'an*, edited by Jane D. McAuliffe, 215-31. Leiden: Brill, 2004.
Bowley, William. *Zabur aur Git: Isaion Ki Ibadat Ke Liye*. Allahabad, India: Presbyterian Mission, 1842.
Braswell, George. *What You Need to Know about Islam & Muslims*. Nashville: B & H, 2000.

Brockschmidt, Satyaki. *The Harmonium Handbook: Owing, Playing and Maintaining the Devotional Instrument of India*. Nevada City, CA: Crystal, 2003.

Brown, Francis, et al. *Hebrew and English Lexicon of the Old Testament*. Oxford: Clarendon, 1929.

Broyles, Craig. *The Conflict of Faith and Experience in the Psalms: A Form-Critical and Theological Study*. Sheffield, UK: Sheffield Academic, 1989.

Brueggemann, Walter. *Israel's Praise: Doxology against Idolatry and Ideology*. Philadelphia: Fortress, 1988.

Bütler, Robert. "Indigenization of Religious Life." In *Trying to Respond: Essays and Reviews on Islam, Pakistan and Christianity*, edited by Ikram Chaghatai, 369–88. Lahore, Pakistan: Pakistan Jesuit Society, 1994.

———. "Islamic Resurgence in Pakistan and the Church." In *Trying to Respond: Essays and Reviews on Islam, Pakistan and Christianity*, edited by Ikram Chaghatai, 335–56. Lahore, Pakistan: Pakistan Jesuit Society, 1994.

———. "Note on Christian-Muslim Dialogue." In *Trying to Respond: Essays and Reviews on Islam, Pakistan and Christianity*, edited by Ikram Chaghatai, 325–34. Lahore, Pakistan: Pakistan Jesuit Society, 1994.

Caleb, Maqbul. "Christian Sunday Worship in a Punjabi Village." In *Popular Religion in the Punjab Today*, edited by John Webster, 119–26. Delhi: ISPCK, 1974.

Campbell, Ernest. "The Church in the Punjab: Some Aspects of Its Life and Growth." In *The Church as Christian Community: Three Studies of North Indian Churches*, edited by Hayward Victor, 137–220. London: Lutterworth, 1966.

Campbell, J. Mary. *The Power-House at Pathankot: What Some Girls of India Wrought by Prayer*. Lucknow, India: WCTUI, 1918.

Carey, Freda. "Theological Education by Extension in Pakistan." *Ecumenical Review* 64 (2012) 160–68.

Carre, Ernest. *Praying Hyde: A Present Day Challenge to Prayer*. London: Pickering, 1930.

Christopher, Paul. "Sialkot Convention." In *Oxford Encyclopaedia of South Asian Christianity*, edited by Roger Hedlund, 628. Oxford: Oxford University Press, 2012.

Church Missionary Society Archives, Birmingham University Library. CMS Archives: Jan 1875 CII/04/7/10.

Clark, Henry. *Robert Clark of the Panjab, Pioneer and Missionary Statesman*. London: Melrose, 1907.

Clark, Robert. *A Brief Account of the Thirty Years of Missionary Work of the Church Missionary Society in the Punjab & Sindh, 1852–1882*. Lahore: Albert, 1883.

Cox, Jeffrey. *The British Missionary Enterprise since 1700*. Abingdon, UK: Routledge, 2008.

———. "George Alfred Lefroy, 1854–1919, a Bishop in Search of a Church." In *After the Victorians: Private Conscience and Public Duty in Modern Britain*, edited by S. Pedersen et al., 55–76. London: Routledge, 1994.

———. *Imperial Fault Lines: Christianity and Colonial Power in India, 1880–1940*. Stanford: Stanford University Press, 2002.

Culshaw, Wesley. "Bible Translation in Hindi, Urdu and Hindustani." *Bible Translator* 13 (1962) 65–71.

Daniell, David. *The Bible in English: Its History and Influence*. London: Yale University Press, 2003.

Das Jain, Banarsi. "Panjabi." In *Encyclopedia of Literature*, edited by Joseph Shipley, 552–56. New York: Philosophical, 1946.

Dogar, Vidyasagar. "The Christian Community in Punjab: An Analogy." *Religion and Society* 38 (1991) 3–17.
———. "Punjabi Psalms/Psalter." In *Oxford Encyclopaedia of South Asian Christianity*, edited by Roger Hedlund, 576. New Delhi: Oxford University Press, 2012.
———. *Rural Christian Community in North West India*. Delhi: ISPCK, 2001.
Doyle, Michael. "Translation and the Space Between." In *Translation Theory and Practice, Tension and Interdependence*, edited by Mildrad Larson, 13–26. New York: ATS, 1991.
Ekbal, Nikhat. *Great Muslims of Undivided India*. Delhi: Kalpaz, 2009.
Elias, Jamal. *Death before Dying: The Sufi Poems of Sultan Bahu*. Los Angeles: University of California Press, 1998.
Elkayam, Asher. *The Qur'an and Biblical Origins: Hebrew, Christian and Aramaic Influences in Striking Similarities*. Bloomington, IN: Xlibris, 2009.
Evans, Edward. "Coming to Faith in Pakistan." In *From the Straight Path to the Narrow Way: Journeys of Faith*, edited by David H. Greenlane, 167–88. Milton Keynes: Authentic, 2006.
Everaert, Christine. *Tracing the Boundaries between Hindi and Urdu*. Leiden: Brill, 2010.
Fair, Christine. *The Madrassah Challenge: Militancy and Religious Education in Pakistan*. Washington, DC: United States Institute of Peace Press, 2008.
Faiz, Ahmed. *100 Poems by Faiz Ahmed Faiz*. Translated by Sarvat Rahman. New Delhi: Abhinav, 2002.
Farrell, Gerry "Harmonium (India)." In *Continuum Encyclopedia of Popular Music of the World*, edited by John Shepherd, 307–8. New York: Continuum, 2003.
Forrester, Duncan. *Forrester on Christian Ethics: Collected Writings on Christianity, India, and the Social Order*. Burlington: Ashgate, 2010.
Franken, Hendricus. *The Mystical Communion with JHWH in the Book of Psalms*. Leiden: Brill, 1954.
Fry, Euan. "Training Nationals as Bible Translators." *Bible Translator* 23 (1972) 430–35.
Gabriel, Mark. *Islam and the Jews*. Florida: Frontline, 2003.
Gabriel, Theodore. *Christian Citizens in an Islamic State: The Pakistan Experience*. Ashgate: Aldershot, 2007.
Garlow, James. *A Christian's Response to Islam*. Colorado Springs: Cook, 2002.
Geaves, Ron. *Islam Today: An Introduction*. London: Continuum, 2010.
Glassé, Cyril. *Concise Encyclopedia of Islam*. San Francisco: Harper & Row, 1989.
Glassman, Eugene. "Bible Translation for Muslim Audiences." *Bible Translator* 33 (1982) 439–45.
Godfrey, Philips. *The Outcastes Hope*. London: CMS, 1912.
Goh, Robbie. *Christianity in Southeast Asia*. Singapore: ISAS, 2005.
Goldingay, John. *Psalms: 1–41*. Grand Rapids: Baker, 2006.
Gordon, Andrew. *Our India Mission: A Thirty Years' History of the Indian Mission of the United Presbyterian Church of North America, together with Personal Reminiscences*. Philadelphia: Gordon, 1886.
Gill, Azam. "Will Rebranding Christians Make Their Lives Any Easier in Pakistan?" *Tribune Express*, September 7, 2016. https://tribune.com.pk/article/40072/will-rebranding-christians-make-their-lives-any-easier-in-pakistan.
Hammerle, Arife. *Sufi Grace: Sacred Wisdom Heart to Heart*. Bloomington: AuthorHouse, 2009.
Hanif, N. *Biographical Encyclopaedia of Sufis: South Asia*. New Delhi: Sarup, 2000.

# Bibliography

Harding, Christopher. *Religious Transformation in South Asia: The Meanings of Conversion in Colonial Punjab*. Oxford: Oxford University Press, 2008.

Harris, Laird, et al. *Theological Wordbook of the Old Testament*. 2 vols. Chicago: Moody, 1980.

Hassan, Imad. *Shajara Code Decoded*. Milton Keynes: Author, 2009.

Hassan, Mohammad. *Nazir Akbarabadi*. New Delhi: Sahitya, 1973.

Hayyim, Sulayman. *Farhang I Yakjildi I Farsi-Ingilisi*. Tehran: Beroukhim, 1953.

Hedlund, Roger. "Pakistan." In *Evangelical Dictionary of World Missions*, edited by Scott Moreau, 718–19. Carlisle, UK: Paternoster, 2000.

Henry, Haris. "The Dialogue of Civilisations, Peace Building beyond Religious Bigotry: A Christian Perspective." *Al-Mushir* 45 (2003) 73–85.

Heston, Wilma. "Punjab." In *South Asian Folklore: An Encyclopaedia*, edited by M. Mills et al., 495–98. London: Routledge, 2003.

Hidayatullah, R. *Quran-e-Majid: Punjabi Tarjume Te Tafsir Nal*. Lahore, Pakistan: Punjabi Adabi, 1986.

Horovitz, Forfatter. "Zabur." In *The Encyclopaedia of Islam*, edited by P. Bearman et al., 372–73. Leiden: Brill, 2002.

Huda, Qamar-Ul. *Striving for Divine Union: Spiritual Exercises for Suharwardi Sufis*. London: Routledge, 2003.

Hughes, Thomas. *A Dictionary of Islam*. London: Allen, 1895.

Hussain, Maulvi. *Tafsir Muhammadi*. Lahore: Faqir, 1904.

Hyder, Syed, and Carla Petievich. "Qawwali Songs of Praise." In *Islam in South Asia in Practice*, edited by Barbara Metcalf, 93–100. Princeton: Princeton University Press, 2009.

*Injil Sharif Yani Sade Khudawand Te Najat Dain Walay Yesu Masih Da Nawa Ehad Nama* [Injil Sharif, i.e., The New Testament of Our Lord and Saviour Jesus Christ]. Lahore: BFBS, 1912.

Jacobsen, Douglas. *The World's Christians: Who They Are, Where They Are, and How They Got There*. Oxford: Wiley-Blackwell, 2011.

Jafri, F. "Urdu Ghazal." In *Encyclopaedia of Indian Literature*, edited by Amaresh Datta, 1395–97. New Delhi: Sahitya, 2005.

Jairazbhoy, Nazir. *The Rāgs of North Indian Music: Their Structure & Evolution*. Bombay: Prakashan, 1995.

Jinkins, Michael. *In the House of Lord: Inhabiting the Psalms of Lament*. Collegeville: Liturgical, 1998.

Joint Committee of the Survey of Christian Literature for Moslems, et al. *Christian Literature in Moslem Lands: A Study of the Activities of the Moslem and Christian Press in all Mohammedan Countries*. New York: Doran, 1923.

Juynboll, Gautier. "Sunna." In *Encyclopaedia of the Qur'an*, edited by Jane D. McAuliffe, 163–66. Leiden: Brill, 2004.

Kanda, Kishan. *Masterpiece of Urdu Ghazal: From the 17th to the 20th Century*. New Delhi: Sterling, 1992.

Kanda, Kishan. *Masterpiece of Urdu Rubaiyat*. New Delhi: Sterling, 1994.

Kendrick, Graham. "Worship in the Key of G." In *Christianity*, edited by R. Dickinson, 26–31. London: CCP, 2013.

Khan, Fateh. *God Created the Universe with the Purpose to Serve Humankind*. Peshawar, Pakistan: Khyber, 2009.

Khatib, Mohammad. *The Bounteous Koran: A Translation of Meaning and Commentary.* London: Macmillan, 1984.

Khimjee, Husein. *The Attributes of God in the Monotheistic Faiths of Judeo-Christian and Islamic Traditions.* Bloomington: Universe, 2011.

Kim, Sebastian, and Kirsteen Kim. *Christianity as a World Religion.* London: Continuum, 2008.

Kohli, Singh. "Sufism (Punjabi)." In *Encyclopaedia of Indian Literature*, edited by Amaresh Datta, 4207-8. New Delhi: Sahitya, 1987.

Kuttianiamattathil, Jose. "Contextual Theological Reflection in Pakistan." In *Asian Christian Theologies: A Research Guide to Authors, Movements, Sources*, edited by J. England et al., 408-56. New York: Orbis, 2002.

Lalljee, Yousuf. *Know Your Islam.* New York: Tehrike Tarsile Quran, 2003.

Laney, Carl. "A Fresh Look at the Imprecatory Psalms." In *Vital Biblical Issues: Examining Problem Passages of the Bible*, edited by Roy Zuck, 30-39. Grand Rapids: Kregel, 1994.

Larson, Warren. *Islamic Ideology and Fundamentalism in Pakistan: Climate for Conversion to Christianity?* Lanham, MD: University Press of America, 1998.

Leaman, Oliver. "Hadith." In *The Qur'an: An Encyclopaedia*, edited by Oliver Leaman, 223-29. Abingdon, UK: Routledge, 2006.

Lefebvre, Alain. *Kinship, Honour and Money in Rural Pakistan.* Richmond, UK: Curzon, 1999.

LeMon, Joel. "Saying Amen to Violent Psalms: Patterns of Prayer, Belief and Action in the Psalter." In *Sounding of the Theology of Psalms: Perspective and Methods in Contemporary Scholarship*, edited by Roy Jacobson, 93-109. Minneapolis: Augsburg Fortress, 2011.

LeVine, Mark. "Heavy Metal Muslims: The Rise of a Post-Islamist Public Sphere." In *What Happened to the Islamists? Salafis, Heavy Metal Muslims and the Lure of Consumerist Islam*, edited by Oliver Roy, 199-232. New York: Columbia University Press, 2012.

Lewis, Franklin. "Rubai." In *The Princeton Encyclopaedia of Poetry and Poetics*, edited by Roland Greene, 1227-28. New Jersey: Princeton, 2012.

Limburg, James. *Psalms.* Louisville: John Knox, 2000.

Lobel, Diana. *Between Mysticism and Philosophy: Sufi Language of Religious Experience in Judah Ha-Levi's Kuzari.* New York: State University of New York Press, 2000.

Lochtefeld, James. *The Illustrated Encyclopedia of Hinduism.* New York: Rosen, 2002.

Lodahl, Michael. *Claiming Abraham: Reading the Bible and the Qur'an Side by Side.* Grand Rapids: Brazos, 2010.

Loehlin, Clinton. "The Gurmukhi Punjabi Old Testament." *Bible Translator* 4 (1953) 66-70.

Loh, I-To. "Music, Asian Christian." In *A Dictionary of Asian Christianity*, edited by Scott Sunquist, 569-74. Grand Rapids: Eerdmans, 2001.

Longman, Tremper. *How to Read the Psalms.* Leicester: InterVarsity, 1988.

Louie, Sam. *Asian Honor: Overcoming the Culture of Silence.* Bloomington, IN: West Bow, 2012.

Luzbetak, Louis. "Contextual Translation: The Role of Cultural Anthropology." In *Bible Translation and the Spread of Church: The Last 200 Years*, edited by Philip Stine, 108-19. Leiden: Brill, 1992.

# Bibliography

Lytle, David. *Zabur Punjabi Nazm Men Tarjuma Kiya Gaya* [Psalms translated in Punjabi verse]. Benares, India: Medical Hall, 1892.
Mackenzie, Colin. *Life in the Mission, the Camp, and the Zenana*. London: Harrison, 1853.
Madras, Henry. "The Mass Movement towards Christianity in the Punjab." *International Review of Missions* 2 (1913) 442–53.
Maini, Tridivesh. *South Asian Cooperation and the Role of the Punjabs*. New Delhi: Saddharth, 2007.
Makins, Marion, ed. *Collins Concise Dictionary*. Glasgow: HarperCollins, 1995.
Malik, Iftikhar. *Culture and Customs of Pakistan*. London: Greenwood, 2006.
———. "Religious Minorities in Pakistan." In *Minority Rights Group International*, edited by Salima Thawer, 1–36. London: MRGI, 2002.
Malik, Saeed. *A Perspective on the Signs of Al-Quran: Through the Prism of the Heart*. Charleston, SC: BookSurge, 2010.
Manav, Phool Chand. "Joshua Fazal-ul-Din." In *Encyclopaedia of Indian Literature: Devraj to Jyoti*, edited by Amaresh Datta, 1868. Delhi: Sahitya, 1988.
Manon, Rajendra. *The Miracle of Music Therapy*. Delhi: Pustak, 2005.
Mansoor, Sabiha. *Punjabi, Urdu, English in Pakistan: A Sociolinguistic Study*. Lahore, Pakistan: Vanguard, 1993.
Marlow, Louise. "Kings and Rulers." In *Encyclopaedia of the Qur'an*, edited by Jane D. McAuliffe, 90–95. Leiden: Brill, 2002.
Marshall, Paul, and Nina Shea. *Persecuted: The Global Assault on Christians*. Nashville: Nelson, 2013.
Martin, Josephine. *A Father to the Poor*. Philadelphia: UPBFM, 1931.
*Masihi Git Ki Kitab* [Christian hymn book]. Agra: CMS, 1914.
*Masihi Git Ki Kitab: Ibadat Ke Liye* [Christian hymn book: For worship]. Lucknow, India: American Methodist, 1866.
*Masihi Git Kit Kitab Sath Ragon Ke* [Christian hymn book with melodies]. London: Novello, 1916.
Massey, James. "Indian Christian Response to Bhakti." In *Shri Krishna Caitanya and the Bhakti Religion*, edited by E. Weber et al., 135–45. Frankfurt: Lang, 1988.
———. "Literary Heritage of Punjabi Christians: An Analysis." In *Religion and Society* 38 (1991) 26–36.
———. *Panjab: The Movement of the Spirit*. Geneva: WCC, 1996.
———. "Punjabi Christian Writer's Response to the Gospel." In *Oxford Encyclopaedia of South Asian Christianity*, edited by Roger Hedlund, 574–75. New Delhi: Oxford University Press, 2012.
McClintock, Wayne. "A Sociological Profile of the Christian Minority in Pakistan." *Missiology: An International Review* 20 (1992) 343–53.
Mcgaw, Francis. *Praying Hyde*. Minneapolis: Bethany, 1970.
McGinnis, Ray. *Writing the Sacred: A Psalm-Inspired Path to Appreciating and Writing Sacred Poetry*. Kelowna, BC: Northstone, 2005.
Mendes, Blascovich. "Tools of Inter-Religious Dialogue and Contemporary Challenges." *AlMushir* 39 (1997) 95–98.
Milligan, Anna. *Facts and Folks in Our Fields Abroad*. Philadelphia: UPBFM, 1921.
Mir, Farina. *The Social Space of Language: Vernacular Culture in British Colonial Punjab*. Berkeley: University of California Press, 2010.
*The Mishnah*. Translated by Herbert Danby. London: Oxford University Press, 1933.

Moghal, Dominic. "Alienation of the Local People: The Future of Religious Minorities in Pakistan." *Al-Mushir* 37 (1995) 25–41.

Mohiuddin, Yasmeen. *Pakistan: A Global Studies Handbook*. Santa Barbara, CA: ABC-CLIO, 2007.

Montefiore, Claude. "Mystic Passages in the Psalms." *Jewish Quarterly Review* 1 (1889) 143–63.

Moorthy, Vijaya. *Romance of the Raga*. New Delhi: Fine Art, 2001.

Morgan, Diane. *Essential Islam: A Complete Guide to Belief and Practice*. Santa Barbara, CA: Greenwood, 2010.

Murdoch, John. *Indian Missionary Manual*. London: Nisbet, 1895.

———. *Indian Year-Book for 1861: A Review of Social, Intellectual and Religious Progress in India and Ceylon*. London: Nisbet, 1862.

Murphy, Eamon. *The Making of Terrorism in Pakistan: Historical and Social Roots of Extremism*. Abingdon, UK: Routledge, 2013.

Nanda, Serena, and Richard L. Warms, eds. *Cultural Anthropology*. London: Wadsworth, 1998.

Nayyar, Adam. "Punjab." In *The Garland Encyclopedia of World Music: South Asia; The Indian Subcontinent*, edited by Allison Arnold, 762–72. London: Garland, 2000.

Nazir-Ali, Michael, and Christopher Stone. *Understanding My Muslim Neighbour*. Norwich, UK: Canterbury, 2002.

Nazir-Ali, Michael. *Conviction and Conflict: Islam, Christianity and World Order*. London: Continuum, 2006.

———. *Frontiers in Muslim-Christian Encounter*. Oxford: Regnum, 1987.

———. "The Good Fight." Interview with Huw Spanner. *Third Way* magazine website, November 2011. https://thirdway.hymnsam.co.uk/editions/nov-2011-/high-profile/the-good-fight.aspx.

———. *Islam: A Christian Perspective*. Philadelphia: Westminster, 1983.

———. *Triple Jeopardy of the West: Aggressive Secularism, Radical Islamism and Multiculturalism*. London: Bloomsbury, 2012.

———. *The Unique and Universal Christ: Jesus in a Plural World*. Milton Keynes, UK: Paternoster, 2008.

Neil, Stephen. *A History of Christianity in India, 1707–1858*. Cambridge: Cambridge University Press, 2002.

Neuwirth, Angelika. "Qur'anic Readings of the Psalms." In *The Qur'an in Context: Historical and Literary Investigations into the Qur'anic Milieu*, edited by A. Neuwirth et al., 733–78. Leiden: Brill, 2010.

Newton, John. *History of the American Presbyterian Mission in India*. Allahabad, India: Allahabad, 1886.

———. "An Indian Catholic Church." In *Report of the Punjab Missionary Conference Held at Lahore*, edited by the Committee of Compilation, 299–317. Lodiana, India: Presbyterian Mission, 1863.

Nigosian, Solomon. *Islam: Its History, Teaching, and Practices*. Bloomington: Indiana University Press, 2004.

O'Brien, John. *The Construction of Pakistani Christian Identity*. Lahore, Pakistan: Research Society, 2006.

———. "The Quest for Pakistani Christian Identity: A Narrative of Religious Others as Liberative Comparative Ecclesiology." In *Church and Religious "Other,"* edited by Gerard Mannion, 78–103. London: Clark, 2008.

Parker, Arthur. *Children of the Light in India: Biographies of Noted Indian Christians.* New York: Revell, 1929.
Pattison, Stephen. *Shame: Theory, Therapy, Theology.* Cambridge: Cambridge University Press, 2000.
Perkins, Howell. "Caste Distinctions in India." *Church Missionary Intelligencer: A Monthly Journal of Missionary Information* 7 (1871) 301–10.
Pervez, Shoaib. *Security Community in South Asia: India-Pakistan.* Abingdon, UK: Routledge, 2013.
Peters, Francis. "Allah." In *The Oxford Encyclopaedia of the Modern Islamic World*, edited by John Esposito, 76–79. New York: Oxford University Press, 1995.
Philippon, Alix. "When Sufi Tradition Reinvents Islamic Modernity: The Minhaj-ul-Qur'an, a Neo-Sufi Order in Pakistan." In *South Asian Sufis: Devotion, Deviation and Destiny*, edited by B. Clinton et al., 111–22. London: Continuum, 2012.
Pickett, Jarrell. *Christian Mass Movement in India: A Study with Recommendations.* Cincinnati: Abingdon, 1933.
Pickthall, Marmaduke. *The Glorious Koran: With English Translation, Introduction and Notes.* London: Unwin, 1976.
Platts, John. *A Dictionary of Urdu, Classical Hindi, and English.* Oxford: Oxford University Press, 1960.
Popley, Herbert. *The Music of India.* Madras: SPCK, 1921.
Powell, Avril. "Pillar of a New Faith: Christianity in Late-Nineteenth-Century Punjab from the Perspective of a Convert from Islam." In *Christians and Missionaries in India*, edited by Robert Frykenberg, 223–55. London: Routledge, 2003.
Presbyterian Historical Society Philadelphia. PCUSA Archives: 1881, RG 360/III/6705.
Presbyterian Historical Society Philadelphia. PCUSA Archives: 1896–1954, RG 53/3.
Presbyterian Historical Society Philadelphia. PCUSA Archives: 1905, RG 360/III/6562.
Presbyterian Historical Society Philadelphia. PCUSA Archives: 1905, RG 360/III/6554.
Presbyterian Historical Society Philadelphia. PCUSA Archives: Missionary Correspondence/WMM/October 1892.
Presbyterian Historical Society Philadelphia. PCUSA Archives: Missionary Correspondence/WMM/March 1891.
Presbyterian Historical Society Philadelphia. PCUSA Archives: Missionary Correspondence/WMM/June 1892.
Pressly, Frank Y. "The Punjabi Zabur: Its Composition, Use, and Influence." MTh thesis, Columbia Theological Seminary, 1954.
Pritchett, Frances. *Nets of Awareness: Urdu Poetry and Its Critics.* Los Angeles: University of California Press, 1994.
Prtichett, Frances. "Qissa." In *South Asian Folklore: An Encyclopaedia*, edited by M. Mills, 502–3. London: Routledge, 2003.
*Punjabi Zabur: Desi Ragan Vich* [Punjabi psalms in local tunes]. Benares, India: Medical Hall, 1908.
Puri, Lekh. "Bulleh Shah in Punjabi Poetic Tradition." In *Crossing Boundaries*, edited by Geeti Sen, 126–38. New Delhi: Orient, 1997.
Qadeer, Mohammad. *Pakistan: Social and Cultural Transformations in a Muslim Nation.* Abingdon, UK: Routledge: 2006.
Qurban, Harrison. *Urdu Ke Masihi Shuara* [Christian poets of the Urdu language]. Saharanpur, India: Mehboob, 1983.

Qureshi, Irna. "Destigmatising Star Texts-Honour and Shame among Muslim Women in Pakistani Cinema." In *South Asian Media Cultures: Audiences, Representations, Contexts*, edited by Shukuntala Banaji, 181–98. London: Anthem, 2010.

Qureshi Regula, and Hiromi Sakata. "Music in Pakistan: An Introduction." In *The Concise Garland Encyclopaedia of World Music*, edited by Ellen Koskoff, 1047–48. Abingdon, UK: Routledge, 2006.

———. "'Muslim Devotional': Popular Religious Music and Muslim Identity under British, Indian and Pakistani Hegemony." *Asian Music* 24 (1992) 111–21.

———. *Sufi Music of India and Pakistan: Sound, Context, and Meaning in Qawwali*. Cambridge: Cambridge University Press, 1986.

Racy, Ali. "Music." In *The Oxford Encyclopaedia of the Modern Islamic World*, edited by John Esposito, 180–83. New York: Oxford University Press, 1995.

Rahbar, Daud. *God of Justice: A Study in the Ethical Doctrine of the Qur'an*. Leiden: Brill, 1960.

Rahman, Tariq. "Government Policies and the Politics of the Teaching of Urdu in Pakistan." *Annual of Urdu Studies* 17 (2002) 95–124.

———. "Languages and Education." In *A History of Pakistan and its Origins*, edited by Christopher Jaffrelot, 252–57. London: Anthem, 2002.

———. *Language and Politics in Pakistan*. Karachi, Pakistan: Oxford University Press, 1998.

———. *Language, Ideology and Power*. Karachi, Pakistan: Oxford University Press, 2002.

———. "Language, Knowledge and Inequality." In *Linguistic Structure and Language Dynamics in South Asia*, edited by Anvita Abbi, 185–96. Delhi: Motilal, 2001.

———. "Language Policy, Multilingualism, and Language Vitality in Pakistan." In *Trends in Linguistics: Lesser-known Languages of South Asia*, edited by A Saxena et al., 73–104. Berlin: Mouten, 2006.

———. "Language, Politics and Power in Pakistan: The Case of Sindh and Sindhi." *Ethnic Studies Report* 17 (1999) 21–34.

———. "Punjabi During British Rule." *Journal of Punjab Studies* 14 (2007) 27–39.

Rasool, Naz, and Sabiha Mansoor. "Contemporary Issues in Language, Education and Development in Pakistan." In *Global Issues in Language, Education and Development: Perspectives from Postcolonial Countries*, edited by Naz Rasool, 218–42. Clevedon, UK: Multilingual, 2007.

Reck, David. "India." In *World's Music: An Introduction to the Music of the World's Peoples*, edited by J. Titon et al., 179–202. Belmont, CA: Schirmer, 2009.

Riddell, Peter. "Entitled to God: Copyrighting 'Allah' in Malaysia Stir Strife." *Touchstone: A Journal of Mere Christianity* 23 (2010) 42–43.

———. "Islamization, Civil Society and Religious Minorities in Malaysia." In *Islam in Southeast Asia: Political, Social, and Strategic Challenges for the 21st Century*, edited by K. Nathan et al., 162–90. Singapore: ISAS, 2005.

———. "Music." In *The Qur'an: An Encyclopaedia*, edited by Oliver Leaman, 433–34. Abingdon, UK: Routledge, 2006.

———. "The Suffering Church: Two Murdered in Pakistan." *Touchstone: A Journal of Mere Christianity* 23 (2010) 7.

Rumalshah, Mano. "Contemporary Challenges to the Religious World in Pakistan." *Al-Mushir* 39 (1997) 45–54.

Ruthven, Malise. *Islam: A Very Short Introduction*. New York: Oxford University Press, 2012.

Sabourin, Leopold. *The Psalms: Their Origin and Meaning.* Vol. 1. New York: Alba, 1969.
Sadiq, Yousaf. "Bible Translation in Pakistan." In *Oxford Encyclopaedia of South Asian Christianity*, edited by Roger Hedlund, 90–91. New Delhi: Oxford University Press, 2012.
———. "The Book of Psalms as Bridge-Building between Christians and Muslims." *Evangelical Quarterly: An International Review of Bible and Theology* 90 (2019) 303–16.
———. "How Should We Respond to the Persecution of Christians? Practical Steps for Strengthening the Church." *Lausanne Global Analysis* 8 (2018) 90–91.
———. "Jesus' Encounter with a Woman at the Well: A South Asian Perspective." *Missiology: An International Review* 46 (2018) 363–73.
———. "A Precious Gift: The Punjabi Psalms and the Legacy of Rev. Dr. Imam-ud-Din Shahbaz." *International Bulletin of Missionary Research* 38 (2013) 36–39.
*Sahih Muslim: Being Traditions of the Sayings and Doings of the Prophet Muhammad as Narrated by His Companions and Compiled under the Title al-Jami-us-Sahih by Imam Muslim.* Translated by Abdul H. Siddiqi. Four Volumes, Lahore, Pakistan: S. M. Ashraf, 1995.
Salmon, Ruth. *The Punjab Then and Now.* London: CMS, 1950.
Samat, Talib. *The 99 Most Eminent Names of Allah.* Kuala Lumpur, Malaysia: Utusan, 2001.
Samiuddin, Abida, ed. *Encyclopaedic Dictionary of Urdu Literature.* Vol. 1. New Delhi: Global, 2007.
Satthianadhan, Samuel. *Sketches of Indian Christians.* London: CLSI, 1896.
Sauli, Arnaud. "Circulation and Authority: Police, Public Space and Territorial Control in the Punjab, 1861–1920." In *Society and Circulation: Mobile People and Itinerant Cultures in South Asia*, edited by C. Markovits et al., 164–215. London: Anthem, 2003.
Schippers, Arie. "Psalms." In *Encyclopaedia of the Qur'an*, edited by John McAuliffe, 314–17. Leiden: Brill, 2004.
Schökel, Alonso. *A Manual of Hebrew Poetics.* Rome: Biblico, 1988.
Sells, Michael. "Dhikar." In *The Oxford Encyclopaedia of the Modern Islamic World*, edited by in John Esposito, 372–73. New York: Oxford University Press, 1995.
Sengupta, Pradip. *Foundations of Indian Musicology.* New Delhi: Abhinav, 2000.
Shah, Giriraj. *Glory of Indian Culture.* New Delhi: Diamond, 2002.
Shahi, Gohar. *The Religion of God.* Bloomington, IN: Balboa, 2012.
Shahid, Salamat. *Classical Music of the Sub-Continent.* Karachi, Pakistan: Fazleesons, 1999.
Sharma, Manorma. *Music Aesthetics.* New Delhi: APH, 2007.
———. *Musical Heritage of India.* New Delhi: APH, 2007.
Sharma, Raj. *History of Christian Missions: North India Perspective.* Delhi: Mittal, 1988.
Shirazi, Faeghen. "Men's Facial Hair in Islam: A Matter of Interpretation." In *Hair: Style, Culture and Fashion*, edited by G. Biddle Perry et al., 111–22. Oxford: Berg, 2008.
*Sialkot Convention Geet Ki Kitab* [Sialkot convention hymn book]. 60th ed. Lahore, Pakistan: Naulakha, 2019.
Siddiqi, Farhan. *The Politics of Ethnicity in Pakistan: The Baloch, Sindhi and Mohajir Ethnicity.* Abingdon, UK: Routledge, 2012.
Singh, Harbans. "Punjabi." In *Medieval Indian Literature: An Anthology*, edited by Kavalam Paniker, 417–52. New Delhi: Sahitya, 1997.

Singh, Harbans, and N. Gerald Barrier, eds. *Punjab Past and Present: Essays in Honour of Dr. Ganda Singh*. Patiala, India: Punjabi University, 1973.
Singh, Munshi. *The Panjabi Dictionary*. Lahore: Ghulab, 1895.
Singh, Sardar. *Faith and Philosophy of Sikhism*. Delhi: Singhal, 2009.
Spate, Oslar. "Punjab." In *Chambers Encyclopaedia*, edited by George Newness, 374–77. London: Newness, 1964.
Spencer, Harold. "Musalmani Vernacular Gospels Used in India." *Bible Translator* 4 (1953) 162–65.
Stacy, Vivian. "How the Bible Came." *St. Francis Magazine* 3 (2007) 1–15.
Steer, Roger. *Good News for the World*. Oxford: Monarch, 2004.
Stewart, Robert. *Life and Work in India: An Account of the Conditions, Methods, Difficulties, Results, Future Prospects and Reflex Influence of Missionary Labor in India . . .* Philadelphia: Pearl, 1899.
Stock, Frederick. *People Movements in the Punjab: With Special Reference to the United Presbyterian Church*. Pasadena, CA: Carey, 1975.
Strohmer, Charles. "Taliban Neighbors: Christian Witness in Pakistan." *Christian Century* 126 (2009) 10–12.
Synod Church of Pakistan. *Dua-e-Aam Kalisia-e-Pakistan* [The Book of Common Prayers, Church of Pakistan]. Karachi, Pakistan: Bhagtani, 1985.
Talbani, Aziz. "The More Things Change the More They Stay the Same." In *Education and Society*, edited by Joseph Zajda, 133–50. Albert Park, Australia: Nicholas, 1995.
Talib, Mohammed. *Universal Peace: To Unite a Universal Brotherhood*. N.p.: Lulu, 2005.
*Tenth Anniversary Memorial: Young People's Christian Union of the United Presbyterian and Associate Reformed Presbyterian Churches of North America, 1889–1899*. Pittsburgh: UPBP, 1899.
Thielemann, Selina. *Divine Service and the Performing Arts in India*. New Delhi: APH, 2002.
———. *Sounds of the Sacred: Religious Music in India*. New Delhi: APH, 1998.
Thomas, Kenneth. "The Use of Arabic Terminology in Biblical Translation." *Bible Translator* 40 (1989) 101–8.
Thomas, Paul. *Christians and Christianity in India and Pakistan: A General Survey of the Progress of Christianity in India from Apostolic Times to the Present Day*. London: Allen & Unwin, 1954.
Thompson, Gordon. "Gujarat." In *The Concise Garland Encyclopedia of World Music*, edited by Ellen Koskoff, 1014–22. London: Routledge, 2008.
Timothy, Fr. "Catholicism in the Punjab." In *Popular Religion in the Punjab Today*, edited by John Webster, 74–77. Delhi: ISPCK, 1974.
Tomes, Roger. "Sing to the Lord a New Song." In *Psalms and Prayers: Papers Read at the Joint Meeting of the Society of Old Testament*, edited by B. Becking et al., 237–52. Leiden: Brill, 2007.
*The Translation of the Meaning of Sahih Al-Bukhari*. 9 vols. Translated by Mohammad M. Khan. Medina, Saudi Arabia: Dar Ahya Us-Sunnah, 1971.
Travers, Michael. *Encountering God in the Psalms*. Grand Rapids: Kregel, 2003.
Tucker, Dennis. "Democratization and the Language of the Poor in Psalms 2–89." *Horizons in Biblical Theology* 25 (2003) 161–78.
Turner, Colin. "Rizq." In *The Qur'an: An Encyclopaedia*, edited by Oliver Leaman, 552. Abingdon, UK: Routledge, 2006.

# Bibliography

Ullmann, Julius. *Ragmala Yane Zabur Aur Git Ki Kitab Ke Un Giton Ke Rag Jo Aksar Malum Nahi Hain* [Ragmala, i.e., tunes of songs in Zabur aur Git hymn book that are often not known]. London: Clowes, 1872.

Union Theological Seminary. *Alumni Catalogue of the Union Theological Seminary in the City of New York, 1836-1936.* New York: Union, 1937.

United Presbyterian Church of North America (UPCNA). *Annual Report of the Board of Foreign Missions of the United Presbyterian Church of North America.* Philadelphia: UPBFM, 1931.

———. *Annual Report of the Board of Foreign Missions of the United Presbyterian Church of North America.* Philadelphia: UPBFM, 1909.

———. *Handbook on Foreign Missions of the United Presbyterian Church of North America.* Philadelphia: BFMBDWMS, 1925.

United Presbyterian Church of the United States of America (UPCUSA). *Minutes of the Forty-Eighth General Assembly of the United Presbyterian Church of the United States of America*, vol. XI, no. 3. Pittsburgh: UPBP, 1906.

———. *Minutes of the Forty-Seventh General Assembly of the United Presbyterian Church of the United States of America*, vol. XI, no. 2. Pittsburgh: UPBP, 1905.

———. *Minutes of the Thirty-Fifth General Assembly of the United Presbyterian Church of the United States of America*, vol. VIII, no. 2. Pittsburgh: UPBP, 1893.

———. *Minutes of the Thirty-Seventh General Assembly of the United Presbyterian Church of the United States of America*, vol. VIII, no. 4. Pittsburgh: UPBP, 1895.

———. *Minutes of the Thirty-Sixth General Assembly of the United Presbyterian Church of the United States of America*, vol. VIII, no. 3. Pittsburgh: UPBP, 1894.

———. *Triennial Report of the Board of Foreign Missions of the United Presbyterian Church of North America.* Philadelphia: BFM, 1925.

———. *Triennial Report of the Board of Foreign Missions of the United Presbyterian Church of North America, 1916-1918.* Philadelphia: UPBFM, 1919.

Victor, Arthur. "Impact of Punjabi Culture on Punjabi Christian Literature." *Religion and Society* 38 (1991) 37-46.

Waardenburg, Jacques. "The Early Period 610-650." In *Muslim Perceptions of Other Religions: A Historical Survey*, edited by Jacques Waardenburg, 3-17. New York: Oxford University Press, 1999.

Walbridge, Linda. "The Christians of Pakistan: The Interaction of Law and Caste in Maintaining 'Outsider' Status." In *Nationalism and Minority Identities in Islamic Societies*, edited by Maya Shatzmiller, 108-26. Montreal: McGill-Queen's University Press, 2005.

———. *Christians of Pakistan: The Passion of Bishop John Joseph.* New York: Routledge, 2003.

Walford, Nancy. *Introduction to the Psalms: A Song from Ancient Israel.* Danvers, MA: Chalice, 2004.

Webster, John. "Gordon, Andrew." In *Biographical Dictionary of Christian Missions*, edited by Gerald Anderson, 251-52. New York: Macmillan, 1998.

———. *A Social History of Christianity: North-West India since 1800.* New Delhi: Oxford University Press, 2007.

Wegner, Paul. *The Journey from Texts to Translations.* Grand Rapids: Baker, 1999.

Weiss, Anita. "Population Growth, Urbanization, and Female Literacy." In *The Future of Pakistan*, edited by Stephen Cohen, 236-48. Washington, DC: Brookings Institution, 2011.

Wenham, Gordon. *Psalms as Torah*. Grand Rapids: Baker Academic, 2012.
Westermeyer, Paul. *Let Justice Sing: Hymnody and Justice*. Collegeville: Liturgical, 1998.
Wikeley, James. *Punjabi Musalmans*. Lahore, Pakistan: Book House, 1968.
Young, William. *Days of Small Things? A Narrative Assessment of the Work of the Church of Scotland in the Punjab in "The Age of William Harper, 1873–1885."* Rawalpindi, Pakistan: CSC, 1991.
———. *Handbook of Source-Materials for Students of Church History up to 650 A.D.* Madras: CLS, 1969.
———. *Sialkot Convention Hymn Book: Notes on Writers and Translators*. Daska, Pakistan: [publisher not identified], 1965.
Youngson, John. *Forty Years of the Panjab Mission of the Church of Scotland, 1855–1895*. Edinburgh: Clark, 1896.
*Zabur: Desi Ragan Vich*. Lahore: Nol Kishore, 1909.
*Zabur: Punjabi Nazm Te Desi Ragan Vich*. Lahore, Pakistan: PRBS, 1970.
Zaidi, Abbas. "A Postcolonial Sociolinguistics of Punjabi in Pakistan." *Journal of Postcolonial Cultures and Societies* 1 (2010) 22–55.
Zanaty, Anwer. *Glossary of Islamic Terms*. Cairo: Shams, 2006.
Zarabozo, J. *What Is Islam*. Riyadh, Saudi Arabia: MIA, 2007.
Ziai, Aslam. "Focus on Translators: A Challenging Task in Pakistan." *Bible Translator* 41 (1990) 244–47.

# Subject Index

Abbottabad, 54
Adolph Rudolph, 5
Agra, 40, 57
*Ahl-e-Kitab*, 84
Ahmadiya, 92
Al-Masudi, 88
*Al-Rahman Al-Rahim*, 97
*Al-Shafia Al-Sajjaidya*, 86
Alonso Schökel, 90
American Methodist Press, 5
American Mission Press, 34
Amritsar Mission, 31, 33
Amritsar, 30–31, 33, 40, 57
Andrew Gordon, 3, 6–8, 20, 22, 30–32, 34, 37, 61–62
Anglicans, 31, 75, 104
Anglo-Indian, 4
Anita Weiss, 3
Anna Milligan, 35–36
Arabic, 3, 79, 83, 114
Archie D'Souza, 104
Arthur Herbert, 18
Arthur Parker, 32
Arthur Victor, 132
Asceticism, 90
Asia Bibi, 102–3
Asimi A.D., 136
*Asma-ul-husna*, 133
Athanasius, 101
Attitude toward missionaries, 62

Auld Lang Syne hymn, 18
Avril Powell, 31
Azhar Alam, 130
Aziz-ul-Haq, 7, 157

Babu Sadiq, 16, 35
Bannu, 115
Baptist Missionary Society, 58
Baptists, 75, 132
Barelvi, 93
Barkat Ullah, 119
Batala, 115
Beas, 3
Benares, 6, 13, 27, 35
Berlin Mission, 5
Bettie Addleton, 98
*Bhajan*, 10, 18
*Bhajana*, 19–20
*Bhakti*, 19
Bhalwal, 36
Bible translation, 118–21
Biblical Hebrew, 8, 81, 90–91, 97–98, 100–102, 104, 121–22, 130, 133, 135
Blasphemy Laws, 65–67, 102–103
Boarding School Sialkot, 9
Bollywood wedding, 73
Bonnie Mendes, 136
Book of Common Prayer, 72–73
Brethrens, 75, 132

Bridge-building, *See* Psalms as bridge-building
British and Foreign Bible Society, xvi, 58, 107, 114, 121–123
  Punjab auxiliary, 58, 114–123
British Library, xvii
Bulleh Shah, 88–91, 98, 100

Cadbury Research Library, xvii
Calvary Chapel Norbury (London, UK), 40, 130
Cambridge University, xvi
Camila Adang, 88, 99
Canadian School of Missions, 26
Canon Hares, 116, 119
Canon Jawahir Masih, 120
Captain John Mill, 3
Caste, 55–56, 60, 131
Catholic Bible Commission Pakistan, 113
Center for Muslim-Christian Studies, xvii
Chandu Ray, 114, 118, 120, 123
Charismatics, 75, 132
Chaughatia, 7
*Chaupai*, 43, 131
Chennab, 3
*Chimta*, 50
Chorus, 41, 75
Christian-Muslim Relations and Psalms, ix, 84–105
Christians in Pakistan
  Christian institutions, 8
  Discriminated, 65–67, 103–5
  Persecuted, 65–67
  Suffering for Christ, 65–67
Christian Talent Society, 40, 130
Christian Training Institute, 37
Christopher Harding, 59–60
Church Missionary Society, xvii, 30–33, 57
Church of England, 31, 57, 115,
Church of Pakistan, 74–75
Church of Scotland, xvii, 2, 116, 121
Clarkabad, 121
Clementine, 18
Clinton Loehlin, 95
CMS Industrial Press, 57

Common Bible, 112
Communion with God, 90, 98
Contextualization, xvi-xvii, 51, 131
Cornerstone Asian Church (Mississauga, Canada), 40
Covid-19 Pandemic, 68–70, 76, 98
Criticism on Bible, 109–110, 113, 127
Crowther Center Library, xvii
Cultural identity, 142
Cyril Glassé, 85

*Daf*, 92
Dalits, vii
Daskawie, 120
Daud Singh, 119
David Smith Lytle, 11–12, 21–24, 27, 35, 46
Day of Ascension, 72
Day of Judgement, 96
Delhi, 39–40
Deoband, 93
*Dervish*, 90
Devanagari Script, 90
Dhariwal, 54
*Dhawq*, 91
*Dholak*, 50, 94
Ditt, 7–8, 60
*Dohras*, 41
Drew Theological Seminary, 26
Dungwreth,119, 121

Eastern Melodies, 18–22, 75
Eastern Punjabi, 114
Ecumenical Bible translation, 112
Edwin Smith, 121, 123
Emma Dean Anderson, 11, 24–28, 37–38
Ernest Mall, 81
Europe, viii
Evarist Pinto, 112

Faisalabad, 27, 37
*Fakir*, 90
Farid, 91, 100
Farina Mir, 113
  Farukhabad Mission, 5
Feroze Khan Tarar, 120, 123
Follow Me hymn, 18

# Subject Index

Forman Christian College Lahore, 8
Formulaic devices, 97–98
Francis Tanveer, 76
Frank Pressly, 16, 35
Freda Carey, 107, 126
Fredrick Stock, 16–18

Gandhi, 25
Gauhar Masih, 117, 120–22, 138
Genevan Psalter, viii
George Braswell, 33
Gerhard Böwering, 83, 97
Ghazal, 41–42
Ghulam Qadir Masihi Printer, 114
Gojra, 116
Gordon College Rawalpindi, 7
Gordon Wehnam, 133
Gordon-Conwell Theological Seminary, xvii
Gordon, Andrew. *See* Andrew Gordon
Government Support for Urdu, 62–63, 76, 118
Graham Bailey, 116, 119, 140
Graham Kendrick, 64
Grierson, 118
Gujarati Language, 19
Gujranwala Theological Seminary, xvii, 37
Gujranwala, 24, 26, 54, 126
Gurdaspur, 34–36
Gurmukhi Punjabi Bible, 137–38
Gurumukhi Script, 114

*Hadith* on the Psalms, 86–87
Hanafi, 93
Harmonium, 50, 65, 94
Harold Spencer, 134
Harris Stewart, 120, 123
Harrison Qurban, 29
Henrietta Cowden, 11, 17, 21, 26–28, 35, 46, 54
Herbert Danby, 71
Hindu deities, 49
Hindustani Choral Book, 5
Hindustani language, 59
Holy Communion, 61, 72
Huguenots, viii
Hunter Memorial Church, 3
Hunter Pura, 3
Hunter, Thomas. *See* Thomas Hunter.

I. D. Shahbaz. *See* Imam-ud-Din Shahbaz
Ibn Qutayba, 87, 99
Ibn Rabban, 88
Illinois, 24
Ilyas Masih, 130
Ilyas Mughal, 130
Imad-ud-Din Lahiz, 31–32
Imam-ud-din Shahbaz
    Birthplace, 30
    Christian odes, 43–46
    Conversion and baptism, 28–33
    Doctor of divinity, 36
    Family, 36
    Impact of his work, 38–39
    Last Days, 35–36
    Lost sight, 16, 35, 38
    Mentioned in media, 40
    Modern Milton, 35
    Pen name, 29
    Poetic Styles, 41–43
    Poetic Themes, 43–46
    Poetry in *Nur Afshan*, 34
    Served with Church Missionary Society, 33–34
    Trained at Amritsar Mission, 33
    Visionary and Inspirational Man, 36–38
    Work in Gurdaspur, 34–35
    Work on Punjabi *Zabur*, viii, 16–20, 35–36
    Work on Urdu Metrical Psalms, 6–9, 34
Imprecatory Psalms, 99, 134
Inayat Bernard, 40, 75
Indian Music, 17–19, 28, 49–51
Indian Pakistani Church in Phoenix, USA, 71
Indian Revolt, 3
Indigenous Music, 47–51
Indo-Aryan, 3
Indo-European, 3
Indo-Iranian, 3
Indonesia, 82

Institute of Religion and Society in Bangalore, 40
Interfaith dialogue, 104, 138
Intertextuality and Qur'an, 77, 84–86, 104, 133
Irfan Masih, 66

Jalal-ud-Din, 120
Jalandhar, 40
James Massey, 19, 38, 130
James Wikeley, 83, 93, 134
Jammu, 116
Javed Qureshi, 99
Jeffrey Cox, 55, 59–62, 117, 127, 130
Jhelum, 54
John Hyde, 53–54
John Murdoch, 49
John Newton, 29, 57, 129
John O'Brien, 40, 67
John Webster, 7, 28
John Youngson, 2
Joseph Colony Lahore, 102
Josephine Martin, 11, 17, 21, 26–28, 46
Joshua Fazal-ud-Din, 119–20, 138
Judah Ha-Levi, 91
Julius Ullmann, 5

*Kaisar-i-Hind*, 24
*Kalam-e-Muqadas*, 111–13
Karachi, 2, 75, 103, 112, 126
Karam Dad, 7
Kerala, vii
Keswick Convention, 52
Khalid Mahmood, 40
*Khanun-Werakhum*, 97–98
Khyber, 75
King Solomon, 72
King's College Aberdeen, 3
Kinnaird College, 27
Kirsteen Kim, 67
*Kirtan*, 19
Kishan Kanda, 42–43
*Kitab-e-Muqadas*, 110–12
Krishnaswamy, 120, 140
Kuttianiamattathil Jose, 64

Labhu Mall, 119
Lahore high court, 80

Lahore, xvii, 8, 14, 27, 31, 40, 57–58, 68, 70, 72, 80, 102, 114–15, 119, 121–23, 126
Landour Language School, 12
Language and Class, 59–62
Language Attitude, viii, 114–115, 117, 125–128, 139
Language Hierarchy, viii
Lekh Puri, 90
Liberius Pieterse, 113
Linda Walbridge, 64, 103, 135
Lithographic Press, 23
Louis, Luzbetak, 95
Lucknow, 5
Ludhiana Mission, 4
Ludhiana, 4–5, 34
Lutherans, 75
Lyallpur, 27, 37, 115

Mahanwala, 22
Major Montgomery, 2
Malay Christians, 82
Malaysia, 82
*Manads*, 115–17
Mano Rumalshah, 78
Manorma Sharma, 49–50
Martin, Samuel. *See* Samuel Martin
Martinpur, 9, 54
Mary Jane Campbell,
    Punjabi language skills, 24
    Recipient of *Kaisar-i-Hind*, 24
    Served in Zafarwal, 24
    Taught at Kinnaird College, 47
    Work on the Punjabi Psalms, 11, 21–25, 27, 32, 39, 46, 48
Mary Rachel Martin, 11, 17, 21, 26–27, 46
*Masih*, 7, 43–44, 46
*Masiha*, 46, 98–99
*Masihi Git Ki Kitab*, 5, 57
*Masihi Ishat Khana*, xvii
*Masihi*, 46, 80
*Masnavi*, 42
Mass Movement, 60–62
Massey, James. *See*, James Massey.
Matthew Wimer, xii
Maulana Hidayatullah, 92
Maulvi Muhammad Alim, 7

## Subject Index

Maulvi Muhammad Hussain, 92
*Mazamir*, 4
*Mazmur*, 4
Meditation, 91
Memorial Christian Hospital Sialkot, 2
Methodists, 75, 132
Mian Paulus, 30
Michael Doyle, 79
Michael Nazir-Ali, 82, 85, 109, 131–32, 135–6
Minhaj-al-Quran, 94
Miss Beattie, 115
Miss Hill, 116–17
Mission agencies in India, 56–58, 62, 115–18, 121–22, 131–32
Mission Hospital Sialkot, 2
Missionary strategy in India, 61–62, 75, 171
*Mithi Zuban*, 48
Mohammad Iqbal, 2, 29, 41
Monmouth College, 22
Monmouth, 24
Mother-tongue, 47–51
Muhammad Miraj, 40
Multan, 126
*Munqir and Nakir*, 43–44
Murray College Sialkot, 2, 8
*Musamman*, 43, 131
*Mushaira*, 89
Music in Islam, 92–94
Musical instruments, 27, 50–51, 76, 94,
Muslim apologists and the Psalms, 87–88
Mysticism and Punjabi *Zabur*, 88–91, 93–94, 98, 105, 133, 137

Narowal, 30–31, 34, 40
Nasir Kundan Lal, 120
Negative attitude toward Punjabi language, viii, 110, 115, 118, 125–28, 1139, 42–143
Nesbitt H., 115, 119–20, 122
Nettleton hymn, 18
Newton's Punjabi New Testament, 29
Nol Kishore Printing Press, 14, 114
Nomadic singers, 16
*Nur Afshan*, 34
Nur-ud-Din Jami, 42, 89,

Orality, viii, 88, 133
Outcasts, 55–56, 133

Padri I D Shahbaz award, 133
Pakistan Bible Society, 111–2, 139
Pakistan Christian Recording Ministries, xv
Pakistan Penal Code, 66–67, 102
Palm Sunday, 70–72
Panjab auxiliary of British and Foreign Bible Society, 58, 114–123
Panjabi Manual and Grammar, 26
Parallelism, 90, 133
Partition of India, 52, 115–16, 126, 137
Pasrur, 11, 26, 54
Pathankot, 25, 27, 54
Patras Masih, 103
Paul Christopher, 52
Paul Marshall, 102
Paul Miller, 115
Paul Wegner, 79
Pennsylvania, xvii, 22
Pentecostals, 76, 132
People of the Book, 84
Peter Riddell, ix, xi, 82, 93, 102
Pittsburgh Theological Seminary, xvii
Prem Masih, 7
Presbyterian Church of Pakistan Philadelphia, 130
Presbyterian Historical Society, xvii
Presbyterian Mission Press Allahabad, 4
Presbytery of Gurdaspur, 34
Protestant Urdu Bible, 111–13
Psalm singing pastors, 53
Psalms. *Also See Zabur*
   Acrostic, 90, 104, 133
   Christian-Muslim Relations, 84–105
   Content, 55–56
   Hope, 68–74
   Imprecatory, 99, 134, 150
   Lament, 94, 98–99
   Praise, 94
Psalms as Bridge-building, 84–105
Punjab auxiliary of the British and Foreign Bible Society, 58, 114–23
Punjab Synod Conference, 37

Punjab, vii, 1, 3, 9, 18–19, 34, 39–41, 48, 50–51, 54–55, 57–58, 60–61, 89–90, 114–119, 123, 126–128, 131, 137, 139, 142
Punjabees, 3
Punjabi *Ilm-i-Ilahi*, 25
Punjabi Language, viii, xv, xvii, 1, 3, 10–11, 16, 24, 29, 48–51, 58–61, 76, 88–89, 90–92, 105–7, 114–15, 117, 123–128, 133, 138–143
Punjabi Masihi Church (Surrey, Canada), 40
Punjabi Persian New Testament, xvi, 23, 114
Punjabi Psalter. *See Zabur*
Punjabi wedding, 73–74
Punjabi *Zabur* and the Indian Subcontinent, 38–40

Qadir Bakhsh, 120, 123
*Qawali*, 94, 105, 134
*Qita*, 42–43
Qur'an, viii, 4, 66, 78, 80–82, 84–86, 88, 91–94, 97–101, 104, 112, 133
Qur'anic View on the Psalms, 84–86

Radcliffe commission, 35
Radha Kishan, 17, 20, 50
*Ragas*, 39, 49–50
*Ragmala*, 5
Rahmat Masih, 7
Raiwind, 104, 132
Rajasthani language, 19, 126
Ravi, 3
Rawalpindi, xvii, 7, 104, 116, 154
Robert Butler, 133, 135
Reformed, viii, 16, 75
Refrain, 41, 43, 79, 94
Richard Hoyle, xi
Rimsha Masih, 102
Robbie Goh, 82
Robert Clark, 30–31, 57
Robert Cummings, 11
Robert Stewart, 2, 4–6, 10, 13, 27, 32
Rochester, 132
Roger Hedlund, 54

Roman Catholic Church, 4, 40, 75, 112–13, 132
Roman Catholic Urdu Bible, 112–13
Roman-Urdu Primer, 26
Rosa Bashir-ul-Nissa Sadiq, 36
Royal mosque in Agra, 31
*Rubai*, 42–43
Ruth Pfau, 98

Sabiha Mansoor, 125
Sabzkot, 22
Sacred Heart Cathedral Lahore, 40
*Sahih Muslim*, 86–87
*Sahih-Al-Bukhari*, 86–87, 92
Saint Thomas, vii
Sajid Masih, 103
Salamat Shahid, 49
Salvation Army, 121
Samuel Martin, 6–9, 20, 27, 34
Samuel Satthianadhan, 31
Sangla Hill, 54, 115
Sanskrit, 18, 114
Sargodha, 36, 54
Sarwat Ali, 40
Sattlaj, 3
Scottish Presbyterians, 2
Sebastian Francis Shaw, 40
Sebastian Kim, 64
Serena Nanda, 142
Shabbir Akhtar, 86
Shah Hussain, 98, 100
Shahbaz Bhatti, 102
*Sham-e-Mazamir*, 130
Shama Singh, 36
Shame-based culture, 108–9
Sharif Kunjahi, 92
Sialkot
 Bara Pathar, 52
 Christian Hospital, 2
 Christian Missions, 2–3
 Convention, 52–55
 Economy, 2
 Hymn Book, xvii, 52
 Military location, 1
 Mission, 3, 26
 Surgical Industry, 2
*Siharfi*, 90, 105, 133
Sikhism, 19

## Subject Index 165

Sikhs, 50, 90
Society of St. Paul, 111
Sociolinguistic, viii, 106, 125–128
South Asian Punjabi Christian Diaspora, 40, 71
St. Andrew's Church Ilford (London, UK), 40
Stephen Neil, 3
Stewart, Robert. *See* Robert Stewart.
Stock, Fredrick. *See*, Fredrick Stock.
Stuntz C., 120
Suffering, 67, 76, 94, 99, 135–36
Sufism, 90–93
Sultan Bahu, 89–90
Sunder Singh, 120
Supreme Court of Pakistan, 112
Susan Bassnett, 47
*Swar Sangrah*, 5
Swiss, viii
Synod Church of Pakistan, 71

*Tabla*, 50
Tahir-ul-Qadri, 94
Tariq Rahman, 125–26
Tarkio College, 36
*Tasbih*, 90
Tauqir Amaan Khan, 92
Tej Bhatia, 3, 125
Terry Jones, 112
Thakur Das, 10, 120
Thar Desert, 19
Thomas Fitzpatrick, 30–31
Thomas Fulton Cummings
    Linguist-missionary, 26
    Scholar-Saint, 26
    Work on the Punjabi *Zabur*, 11, 26, 46
Thomas Hughes, 4, 81, 84, 90, 97
Thomas Hunter, 3
Timothy Farrell, xi
Trinity College Cambridge, 31
Trinity International Christian Church (Philadelphia, USA), 40, 130

Union Theological Seminary, 26
United Kingdom, 52, 119
United Presbyterian General Assembly, 13, 23, 26, 35

United Presbyterian Mission, 2–7, 11, 22–26, 28, 34, 52, 56–57
University of Birmingham, xvii
University of Cambridge, xvi
University of Glasgow, xvii
Untouchability, vii, 8, 56, 103
Urdu language, 5, 13, 24, 26, 29, 36, 41, 48, 60–62, 107, 110, 113, 115, 117, 122, 125, 137–38
Urdu Metrical Psalms, 4, 5, 6–9
Uttar Pradesh, 39

Vidyasagar Doger, 39
Vivian Stacy, 113

Walter Brueggemann, 95
Waris Shah, 89
Warren Larson, 104
Wesley Culshaw, 110
Western Melodies, viii, 4, 6, 13, 18–19
Western Meters, 6, 59
Wilfred Bradnock, 114, 118, 120, 123
William Anderson, 24
William Bowley, 4
William Clowes, 5
William Galbraith Young, xvi, 6, 10–13, 16–18, 30, 49, 129
William Harper, xvii
William Hunter, 19
William McKelvey, 11, 17, 21, 26–27, 46
Wycliffe Singh, xvii

Xenia Theological Seminary, 22

Youhanabad, 72
Youngson, John. *See* John Youngson.

*Zabur* (Psalms)
    1892 edition, 12–14, 23–24, 36–27, 49, 67, 81, 129, 140
    1908 edition, 13–15, 17, 20, 23–27, 35, 81–83, 139–41
    Amidst Covid-19 Pandemic, 68–70
    Committee, 10–11
    Devotional use, 64
    In Christian-Muslim relations, 85–105

*Zabur* (Psalms) (continued)
   In Indian Subcontinent, 38–40
   In times of persecution, 65–67
   Liturgical use, 70
   Memorization, 64, 68, 129, 132
   Mentioned in Quran, 4
   Personal and Communal Piety, 64–65
   Poetic Features, 41–43
   Poetic Themes, 43–46
   Preparation, 14
   Reasons delayed their preparation, 59–63
   Reasons for success, 47
   Symbol of unity, 74–76
   Text Analysis, 16

*Zabur aur Git*, 4
*Zabur o Git*, 57
Zafarwal, 24, 30, 32, 34, 116
Zenana Missionary Society, 13, 24, 36, 116
Ziai Aslam, 110–11, 122, 138

# Scripture Index

| Psalms | | | |
|---|---|---|---|
| 16:7–8 | 81 | 9 | 80 |
| 20:1–2 | 72 | 11 | 96 |
| 24:7–8 | 71 | 14 | 96 |
| 45:10–11 | 73 | 18 | 80 |
| 46:1–2 | 69 | 19 | 95 |
| 55:16–18 | 67 | 28 | 80 |
| 91:9–12 | 68 | 37 | 96 |
| 111:4–5 | 70 | 41 | 80 |
| 121:1–2 | 70 | 48 | 80 |
| 1:6 | 81 | 56 | 80 |
| 2:6 | 81 | 60 | 101 |
| 16:1 | 65 | 62 | 80 |
| 22:27 | 81 | 65 | 80 |
| 33:2 | 81 | 68 | 96 |
| 34:7 | 81 | 74 | 80 |
| 47:2 | 81 | 80 | 80 |
| 63:7 | 91 | 82 | 96 |
| 72:17 | 72 | 85 | 80 |
| 77:13 | 91 | 86 | 97 |
| 78:4 | 81 | 89 | 95 |
| 107:2 | 81 | 95 | 80 |
| 119:97 | 91 | 97 | 101 |
| 126:1 | 81 | 103 | 101 |
| 136:1 | 81 | 104 | 96 |
| 143:5 | 91 | 105 | 80 |
| 7 | 96 | 106 | 96 |
| 8 | 90 | 109 | 95 |
| | | 112 | 96 |

**Psalms (continued)**

| | | | | | |
|---|---|---|---|---|---|
| 116 | 80 | 146 | 96 |
| 132 | 96 | 148 | 95 |
| 135 | 95 | 149 | 80 |
| 138 | 80 | | |
| 140 | 96 | **Matthew** | |
| | | 25:6 | 73 |

www.ingramcontent.com/pod-product-compliance
Lightning Source LLC
Chambersburg PA
CBHW071454150426
43191CB00008B/1339